Indian Manufacturing Sector in Post-Reform Period

Sumit Kumar Maji · Arindam Laha ·
Debasish Sur

Indian Manufacturing Sector in Post-Reform Period

An Assessment of the Role of Macroeconomic
and Firm-Specific Factors in Determining Financial
Performance

Sumit Kumar Maji
Department of Commerce
The University of Burdwan
Burdwan, West Bengal, India

Arindam Laha
Department of Commerce
The University of Burdwan
Burdwan, West Bengal, India

Debasish Sur
Department of Commerce
The University of Burdwan
Burdwan, West Bengal, India

ISBN 978-981-19-2665-5   ISBN 978-981-19-2666-2   (eBook)
https://doi.org/10.1007/978-981-19-2666-2

This Palgrave Macmillan imprint is published by the registered company Springer Nature Singapore Pte Ltd.
The registered company address is: 152 Beach Road, #21-01/04 Gateway East, Singapore 189721, Singapore

PREFACE

It is theoretically established that the manufacturing sector acts as the dominant driver of economic growth, development and employment opportunity of a country. With the outset of liberalization measures in the Indian economy since mid-80s, the possibility for growth of the Indian manufacturing firms has multiplied on one hand and on the other hand the firms in the manufacturing sector are equally exposed to the externalities stemming from the dynamism of industry-specific and macroeconomic factors. To survive in the competitive economic environment in the post-liberalization era there was a pressing demand to revamp the level of efficiency and financial performance of the manufacturing firms. Thus, it is of prime significance to comprehend the divergent factors (such as microeconomic, industry-specific and macroeconomic factors) which are capable of determining the level of efficiency and the financial performance of the firms. In this context, the book sheds some light on the growth of the Indian manufacturing sector, identifies the microeconomic and macroeconomic factors affecting the level of efficiency, profitability and the interrelationship between macroeconomic variables and stock market performance of the firms belonging to various sectors within the broad Indian manufacturing industry. The book is divided into a total of seven chapters. In Chapter 1 the importance of the manufacturing sector in the context of an economy and the essentiality of the consideration of the different factors in explaining the financial performance are introduced. Chapter 2 deals with the evolution of industrial policies in India. In Chapter 3, a systematic review of the existing research studies is made in order to identify the various factors affecting financial performance of firms. Chapter 4 is dedicated to ascertain the level of efficiency of the firms operating in different manufacturing sub-sectors and their determinants. Chapter 5 analyses the profitability of the firms as well as the implications of various microeconomic and macroeconomic factors on such profitability. In Chapter 6, the long-run and short-run causal relationships between the major macroeconomic variables and the sectoral stock indices are assessed. Finally, Chapter 7 makes a summary of the findings of the study and concluding observations. This chapter also attempts to identify the policy implications of the study.

Burdwan, India   Sumit Kumar Maji
                                                       Arindam Laha
                                                       Debasish Sur

CONTENTS

About the Authors

Dr. Sumit Kumar Maji is Assistant Professor in the Department of Commerce, The University of Burdwan, West Bengal, India. He has completed his M.Com from The University of Burdwan in 2010 and was awarded University Gold Medal and Tarunendra Bose Gold medal for his academic excellence. Dr. Maji has received a Doctorate degree from The University of Burdwan in 2019. He is actively engaged in research and has published a number of research articles in various Scopus listed, Web of science listed and UGC Care listed Journals and Edited volumes of national and international repute published from IGI Global, Inderscience, Emerald, Sage, Publishing India, Taylor & Francis etc. Dr. Maji has also completed research projects funded by The University of Burdwan and ICSSR, New Delhi. He has also participated and presented research papers in different seminars and conferences in India. Dr. Maji has been awarded the South-South and Triangular Fellowship by ILO for attending the academy on Social and Solidarity Economy, 2017 held in Seoul, South Korea. He has also obtained the prestigious IAA Young Researcher Award from Indian Accounting Association in 2021.

Prof. Arindam Laha has been teaching Economics at the Department of Commerce, The University of Burdwan, West Bengal, India for the last 12 years. He has written one book and has published a number of research articles in internationally reputed journals of

Social Sciences viz., *Pakistan Development Review, Bangladesh Development Studies, International Journal of Public Administration, Finance India, Indian Journal of Agricultural Economics* and also in various edited volumes published by Routledge Publication, Emerald Publishing, Cambridge Scholars Publishing, IGI Global. He has been awarded ILO's South-South Triangular Cooperation scholarship.

Prof. Debasish Sur is Professor at the Department of Commerce of The University of Burdwan, West Bengal. He has over 24 years of teaching experience at the post-graduate level. Professor Sur has so far contributed more than 100 papers in reputed professional and academic journals such as *Finance India, International Journal of Risk Assessment and Management, International Journal of Management Concepts and Philosophy, Management and Labour Studies, Asia-Pacific Journal of Management Research and Innovation,* etc. He already has four books to his credit. He also engages himself as reviewer in reputed international publishing houses like Palgrave Macmillan, Emerald, Taylor and Francis, Springer, etc.

Abbreviations

ADF	Augmented Dickey–Fuller Test
ARDL	Auto Regressive Distributed Lag Model
BM	Basic Materials
BSE	Bombay Stock Exchange
CDGS	Consumer Discretionary Goods and Services
COP	Crude Oil Price
COR	Capital–Output Ratio
CRS	Constant Returns to Scale
EBIT	Earnings Before Interest and Taxes
ECT	Error Correction Term
EGM	Evidence Gap Map
EPU	Economic Policy Uncertainty
FDI	Foreign Direct Investment
FEM	Fixed Effect Model
FMCG	Fast Moving Consumer Goods
FPI	Foreign Portfolio Investment
FPIR	Foreign Portfolio Investment Ratio
GDP	Gross Domestic Product
GFCF	Gross Fixed Capital Formation
GP	Gold Price
HC	Healthcare
IC	Intellectual Capital
IDRA	Industries Development and Regulation Act
IIP	Index of Industrial Production
IMF	International Monetary Fund
IND	Industrials

INT	Rate of Interest
IPR	Industrial Policy Resolutions
MRTP	Monopoly Restrictive Trade Practices
MS	Money Supply
NPA	Non-Performing Assets
OECD	Organization for Economic Cooperation and Development
OPEC	Organization for Petroleum Exporting Countries
PCA	Principal Component Analysis
PF	Price Factor
PP	Philips–Perron Test
PPP	Public–Private Partnership
PSU	Public Sector Undertaking
R&D	Research & Development
RBI	Reserve Bank of India
REER	Real Effective Exchange Rate
REM	Random Effect Model
ROA	Return on Asset
UECM	Unrestricted Error Correction Model
VAIC	Value Added Intellectual Coefficient
VAR	Vector Auto Regression
WPI	Wholesale Price Index

LIST OF FIGURES

LIST OF TABLES

CHAPTER 1

Introduction

Abstract Manufacturing sector is regarded as the prime driver of economic growth and development for a country. Presence of a strong manufacturing sector is quintessential in generating adequate employment opportunity in an economy. With a gradual opening up of the Indian economy since mid-80s, the opportunity for growth for the Indian manufacturing firms has multiplied on one hand. On the other hand, the firms have to face the externalities emanating from the exposure to the industry-specific and macroeconomic factors. In a liberalized economic environment, the competition becomes fierce. In the wake of such enormously competitive environment, the firms belonging to the Indian manufacturing sector has to operate efficiently and more importantly profitably to sustain in the long run. Therefore, it is of utmost importance to understand the diversified factors which are capable of affecting the level of efficiency and the financial performance of the firms. The various factors which affect a firm normally get classified into three broad categories such as microeconomic, industry-specific and macroeconomic factors. Irrespective of the policy regime, these three factors have remained at the core of the financial performance analysis of the firms belonging to the Indian manufacturing sector. But with the opening up of the economy, the industry-specific and macroeconomic factors became even more important. Thus, the formulation of the business strategies in the post-liberalized business environment requires special consideration of all these factors together. In this introductory chapter the need of the manufacturing sector and the various microeconomic, industry-specific and macroeconomic determinants of the financial performance of the firm pertaining to the diverse manufacturing sector have been emphasized. This chapter also underscores the innovativeness of the book at the end of this chapter.

Keywords Manufacturing · Economic growth · Employment · Microeconomic factors · Macroeconomic factors

1.1   NEED FOR MANUFACTURING SECTOR

In an economy, different sectors can be classified into three broad categories: primary, secondary and tertiary sectors. Out of these three, agriculture and its allied activities are considered as the primary sector in the economy. The second important sector in the economy is the industry which incorporates the activities connected with 'Mining & Quarrying', 'Manufacturing', 'Electricity, Gas and Water Supply' and 'Construction'. This sector is also known as the secondary sector. Lastly, the activities related to 'Trade, Hotels, Transport, Communication and Services related to Broadcasting', 'Financial, Real Estate and Professional Services', 'Public Administration, Defence and Other Services' are included in the category of 'Service' or 'Tertiary' sector.

The contribution of the different sectors to the national economy may not be uniform across countries of the world.[1] One common feature that can be observed throughout the world is that the contribution of the service sector to the GDP is found to be the highest, followed by the industry and agriculture. Another distinguishing feature of changing dynamics of sectoral contribution is that the contribution of the agriculture to the GDP reduces significantly across the globe whereas the service sector's contribution to it is on the rise with the passage of time.

---

[1] For example the contributions of agriculture, industry and services for China during 2017 were 7.5%, 39.9% and 52.7%, respectively. Similarly, if we look at the US economy the contribution of agriculture, industry and services were found to be 0.92%, 18.21% and 77.37%, respectively, and the same for the world as a whole were 3.43%, 25.44% and 65.03%, respectively, during 2017 (Statistica).

In India[2] also, the contributions to the GDP made by the agriculture (including forestry and fishing), industry and service sectors were approximately 16.1%, 29.6% and 54.30%, respectively, in 2018–2019 and the growth in the Indian service sector has been continuously stepping up in an unprecedented manner over the last one and half decades.

As far as the manufacturing sector is concerned, the global trend suggests that in many of the Western developed OECD countries of the globe, the share of manufacturing sector in the national income has reduced remarkably over the last three decades or so. It is popularly known as the deindustrialization phenomena (Christopherson et al., 2014). Such a process of deindustrialization is mainly driven by certain factors like availability of low-priced manufactured goods from other countries (like China), lack of innovation and investment, excessive import dependence and off shoring manufacturing plants in low cost countries. In addition to these, the rapid technological progress in the erstwhile industrially developed countries has made a significant contribution towards reducing the demand of labour in the manufacturing sectors in these economies. However, many experts consider this deindustrialization as a positive phenomenon because these Western countries were supposed to specialize and focus more on the knowledge-based services sectors rather than focusing on the manufacturing (Christopherson et al., 2014). The concept of reliance on the service sector for fostering economic growth and development is also very fragile in nature. The financial crisis of 2008–2009 has shown that the service sector especially the companies providing the financial services are dreadfully exposed to the external shocks. Therefore, it is extremely important for the economies of the globe to rectify the imbalance of exorbitant trust in the service sector and to stimulate the manufacturing sector to make the growth process resilient. It is true that as the industrial development process continues, the agricultural contribution to the national income will keep on reducing. The agricultural sector has a tremendous potential to engage huge number of people in work. However, with the reduction of the share of the agriculture, there will be a shift of workforce from the agriculture sector to the industry and services. Although the service sector is growing at a very fast pace all over the globe, this sector is

---

[2] https://www.indiabudget.gov.in/economicsurvey/doc/vol2chapter/echap01_vol2.pdf.

exceedingly lenient towards skilled workforce. Thus, the growth of service sector will not provide much scope for generating adequate employment opportunity to mop up the huge workforce.

Manufacturing sector can be considered as the engine of growth and development in majority of the countries of the globe, except in some oil-rich nations (Haraguchi et al., 2017). The existence of a strong manufacturing sector in an economy offers manifold advantages. Firstly, the productivity growth of the manufacturing sector is much higher as compared to that of any other sector in the economy primarily due to higher levels of capital accumulation and economies of scale. Such a potentiality of achieving a higher rate of growth in productivity makes this sector as the engine of growth (Kaldor, 1967). Further, the momentum of increase in productivity of the manufacturing sector is found to be more in a poor country which underlines the proclivity of this sector for unconditional convergence with the technological frontier (Rodrik, 2016). Secondly, the manufacturing sector can only provide large-scale employment opportunities to all classes of workforce. Thirdly, the rate of technological progress is much higher in the manufacturing industry as compared to the other sectors in the economy and such a high rate of technological progress in turn accelerates the overall technological development in the economy as a whole. Fourthly, the growth in the manufacturing sector has multiplier forward and backward linkage effects. The development in the manufacturing output propels the growth of output in the backward linked sectors such as mining and quarrying. It also expedites the output growth through forward linkages in the other manufacturing sub-sectors. Fifthly, growth in primary and secondary sectors of the economy also enhances the growth prospects of the tertiary sector. It implies that with the increase in the per capita income gleaned from secondary sector, the demand for the services steps up through forward linkage effect (Bhattacharya & Mitra, 1989). Sixthly, with the development of manufacturing sector and with its forward and backward linkages the income level in the economy increases which in turn creates additional demand for the goods and services. With more demand in the economy more production and delivery of services takes place and so on. Eventually, it creates a virtuous cycle in the economy.

However, the growth that the Indian economy has so far experienced in the last three decades was primarily driven by the service sector (Kotwal et al., 2011). The contribution of the service sector to the GDP and the growth of service sector have increased tremendously since early 1970s whereas the contribution of the manufacturing sector to the GDP has remained stagnant in India. The growth of economy based on the contribution of the manufacturing sector is of utmost importance for emerging economies like India to tackle the problem of massive unemployment. Many countries in Asia, such as the Philippines, Indonesia, South Korea, Japan, Taipei, Singapore and especially China have been able to develop their economies by heavily promoting the manufacturing sector (Bollard et al., 2013; Felipe et al., 2018). The crucial problem associated with the service sector-led growth is that such a growth is not being able to create adequate number of employment opportunities for all classes of the labour force because service sector is essentially skill and technology intensive rather than labour dependent. It is the manufacturing sector which is capable of employing large number of low-skilled labour forces (Rodrik, 2016). The importance of the manufacturing sector can easily be understood from the fact that out of the total employed workforce in different sectors in India, 66.91 million (16.8%) were employed in the secondary sector during the year 1999–2000 (Dasgupta & Singh, 2005). Although the share of employment in the manufacturing sector surged to 25.58% during 2019,[3] considering the large number of aspiring young people in the job market, the growth of the employment opportunity needs to be multiplied. Though India has a huge employable workforce, the job opportunities are very less which not only affects the economic growth but also widens the inequality further (Rajan, 2006b). The private entrepreneurs are also getting more attracted towards the service sectors rather than manufacturing as evidenced by the large number of service start-ups mushrooming day by day.

To alter this job-less growth story of India, it is of great importance that the labour-intensive manufacturing industry needs to be promoted (Rajan, 2006b). Although, it is argued in the recent literature that the manufacturing sector has lost its importance as the engine of growth and employment (Rodrik, 2016b) in developed economies especially on account of the high level of skill requirement due to technological development in the manufacturing sector (Ghani & O'Connell, 2016). However, in developing economies, employment opportunities always increase as the manufacturing sector grows (Haraguchi et al., 2017).

---

[3] https://data.worldbank.org/indicator/SL.IND.EMPL.ZS?locations=IN.

Another important issue is that the imports of the manufacturing products in India have stepped up remarkably in the last decade especially on account of the availability of the cheap Chinese products. The imports of basic goods,[4] capital goods,[5] intermediate goods[6] and consumer goods[7] have burgeoned manifold during the period 2004–2005 to 2010–2011 (Singh, 2012). Although it is to be kept in mind that REER has remained more or less stable during this period[8] of time. To go into further details, the imports of manufacturing sub-sectors such as food products and beverages, tobacco products, wearing apparel, chemical and chemical products, leather items, rubber and plastic products, machinery and equipment, motor vehicles, trailers and semi-trailers, transport equipment, medical precision and optical instruments, publishing, printing and reproduction of recorded media, wood and wood products have augmented outstandingly during the period 2004–2005 to 2010–2011.[9] Such an increase in the import of manufacturing output is not good from the point of view of the Indian economy. Perhaps because of these reasons the Government of India had introduced the National Manufacturing Policy in 2011 to rejuvenate the manufacturing sector in India (Felipe et al., 2018). In addition to this, various other sector-specific policies, such as National Textile Policy in 2000, National Policy on Electronics in 2012 and National Capital Goods Policy in 2016 were also adopted from time to time to boost the manufacturing sector. In this regard, the ambitious 'Make in India' initiative was undertaken by the Indian Government in September 2014 to strengthen the Indian manufacturing industry as well as to create adequate job opportunities and also to promote the

[4] Some of the important basic goods are aluminium and aluminium products, copper and copper products, cement.

[5] Some of the important capital goods are welding Machines, cooling towers, air conditioners, industrial machinery, agricultural machinery, computer and computer peripherals, turbine, cranes, elevators and lifts, solar power system, construction equipment, textile machinery, health care and surgical equipment, inverters and UPS, etc.

[6] Some of the important intermediate goods are auto ancillary, glasses, integrated circuits, picture tubes, etc.

[7] Some of the important consumer goods are tyres and tubes, leather products, mixers and grinders, pressure cookers, ceramic sanitary items, telephone instruments, washing machine, apparels, watches, refrigerators, mobile phones and accessories.

[8] REER in March 2005 was 97.80 which increased to 98.31 in March 2011 (2004–2005 as the base year).

[9] For details see Singh (2012).

overall economic growth. However, it is a matter of appreciation that there has been an increase in the domestic production in respect of almost all the manufacturing industry sub-groups and the export in respect of textile, radio, television and communication equipment and basic metals sectors has also improved remarkably during the last decade.[10]

1.2 Financial Performance Indicators of the Manufacturing Sector and Their Linkages with Economic Factors: A Conceptual Framework

The promotion of the manufacturing sector is important for spurring economic growth and employment opportunity. But for long-run endurance, the firms belonging to the manufacturing sector ought to be strong. For this, the firms have to ensure efficient business operation and sound financial performance. It is to be kept in mind that the operating efficiency and the financial performance of the firms are influenced by a host of factors. These factors can be broadly classified into three major domains such as microeconomic factors, industry-specific factors and macroeconomic factors (Hansen & Wernerfelt, 1989). These factors affect the level of efficiency vis-à-vis productivity, profitability and ultimately the share prices of the firms. Different microeconomic factors (such as age of the firm, size of the firm, short-term and long-term debt paying capacity of the firm, openness of the firm, capital structure of the firm, research and innovation capabilities, etc.) are the dominant firm-specific factors which have bearing on the level of efficiency of the firms as well as the profitability of the firms operating in an economy. Figure 1.1 exemplifies the linkage of the different microeconomic, industry-specific and macroeconomic factors in determining the productivity, profitability and share price.

1.3 Microeconomic (or Firm-Specific) Factors

1.3.1 Age of the Firms

Age is a proxy of the experience of a firm. It is a theoretically accepted belief that the level of efficiency and the profitability of the firms get positively affected by the experience of the firm. With the increase in

---

[10] For more details, see Singh (2012).

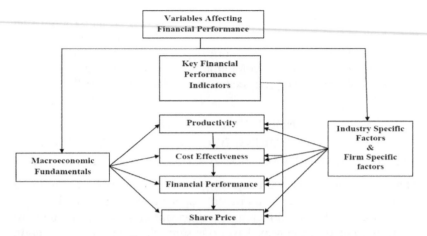

Fig. 1.1 A conceptual framework linking macroeconomic, industry-specific and microeconomic factors on firm performance (*Source* Author's own representation)

the age the learning curve effect comes into existence which enables the firms in operating efficiently and profitably (Agiomirgianakis et al., 2006). However, old firms may suffer from inertia and lack the ability to adapt to the changes emanating from dynamic business environment. Such lack of flexibility of the firms may adversely affect the level of efficiency, profitability and ultimately share prices of the firms.

1.3.2   Size of the Firms

Large size firms are able to reap the advantage of economies of scale (Goddard et al., 2005). The level of efficiency and the financial performance get positively influenced by the age of the firm. The size of the firms is also closely linked with the age of the firms. Therefore, with an increase in age, the size of the firm also enhances by adopting appropriate growth strategy. In addition to this, large size firms are expected to enjoy the power of diversification, greater bargaining power, easy access to cheaper financial resources and formalization of procedure which exerts positive effect on the efficiency, profitability and share price.

1.3.3   Leverage

Capital structure decision is one of the most important decision areas of financial management. Capital structure as indicated by leverage ratio is the combination of the different sources of funds used for the creation of pool of funds to finance various projects. A firm which is more dependent on the external funds is expected to be highly levered or geared. While making the choice of various sources of funds, a firm has to consider risk, cost, control and flexibility associated with the different sources. From the cost perspective, debt is a cheaper source of fund as the interest paid on the debt is a charge against profit as per the prevailing Income Tax Act in India. However, with more and more use of debt in the capital structure of the firm, the financial risk associated with the firm surges significantly as the firm has to meet its fixed financial commitment irrespective of the level of earnings. Moreover, in case of the immediate need of funds, it is easier for the firms to obtain the required funds by the way of debt as acquiring funds by issuing equity is a time taking process. However, a firm should not be too much debt dependent in order to maintain desired flexibility of raising funds for meeting immediate requirements. Further, if a firm relies significantly on the external funds then the owners' control over the firm may get diluted and control may be taken over by the external fund providers. A highly geared firm[11] is expected to be comparatively more efficient and profitable as compared to the low geared firms (Batra & Kalia, 2016). It is theoretically argued that a highly geared firm has to meet the fixed financial commitments and thus it is a binding on the managers of the firms to operate efficiently and in a disciplined fashion so as to meet the fixed financial commitments without facing any difficulty. However, this argument holds good if only the lending institution exerts stringent monitoring system about the end most use of the funds. If the lending institution fails to implement uncompromising monitoring system then the expected improvement in efficiency vis-à-vis profitability may not emerge (Majumdar, 1997).

---

[11] A firm with a high debt/equity ratio.

1.3.4   Liquidity

Along with other firm-specific factors, liquidity which implies the short-term debt paying capability of the firm is also considered to be another important dimension of its financial management. The working capital of a firm is the amount of fund that the firm needs to finance its day-to-day operating activities. Both excessive or shortage of working capital is detrimental to the overall financial health of the firms. Excessive investment in working capital keeps the funds idle and generates no return. Similarly, shortage of working capital adversely affects the day-to-day operation of the firms. Therefore, an appropriate working capital management policy is of supreme significance for ensuing greater efficiency and profitability of the firms (Bhayani, 2010; Chander & Aggarwal, 2008; Voulgaris et al., 2000).

1.3.5   Intellectual Capital

Today we are living in the knowledge era where innovation acts as a precondition to the success of a firm. In this time, the customer choices change at a very rapid pace which gets further intensified by the ever changing technological environment. A firm has to make itself innovation oriented to strive for survival in such a dynamic environment. The firm's innovation capability to a great extent is dependent on the level of Intellectual Capital (IC) that it owns. The concept of IC encompasses three kinds of capital such as Human Capital as represented by the skill, knowledge, ability, experience, morale, motivation, training, ambition, etc., Structural Capital as delineated by the organizational values, culture, ethics, information system, intellectual resources, industrial relation that remains in the organization when the employees leave the organization and Relational Capital as outlined by the stakeholder relation (Edvinsson & Malone, 1997).

1.3.6   Openness of the Firm

International diversification or openness may be defined as the cross-border expansion of the business activities into different locations, regions and markets. Firms generally diversify geographically with an attempt to achieve competitive advantages (Lu & Beamish, 2004). There is a vast body of literature which underlines the positive relationship between the openness vis-à-vis international diversification and the level of financial performance. Such positive relation primarily arises due to the primacy emanating from the exploitation of the market imperfections in the use of its intangibles in various geographies. Penetration into different markets enables the firms to get access to larger customer base which in turn allows the firm to reduce the cost and enhance profit by exploiting the economies of scale. Besides, different geographies are endowed with various kinds of resources and location-specific advantages. Therefore, such advantages may motivate the firms to diversify their business operations internationally. Moreover, other benefits such as economies of learning, innovation, enhanced bargaining power in the factor market and risk mitigation by the way of geographical diversification also arise to the firms which are internationally diversified.

1.4   Industry-Specific Factors

Likewise, supply and demand situation in an industry, indirect tax structure, level of competition within a particular industry, sector-specific Government regulations, existing laws of the land, etc., are the different industry-specific factors which play instrumental role in shaping the efficiency and financial performance of the firms operating in a particular sector.

1.5   Macroeconomic Factors

Last but not the least; macroeconomic factors (such as growth of the economy, inflation, exchange rate, oil price, rate of interest, economic policy uncertainty, money supply, foreign investment, etc.) are equally important in determining the financial performance of the firm. The macroeconomic factors are instrumental in determining firm performance in the context of an integrated open economy. Industry-specific and macroeconomic factors become more pertinent during the post-liberalization period as compared to that in the pre-liberalization era (Majumdar & Bhattacharjee, 2010). Since 1950, the world was experiencing phenomenal growth in the international trade which further started growing exponentially in the 1970s and continued over the last few decades. With the increase in the international trade among the member countries of the world the investment avenues have also amplified remarkably. With the passage of time, economies of the world are now very much interlinked and interconnected. Therefore, the wave of globalization can affect each and every country since we are living in a global village. Though some initiatives were taken in India in implementing outward-looking economic policies in the mid-80s, the wave of globalization was truly magnified during and after 1991. As a result, emerging market economies such as India gradually became the hotspot investment zone for industrialized and developed countries of the world besides China (Hosseini et al., 2011; Wong et al., 2005). As a corollary, the foreign portfolio investment (FPI) and foreign direct investment (FDI) have also stepped up manifold in the globe (Goldstein, 1995; Wong et al. 2005). Since then India has been not only experiencing the divergent economic opportunities but also has become exposed to all possible macroeconomic threats.

1.5.1   Economic Growth

Economic growth is the fundamental factor which determines the fate of the firms in any economy. Economic growth basically stipulates the growing market demand of goods and services in an economy. If the economic condition is good and there is adequate purchasing power in the hands of the people, there will be greater demand of goods and services. In order to meet such demand more and more production activities will take place, existing business will expand and new business will come up. Such enhanced demand will further increase the level of the income and with newer job opportunities being created there will be multiplicative effect on the economy resulting in a virtuous cycle.

1.5.2   Exchange Rate

After the collapse of Bretton Woods' system in 1973 there have been remarkable changes in the exchange rate scenario of the world. With the inception of floating exchange rate regime,[12] the international financial transactions have become very complex. Such frequent changes in the exchange rate have made almost all the countries vulnerable to the exchange rate exposure. Exchange rate exposure has a great bearing on the economic growth of a particular country which is indicated by the various economic growth indicators. Solnik (1987), Soenen and Hennigar

---

[12] Under floating exchange rate mechanism the exchange rate changes frequently due to the interplay of the demand and supply situations of foreign currency.

(1988), Ma and Kao (1990), Mukherjee and Naka (1995), Granger, Huang and Yang (2000) and Abdalla and Murinde (1997) postulated that changes in exchange rate levels affect the financial performance of the firms and consequently country's stock market. Ma and Kao (1990) and Mukherjee and Naka (1995) suggested that a currency depreciation will have a favourable impact on export-orientated firms. Devaluation of domestic currency against the foreign currency can have significant impact on the balance of payments position of a country. Though India is under managed floating rate system, the exchange rate is a critical factor as far as the Indian firm performance, stock market and economic growth as a whole are concerned.

1.5.3   Foreign Investment

The extent of FDI and FPI flows into an economy is determined by a host of factors, such as economic growth prospects, inflation, political risk, etc., and such infusion of foreign funds has significant impact on the stock market and overall economic growth. It is expected that the more the inflow of foreign funds, better is the prospects of the economy. Flow of foreign funds in the form of FDI and FPI has notable favourable ramifications on the stock market of a country (Clark & Berko, 1997; Froot et al., 2001). This economic rationale can explain why each and every country is making effort in alluring more funds from the foreign countries.

1.5.4   Inflation

The level of price in an economy has important reverberations on the firm-level efficiency and financial performance. An increase in the price level enhances the cost of production which has a negative impact on the overall operating efficiency, profitability and consequently on share prices of the firm operating in an economy (Apergis & Eleftheriou, 2002; Boyd et al., 2001; Hosseini et al., 2011; Omran & Pointon, 2001). On other hand, a change in the price level influences the prevailing exchange rate of the economy through changes in the purchasing power of the people of the country, which has far-reaching implications on the export and import of that country, industrial production, and ultimately the economic growth. If the output prices rise in the same proportion then the effect of rise in the factor prices gets neutralized. However, Defina

(1991) advocated that during an inflationary situation, the output price does not normally rise in the same proportion and in the same tempo. Moreover, inflation also affects the stock market through the output link as propagated by Fama (1981). Unexpected inflation may also directly affect the stock market negatively through unanticipated innovations in the price level. Inflation uncertainty generally influences the discount rate which ultimately decreases the present value of future corporate cash flows (Malkiel, 1982).

1.5.5   Money Supply and Rate of Interest

Similarly, the extent of money supply and interest rate prevailing in a country has profound effect on the performance of the firms belonging to different industries and the economic growth of the country. The Reserve Bank of India controls the money supply by the way of changing the interest rates and other forms of monetary policy. Such a change in the interest rate affects the perception of the domestic as well as foreign institutional investors and that is reflected in the volatility of the stock market indices. A change in the interest rate has its microeconomic implications on the financing cost of the firms operating in a country and consequently the macroeconomic indicators of such as industrial production and Gross Domestic Product (GDP) get influenced. Increase in the interest rate results in enhanced cost of borrowings of the firm which negatively affects the profitability of the firms. Similarly increased interest rate induces more savings in the economy for which demand in the economy gets affected. Thus the money supply has a dynamic impact on the firms' operating performance and the equity prices (Lastrapes & Selgin, 1995). The appreciation of the rupee value leads to an increase in reserves, money supply and decrease in interest rates (Wilson, 1994).

1.5.6   Oil Price

Oil prices in the international market exacerbate a great influence on the economy of a country. As energy prices surge, production and input costs will generally soar and firm gross profit as well as cash flows will tail off. This perceived risk will further erode the investors' confidence which will incite them to search for alternative investments (Hondroyiannis & Papapetrou, 2001). A hike in the oil price definitely augments the cost of production of the firms, creates inflationary pressure in the economy and generates an imbalance in the balance of payment.[13] If there is an increase in the international oil price, the cost of production of the firms steps up which results in reduction in the earnings of the firm. Besides hike in the oil price also prompts devaluation of the home currency and consequently, import-oriented domestic firms stand to lose due to increased cost and exchange risk exposure while the export-oriented firms will be better off.

1.5.7   *Stock Market Integration*

In an environment of economic integration, stock market operation of a country or more precisely the volatility in the indices of the various Indian stock market indicators can be largely explained by the volatility of the economic growth prospects of various international zones such as Euro Zone, European Union, etc. The international stock market volatility, new developments in the international market, news impending from abroad about the economic policy, etc., can be reflected in the behaviour of stock market indices (Choudhry, 1997; John, 1993). Recent deregulation and liberalization of different markets, improvement and development of communications technology, innovations in financial products and services, increase in the international activities of multinational corporations are the major causes of financial integration among different economies (Jeon & Chiang, 1991). In recent times, the possibility of 'tapering of quantitative easing' policy of the United States and growth prospects of Euro zone have led to the withdrawal of huge amount of FPI from Indian stock market, which has caused a sudden down surge in the Sensex and Nifty. The situation has become vulnerable in the face of volatility in the exchange rate of country, which can be considered as a reflection of poor macroeconomic fundamentals like huge deficit in current account and low foreign exchange reserve of the country. Prior to that during 2008–2009, the US sub-prime crisis affected the economy of almost each and every country of the world including India mirroring the integration of Indian stock market.

---

[13] The international oil demand is huge but the production is controlled by OPEC countries which are again subject to international political diplomacy among the countries of the world.

1.5.8   Economic Policy

In the context of political economy, economic policy of a sovereign country is said to be the manifestation of the philosophy of the political party which comes in power with mandate. Political risk, rule of law, governance system, level of corruption, stability of the Government, socio-economic situation, policy uncertainty, etc., play a crucial role in determining the financial performance of the firms operating in different sub-sectors of the industry as well as the investment potentiality in an economy. In fact, each and every MNC or global company, before making investments in any foreign country assesses the political risk. The countries with higher political risk have less chance of getting foreign fund flows. Moreover, empirical evidences clearly indicate the adverse implications of economic policy-related uncertainty on the stock prices (Antonakakis et al., 2013; Arouri & Roubaud, 2016; Ko & Lee, 2015).

1.6   SELECTION OF SAMPLE FIRMS

For the purpose of analysing the determinants of the firm-level efficiency and profitability of the Indian manufacturing firms, the firm-level data for the period of study 1999–2000 to 2013–2014 were collected from the Capitaline Corporate Database published by Capital Market Publishers Private Ltd. Mumbai, India.[14] In the present study only the Indian manufacturing sector as per National Industry Classification, 2008[15] has been concentrated upon. In order to perform the firm-level analysis, for identifying the list of the different sub-sectors within the broad Indian manufacturing industry, Bombay Stock Exchange (BSE) Manufacturing index[16] obtained from the official website of Asia Index Private Limited[17] was used.

[14] https://www.capitaline.com.

[15] http://mospi.nic.in/sites/default/files/6ec_dirEst/ec6_nic_2008_code.html.

[16] http://www.asiaindex.co.in/indices/equity/sp-bse-india-manufacturing-index#; https://us.spindices.com/documents/methodologies/methodology-sp-bse-thematic-ind ices.pdf.

[17] Asia Index Pvt. Ltd is a partnership between S&P Dow Jones Indices LLC and Bombay Stock Exchange Ltd.

Table 1.1 Sample companies across different sectors belonging to Indian manufacturing industry

BSE Sector	BSE Industry group	BSE Industry sub-group	Population size[18]	Sample size
Basic materials	Steel	Iron and steel and intermediary products	108 (8.75%)	45 (8.74%)
	Cement	Cement and cement products	48 (3.89%)	22 (4.27%)
	Chemical	Commodity and speciality chemical	183 (14.83%)	80 (15.53%)
Consumer discretionary goods and services	Textiles, apparels and accessories	Textile	280 (22.69%)	99 (19.22%)
	Auto components	Auto parts and equipment	101 (8.18%)	48 (9.32%)
Health care	Pharmaceuticals and biotechnology	Pharmaceuticals and biotechnology	165 (13.37%)	68 (13.20%)
Industrials	Electrical equipment	Heavy and other electrical equipment and products	88 (7.13%)	38 (7.38%)
	Construction and engineering	Construction and engineering	103 (8.35%)	47 (9.13%)
	Industrial machinery	Industrial machinery	97 (7.86%)	43 (8.35%)
Fast moving consumer goods	Food products	Packaged and other food products	61 (4.94%)	25 (4.85%)
Total			1234 (100%)	515 (100%)

Source Author's own compilation

At the first step, BSE Sectors were selected purposively, consequently BSE Industry group and sub-group were also chosen purposively from the BSE Manufacturing index[19] construction methodology. Once the industry sub-groups were selected, the lists of the firms from different sub-groups were collected from the official website[20] of BSE, Mumbai,

---

[18] The population size is based on the list of the listed companies under different Industry Sub-Group as on 09/02/2016 as downloaded from BSE website.

[19] http://www.asiaindex.co.in/indices/equity/sp-bse-india-manufacturing-index#; https://us.spindices.com/documents/methodologies/methodology-sp-bse-thematic-ind ices.pdf.

[20] https://www.bseindia.com/corporates/List_Scrips.aspx?expandable=1.

India. Finally, random sampling technique was used to select the companies to avoid any form of selection bias. Proportional sampling method was used in selecting representative samples by making the selection proportionately from each of the sub-groups. Inclusion criteria at the firm level were the availability of the firm-specific data for the period of 15 years from 1999–2000 to 2013–2014. Table 1.1 shows the selection process of the sample companies and the sectoral indices for the purpose of the study.

However, considering the number of the firms which were finally available as per the inclusion criteria, the proportion of the sample in each of the industry sub-groups could not be strictly maintained. Still, the spirit of the proportional sampling method could be retained while determining the final number of the firms from each industry sub-groups. A total number of 515 (41.73%) companies are finally considered for final analysis.

1.7   INNOVATIVENESS OF THE BOOK

The book is expected to make some contribution to the following issues:

The book is of great importance in appraising the level of the efficiency of the firms and the important firm-specific and macroeconomic factors affecting such efficiency so as to enable the managers to make prudent managerial decisions in more informed way.

The book seeks to unearth the different microeconomic and macroeconomic factors affecting the financial performance of the firms which are critical to the managers in executing the operating activities effectively.

The book is also helpful in investigating the crucial macroeconomic variables affecting the sector-specific stock market indices which will enable the existing and prospective investors to make their investment decisions prudently.

Further, the book also makes a modest and unique effort to shed light on the effect of economic policy uncertainty on the sectoral manufacturing stock indices. With the availability of this kind of prior information the global investors will be in a better position to make their investment decisions appositely.

CHAPTER 2

Manufacturing Policies in India: A Disaggregated Analysis

Abstract The industrial policy resolutions are the important policy documents which mandate the strategies adopted by the Government towards the industry. These strategies are at the heart of the overall industrial development and growth of any country. This chapter makes a holistic effort to highlight the various industrial policy resolutions and manufacturing sector-specific policies adopted by the Government of India since independence to foster growth and development. The growth of manufacturing sector during the different plan periods and under alternative industrial policy regimes has also been analysed in this chapter. Efforts were also made to shed some light on the strength of the manufacturing sector in absorbing the shocks emanating from the various macroeconomic crises at different points in time.

Keywords Industrial policy resolutions · Manufacturing · Growth · Crisis · Development

2.1 INTRODUCTION

The manufacturing sector is generally considered as the steering force for creating adequate employment opportunity, reducing regional imbalances and accelerating as well as sustaining the economic growth of a

19

S. K. Maji et al., *Indian Manufacturing Sector in Post-Reform Period*, https://doi.org/10.1007/978-981-19-2666-2_2

country. If India, a densely populated country, wants to establish itself as a responsible global player, the manufacturing sector has to be strengthened to enhance job opportunities to tackle the problem of unemployment (Rajan, 2006b). In realizing the dream of establishing the 'socialistic pattern of the society' since independence, Central Public Sector Enterprises (CPSEs) were set up by the Government of India (GOI) and thereby leaving a very narrow space for the private entrepreneurs to operate. In the post-war period, regulated vis-à-vis planned economy and control over the industries were thought to be the way out for getting rid of the economic backward situation across the globe (Aghion et al., 2006). But with the passage of time the GOI realized that the CPSEs were not capable enough to meet the social objectives that the Government wanted to address. Accordingly, in the next few Industrial Policy Resolutions (IPRs) (of 1948 and 1956) opportunity was delivered to the private sector to provide a level playing field. The IPRs are the important policy documents which mandate the strategies adopted by the Government towards the industry. These strategies will ultimately shape the economic growth of any country. In the socio-economic context of India, the substance of IPRs cannot be undermined. Even though these policy resolutions helped the development of the industry, excessive regulatory interferences (red tapes, protocols, cap on foreign investment, adverse tax regime and Government control) restricted the economy in achieving the anticipated growth rate. Much of the Government regulations were done away in the first phase of globalization in the late 1980s, and later on abolition of the MRTP Act, FERA Act in the New Economic Policy was promulgated on 24 July 1991.

In this backdrop, the Indian economy has witnessed a regime of extreme form of Government control and regulation and later on experienced a liberalized environment over the period of time. This chapter sheds some light on the historical overview of the transition from a regulated environment to a free market economy and the implications of such a transition on the growth of manufacturing sector in India. Explicitly, this chapter probes the growth of manufacturing industry during the different plan periods and under alternative industrial policy regimes. Besides, the chapter recognizes the strength of our economy and manufacturing sector in absorbing the macroeconomic shock by examining the impact of different crises on the growth of manufacturing industry.

2.2 Industrial Policy—An Overview

The period of industrial policy decisions can broadly be divided into two episodes: (i) Period of regulation (1947–1980) and (ii) Period of deregulation (post-1980) (Fig. 2.1).

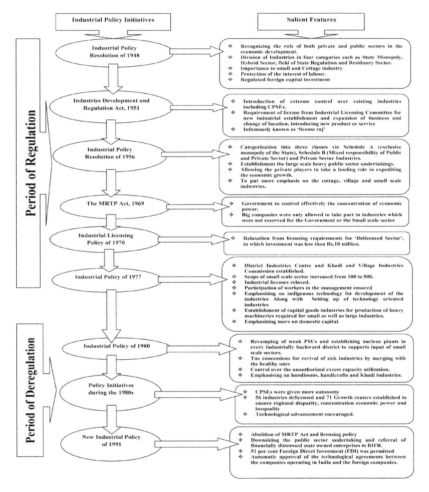

Fig. 2.1 Industrial policy initiatives undertaken from 1947 to 1991 (*Source* Author's own representation)

2.2.1   Period of Regulation (1947–1980)

On gaining independence India walked into the path to frame its industrial policies: first Industrial Policy in 1948 and later on in 1956. These central planning and regulation policies were designed with an objective to control and regulate the private sector, emphasizing on the state owned enterprises, protecting the labour forces and stimulating the small-scale and cottage industries. The introduction of industrial licensing (vide Industries Development and Regulation Act, 1951) was primarily aimed at reducing external reliance by achieving self-sufficiency; diluting the possibility of concentration of economic power in the hands of few private entrepreneurs; reducing the inequality of income and wealth; and ensuring regional balance (Kochhar et al., 2006; Soo, 2006). Yet, the industrial performance till 1970 was observed to be moderate in such a regulated environment and successively followed by a serious decline in the 1970s and 1980s (Bosworth et al., 2007; Chari, 2007). Even Total Factor Productivity (TFP) during the above periods grew negatively (Chari, 2007).

2.2.2   Period of Deregulation (1980 onwards)

Experiences of the slow and fragile rate of industrial growth in the regulation regime paved the way towards a transition to a deregulated liberalized environment (rather a 'pro-market' environment). In the first phase of liberalization, reform measures were initiated by dismantling the requirement of industrial licensing (i.e. de-licensing) for 25 broad industry groups for the purpose of capacity enhancement and product diversification along with reduction of import tariff (Kochhar et al., 2006; Soo, 2006). These liberalization initiatives helped in achieving increased productivity and economies of scale by the introduction of new technology as generated by foreign fund inflow, indigenous R&D and technology embodied in imported goods (Fujita, 1994). The pace of reform measures was intensified with the implementation of 'pro-market' reform initiatives undertaken by the Indian Government in July 1991 (Rodrik & Subramanian, 2005). In addition to the abolition of licensing requirements, reform measures included removal of non-tariff restrictions on the imports of intermediate and capital goods, downsizing the public sector undertaking, disinvestment of some state owned enterprises, allowing Foreign Direct Investment (FDI) in high priority capital intensive and Indian trading companies and approval of the foreign technological agreements (Gupta et al., 2008; Mitra & Ural, 2008). Only a very few industries which are of national and strategic importance were kept under strict regulation. Implications of such liberalization measures got reflected in the growth rate of the economy (Panagariya, 2004b; Soo, 2008) along with a remarkable improvement in the productivity growth in the service sector (Bosworth et al., 2007; Kotwal et al., 2011).

2.3 MANUFACTURING SECTOR-SPECIFIC POLICY INITIATIVES

In order to reinforce the different sectors within the manufacturing industry, to reduce dependence on the import and above all for generating adequate employment opportunities, various manufacturing sub-sector-specific policies were taken up from time to time. For instance, understanding the important role of the textile industry to the national economy and to boost the strength already acquired by this sector vide Textile Policy of 1985, the National Textile Policy, 2000[1] was taken up by the Ministry of Textiles, GOI. Although a number of comprehensive manufacturing sub-sector-specific industrial policies were taken at different points of time, the share of manufacturing sector to the GDP maintained status-quo position at 15% to 16% since 1980 which was considerably lower than that in other emerging Asian economies. For instance, the share of manufacturing sector to the GDP during this period was nearly 30% in China, 36% in Thailand and 31% in South Korea.[2] Therefore, this was the high time to take broader and more far-reaching manufacturing policy so as to enhance the contribution of this sector to the GDP as well as to create huge employment opportunity. In this direction the National Manufacturing Policy, 2011 was undertaken by the Department of Industrial Policy and Promotion under the then Ministry of Industry and Commerce,[3] GOI on 4 November 2011

---

[1] Retrieved from http://texmin.nic.in/sites/default/files/policy_2000.pdf.

[2] *Point of view, National Manufacturing Policy* (2012) by PWC accessed from: https://www.pwc.in/assets/pdfs/industries/industrial-manufacturing/national-man ufacturing-policy-pov.pdf.

[3] https://dipp.gov.in/sites/default/files/po-ann4.pdf.

with the six basic objectives such as increasing the share of the manufacturing to GDP to 25% by 2022, generating 100 million jobs by 2022, skill development of youth, increasing technological depth within the manufacturing sector, enhancing the global competitiveness of manufacturing sector and promoting green manufacturing. Reckoning the fact that the Electronics industry is the largest and fastest growing industry in the Indian manufacturing sector and in tune with other manufacturing sub-sector-specific policies, the National Policy on Electronics[4] was taken up on 19 November 2012 by the Ministry of Communications and Information Technology, GOI with the basic objective of revamping the electronics sub-sector and its export in an ecosystem of innovation. In the wake of the bursting of so-called emerging economy bubble at the end of 2013 and to recover from a very low rate of economic growth. 'Make in India' initiative was also launched in September 2014 to rejuvenate the Indian manufacturing industry and the economy as a whole. Under 'Make in India' initiative, various pro-manufacturing industry policies such as 'Invest India',[5] 'Start-up India', Development of Industrial Corridors, 'Skill India', opening up of FDI in defence, railways and construction, etc., were instituted. Capital Goods (CG) sector is considered as the cornerstone of the growth of the overall manufacturing industry as this sector produces industrial machineries. Therefore, acknowledging its critical role in the growth of the manufacturing sector, a comprehensive policy on Capital Goods sub-sector was taken up in 2016. The key features of the different manufacturing sector-specific policies are presented in Fig. 2.2.

Additionally, also to revamp the policies which were already in existence and to promote other industries, new industrial policies focusing based on the requirement of the different sub-sectors, such as Pharmaceutical Policy, 2017; National Policy on Electronics, 2018 and National Auto Policy, 2018 have been drafted.

---

[4] Retrieved from http://meity.gov.in/writereaddata/files/NPE_Notification.pdf.

[5] Invest India is the national investment promotion and facilitation agency of India which was established as non-profit venture under DIPP, Ministry of Commerce and Industry, GOI.

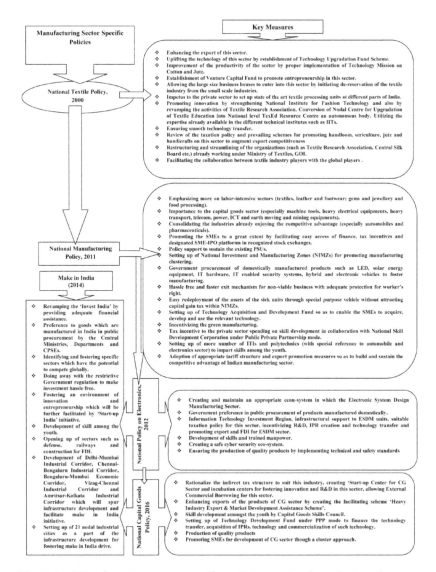

Fig. 2.2 Manufacturing sector-specific policies undertaken during the post-reform period (*Source* Author's own representation)

Indian economy is essentially a mixed economy. Though initially the economy was characterized by central planning, a gradual opening up of the economy to the private players took place. After independence, in order to achieve multiple socio-economic objectives the Planning Commission was established in 1950 which was primarily responsible for framing policies so that economic growth can be fostered, standard of living can be improved, effective utilization of the resources can be made, production can be increased, regional inequality can be removed and employment opportunity can be augmented (Planning Commission, New Delhi). Although the establishment of Planning Commission is considered as one of the most important events in the economic history of India, the adoption of the planning to boost economic development started before the independence in 1944 with the publication of the Bombay Plan[6] (Nayar, 1971). The Bombay Plan projected the investment of Rs.100 billion over a period of 15 years with the prime objective to double the per capita income and to foster heavy industrialization (Nayar, 1971). Accordingly the first five year plan was developed to be achieved for the period 1951 to 1956. The last five year plan was designed for the period 2012 to 2017. The Commission was dissolved in 2015 and since then the task of policy design was handed over to the Niti Ayog. During the several plan periods different socio-economic issues such as health, education, livelihood, unemployment and economic growth were targeted. In a developing country like India, Central Planning played a great role in meeting different socio-economic objectives (Dandekar, 1994; Rudra, 1985).

[6] 'Bombay Plan' is considered to be the first of its kind 15 year plan which provided a blueprint of the objectives that should be attained through economic planning and the pathway of economic development in India (Lokanathan, 1994). Although it was prepared by a group of renowned business personalities (such as J.R.D. Tata, G.D. Birla, Kasturbhai Lalbhai, P. Thakurdas, Sir Ardeshir Dalal, Lala Shriram, D. Shrof, John Matha and others) in 1944, it got wide popularity and recognition across business community including FICCI and the then British Government. In fact the first five year plan was found to be in line with the Bombay Plan (Sanyal, 2011).

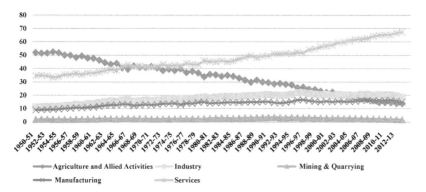

Legend: Agriculture and Allied Activities — Industry — Mining & Quarrying — Manufacturing — Services

Fig. 2.3 Changing contribution of different sectors in GDP (*Source* Author's own representation based on National Accounts Statistics [NAS] data)

2.4   CHANGING LANDSCAPE OF INDUSTRIAL DEVELOPMENT IN INDIA

2.4.1   *Contribution of Industry in GDP*

In the last 15 years, Indian economy is characterized by service-led growth. The sectoral contribution of the GDP[7] (as shown in Fig. 2.3) suggests the following broad trend: a reduction in the contribution of agriculture to the GDP, a steady contribution of the mining and quarrying sector to the GDP, an increase in the share of industry (and particularly that of manufacturing sector) in the GDP and a phenomenal growth of the share of service sector in the Indian GDP.

Figure 2.4 presents the Year on Year (YoY) growth in the GDP, industry, manufacturing and service sectors of India. The YoY growth rate is computed using the following formula: $\frac{(Current\ Year\ Value - Previous\ Year\ Value)}{Previous\ Year\ Value} \times 100$. However, it is apparent that the rate of growth of GDP was low till the 1980s, and even it was observed to be negative in 1957–1958, 1965–1966 and 1979–1980. A

---

[7] The data on GDP of the economy, GDP of the different sectors of the economy such as agriculture and allied activities, manufacturing, mining and quarrying, industry and services were gathered from different issues of Economic Survey, RBI Handbook of Statistics on Indian Economy and Economic and Political Weekly Research Foundation India Time Series Database for the period from 1950–1951 to 2013–2014.

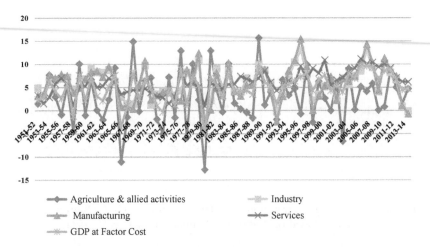

Fig. 2.4 Sectoral year on year growth of GDP, industry, manufacturing and services (*Source* Author's own representation based on NAS data)

distinct improvement in the GDP growth along with industry, manufacturing and service sectors is first noticeable in the late 1980s and later on during 1990–1991. The adaptation of the pro-market economic reform measures undertaken in the 1980s and 1990s facilitated in achieving a noteworthy growth of the industrial sector, especially the manufacturing sector. Service sector registered a consistent positive YoY growth across alternative policy regimes. The experience of the economic crisis in 1965–1966, 1979–1980, 1991–1992 (exchange rate crisis), 1997–1998 (East Asian crisis) and 2008–2009 (financial crisis) had far-reaching implications on the growth prospects of GDP, industry and manufacturing sector in a negative way. Interestingly, the service sector growth was not affected even in times of crisis rather this sector showed its resilience in absorbing the shocks of such crises.

2.4.2   GDP Growth Rate of Manufacturing Sector

In Fig. 2.5 an effort has been made to project the YoY growth of the Indian manufacturing sector in general and registered and unregistered segments in particular. It is apparent from the graphical representation as shown in Fig. 2.5 that the overall growth of the Indian manufacturing

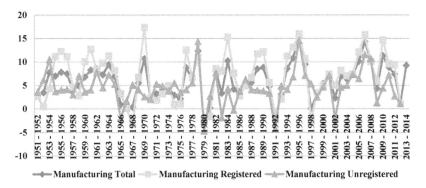

Fig. 2.5 Year on year growth of GDP of manufacturing (Registered and Unregistered) (*Source* Author's own representation based on NAS data)

sector was steady but in 1967–1968 and 1982–1983 it declined significantly. In the wake of East Asian crisis during 1997–1998 and during the economic meltdown of 2008–2009, the growth of overall manufacturing sector declined remarkably. In a similar way the registered and unregistered manufacturing sector growth also dwindled steeply in the same years. But the reduction of the growth rates of the unregistered manufacturing sector was more than that of the registered manufacturing sector in the same periods.

Table 2.1 presents a plan period wise estimation of the economic growth of India in general and the growth of registered and unregistered manufacturing sectors in particular.[8] The growth experiences of the first four plan periods were not at all satisfactory in the manufacturing sector as well as in the economy. A change in the trajectory of growth was observed since the 5th plan period. The GDP growth of the economy registered at 6.61% whereas the manufacturing sector touched double

---

[8] In estimating the rate of growth of manufacturing sector, the following empirical specification of the semi-log model was used.

$$lny_t = \alpha + \beta x_t,$$

where lny_t is the natutral logarithm of the variable, x_t is the time period $= 1, 2, \ldots \ldots n$.

Table 2.1   Plan period wise estimation of growth rate of GDP and manufacturing sector

Plan period	Year	GDP growth rate			
		Economy	Manufacturing		
			Total	Registered	Unregistered
1st plan	1951–1956	4.09[a]	6.46[a]	6.86[a]	6.10[a]
2nd plan	1956–1961	3.97[a]	5.77[a]	7.05[a]	4.50[a]
3rd plan	1961–1966	3.35[b]	6.31[a]	8.10[a]	4.14[a]
4th plan	1969–1974	2.07[b]	3.45[a]	2.91[a]	4.14[a]
5th plan	1974–1979	5.33[a]	7.08[a]	7.75[a]	6.19[a]
6th plan	1980–1985	5.00[a]	6.29[a]	9.71[a]	2.11
7th plan	1985–1990	5.98[a]	6.85[a]	8.51[a]	4.35[a]
8th plan	1992–1997	6.61[a]	10.86[a]	12.28[a]	8.25[a]
9th plan	1997–2002	5.87[a]	4.75[a]	5.29[a]	3.49[b]
10th plan	2002–2007	8.12[a]	8.93[a]	9.86[a]	7.18[a]
11th plan	2007–2012	7.63[a]	8.04[a]	9.78[a]	4.19[a]
Whole period		4.66[a]	5.45[a]	6.35[a]	4.17[a]

Source Author's calculation based on NAS data
Note a and b are statistically significant at 1% and 5%, respectively

digit growth rate for the first time in the 8th plan period. On account of the East Asian Crisis, 1997, the GDP growth rate and the growth rate of the manufacturing sector lessened considerably in the 9th plan period. Another setback in the growth trajectory appeared in the global financial crisis 2008–2009, which affected the growth rate of the economy as well as the growth of manufacturing sector (both registered and unregistered).

The economic reforms in India came about in three phases: debt-driven reforms during the 1980s (1985–1988), crisis-induced reforms during 1991 (1991–1993) and trade-driven reforms from 1998 to 2005 (Sinha, 2019). Table 2.2 exhibits the growth rate of the GDP of the economy and that of the manufacturing sector during alternative liberalization periods. Recognizing the early phase of debt-driven liberalization measures in the late 1980s (Ahluwalia, 2002; Sinha, 2019), the study period is divided into Pre-liberalization period (1971–1972 to 1987–1988) and Post-liberalization period (1988–1989 to 1992–1993). Even if the growth rate of the GDP as a whole stepped up as an outcome of the adaptation of the liberalization measures, registered and unregistered firms in the manufacturing sector and the manufacturing sector in

Table 2.2 Growth rate of GDP and manufacturing sector in pre- and post-reform periods

Reform	Period	GDP growth rate			
		Economy	Manufacturing		
		Total	Total	Registered	Unregistered
Early reform (1985–1988)	Pre (1971–1972 to 1987–1988)	3.98[a]	4.73[a]	5.60[a]	3.68[a]
	Post (1988–1989 to 1992–1993)	4.21[a]	2.97[a]	3.97[a]	1.37[a]
First generation reform (1991–1993)	Pre (1988–1989 to 1992–1993)				
	Post (1993–1994 to 2004–2005[$])	5.92[a]	5.74[a]	6.13[a]	4.95[a]
Second generation reform (1998–2005)	Pre (1993–1994 to 2004–2005[$])				
	Post (2005–2006 to 2013–2014[$])	7.21[a]	7.66[a]	9.22[a]	5.15[a]

Source Author's calculation based on NAS data
Notes a are statistically significant at 1%;
$ The growth rate for registered and unregistered manufacturing were computed for the period from 1992–1993 to 2012–2013 as in the new NAS series with base 2011–2012, such a data for registered and unregistered manufacturing was absent

aggregate exhibited a decline in growth during the first phase of debt-driven post-liberalization period. It proves that the debt induced policy reforms during 1985–1988 failed to exert any positive effect on the growth of the manufacturing sector which corroborates the argument that the early phase of reforms measures were fragile and unsustainable in nature (Panagariya, 2004a).

First generation reform measures that were taken up during 1991–1992 were initiated as a sequel to the foreign exchange crisis in 1991 under the guidelines of IMF and World Bank. The reform measures initiated to tackle the crisis were pro-market in nature and empowered the Indian economy to grow at a rapid pace along with the manufacturing sector (both registered and unregistered). As a matter of fact, the liberalization measures created a conducive environment so as to scale up the manufacturing sector in response to strategic internationalization.

Likewise, the third phase of trade-induced liberalization measures undertaken during 1998–2005 also assisted the Indian manufacturing sector (including both registered and unregistered) and the overall economy as a whole to grow much faster during the post-reform regime as compared to the pre-reform era. Hence, irrespective of the time period, nature and causes of the liberalization measures, the overall effect of the liberalizations initiatives were found to be fruit-bearing for the Indian economy at large.

The manufacturing growth rates experienced a sharp descend following the exchange rate crisis of 1991, East Asian crisis of 1997 and the financial crisis of 2008–2009. Even if the crisis exhibited heterogeneous effect on the prospects of manufacturing sector, recovery of growth rate of the manufacturing sector in the post-crisis period signals the success of the countercyclical policy adopted by the Government to combat such a crisis. The revival of the growth rate after an exchange rate crisis also indicates the effectiveness of the first generation reform measures undertaken by the Government. The effect of the East Asian crisis of 1997 was substantial on the manufacturing sector. Even so, the growth rates of GDP declined marginally by and large because of the noteworthy contribution of service sector to the GDP in 1997–1998 (Table 2.3).

Similarly, the resilience of the Indian economy can also be understood if a comparison of the growth rates is made in between the Pre-financial crisis period (2003–2004 to 2007–2008) and Post-financial crisis period (2009–2010 to 2013–2014). The growth rate of GDP was approximately 9% which was much higher than the so-called Hindu rate of growth. In the same way the growth rates of the manufacturing sector in aggregate, registered manufacturing sector and unregistered manufacturing sector were 10.28%, 11.16% and 8.61%, respectively, during pre-financial crisis period. The growth rate of the GDP declined significantly from 8.60% to 5.89% during the post-financial crisis period. Similarly the growth rate of the manufacturing sector, the registered manufacturing sector and the unregistered manufacturing sector also contracted sharply to 5.74%, 6.69% and 3.51%, respectively, from the earlier period. This situation is also reflected in Fig. 2.5 which reveals that the growth rate declined steadily during the post-crisis period with special reference to the Indian manufacturing sector. Thus, the experience of the financial crisis (2008–2009) demonstrated that it was the worst hit to the

Table 2.3 Growth rate of GDP and manufacturing sector in pre- and post-crisis periods

Period	GDP growth rate			
	Economy	Manufacturing		
		Total	Registered	Unregistered
Pre-Exchange Rate crisis period (1986–1987 to 1990–1991)	6.41[a]	7.00[a]	9.15[a]	3.76[a]
Post- Exchange Rate crisis period (1992–1993 to 1996–1997)	6.61[a]	10.86[a]	12.28[a]	8.24[a]
Pre-Asian crisis period(1992–1993 to 1996–1997)	6.61[a]	10.86[a]	12.28[a]	8.24[a]
Post-Asian crisis period (1998–1999 to 2002–2003)	5.09[a]	5.16[a]	6.18[a]	3.20[b]
Pre-2008–2009 financial crisis period (2003–2004 to 2007–2008)	8.60[a]	10.28[a]	11.16[a]	8.61[a]
Post-2008–2009 financial crisis period (2009–2010 to 2013–2014[#])	5.89[a]	5.95[a]	6.69[b]	3.51

Source Author's calculation based on NAS data
Notes a and b are statistically significant at 1% and 5%, respectively;
The growth rate for registered and unregistered manufacturing were computed for the period from 1992–1993 to 2012–2013 as in the new NAS series with base 2011–2012, such a data for registered and unregistered manufacturing was absent

Indian economy. Hence, the 'decoupling theory[9]' did not work properly for India as against the popular expectations (Subbarao, 2009; Willett, Liang & Zhang, 2011).

2.4.3 Gross Fixed Capital Formation (GFCF) in Manufacturing Sector

Capital stock embraces all durable, reproducible, tangible, fixed goods that are used in the production of other goods and services and that endures for more than the accounting period (Hooley, 1967). It includes residential and non-residential structures, transport equipment, and machinery and other equipment but does not include non-reproducible

[9] Under 'decoupling theory' it is believed that growth in emerging Asian economies is backed by the internal demand and as such free from the contagion impact of the crisis (Siddiqui, 2009).

assets such as natural forests, land and mineral deposits, intangible assets such as patents, software and property rights, inventories of final products and intermediate goods and military.

Capital stock of a nation gets accumulated over the years as a result of annual investments made by the corporate sector and the Government in different fixed assets (Van der Eng, 2009). The productive use of these assets contributes towards the generation of output and income in the economy. The capital stock is used in more than one accounting period in future production (Nomura, 2005). Thus the formation of capital is of special significance in the industrial development of any country.[10] This study examines the growth of capital formation in the manufacturing sector in different plan periods.

The Indian manufacturing sector registered a low formation of capital in the first two plan periods (as shown in Table 2.4). A significant improvement in capital formation is noticed in the 3rd, 5th, 7th and 11th plan periods. As expected, the economic crisis followed by the low level savings and foreign investments resulted in the fall of capital formation in the manufacturing sector. Such a negative growth in the capital forma-tion (in both registered and unregistered sectors) is experienced during the Asian Crisis and Sub-prime crisis period. The average rate of growth of GFCF of the unregistered manufacturing sector (9.76%) was higher as compared to that in the manufacturing sector as a whole (7.27%).

2.4.4   Trend of Capital–Output Ratio of Manufacturing Sector

Capital–Output Ratio (COR) or Capital Intensity (CI) underscores the capital required per unit of output, and can be measured as a ratio of GFCF to the Value of Output (Gupta, 2002). COR is a yardstick of the rate of growth that can be achieved given a level of investment in an economy or in a way the amount of savings required to attain a given level of growth (Ghosh, 1956). An increase of COR posits the starting of economic development of an economy (Rostow, 1990). The data on the gross value of output and gross fixed capital formation in the manu-facturing sector were collected from the Annual Survey of Industries.

---

[10] Higher the capital formation and better the use, higher will be the economic devel-opment of any country. Low rate of savings in a country and limited foreign direct investments results in low level of capital formation which adversely affects the level of economic development of a country (Van der Eng, 2009).

Table 2.4 Growth rate of gross fixed capital formation of manufacturing sector in different plan periods

Plan Period	Year	GFCF Growth Rate		
		Manufacturing		
		Total	Registered	Unregistered
1st plan	1951–1956	0.49	−2.12	55.94[b]
2nd plan	1956–1961	6.01	7.42	−11.24
3rd plan	1961–1966	15.52[a]	15.82[a]	11.99
4th plan	1969–1974	0.69	0.25	2.23
5th plan	1974–1979	6.10[a]	6.51[b]	4.88
6th plan	1980–1985	11.29[a]	15.98[a]	-0.61
7th plan	1985–1990	6.20[b]	3.52	12.27
8th plan	1992–1997	18.11[a]	17.09[a]	21.70[a]
9th plan	1997–2002	−8.30[a]	−9.76[a]	−2.46
10th plan	2002–2007	23.83[a]	27.76[a]	11.88
11th plan	2007–2012	3.88	3.21	7.85
Whole period		7.27[a]	6.96[a]	9.76[a]

Source Author's calculation based on NAS data
Note a and b are statistically significant at 1% and 5%, respectively

Such data on these two variables were only available since 1979–1980. Therefore, the analysis of Capital–Output Ratio was carried out during the period 1979–1980 to 2013–2014.

Figure 2.6 shows that the COR remained stable during 1979–1980 to 1991–1992 which reveals that the first phase of liberalization measures did not have any effect on the COR. The significant positive effect was noticed during 1992–1993 and 1993–1994 with falling of the COR following the introduction of the first generation liberalization measures during 1991. Further, during and beyond the 2nd generation of liberalization, the COR was found to be declining barring 1994–1995. An overall declining trend in the COR during the post-liberalization period (especially in the first and second generations of liberalization) implies the improvement in the efficiency of the Indian industries in utilizing their fixed capital in the production of goods and services. Simply put, it stipulates that the fixed capital was used more efficiently in the post-liberalization period due to the advantages of free movement of factors of production, transfer of technology directly or indirectly and promotion of tertiary education (Rajan, 2006b).

Capital Output Ratio

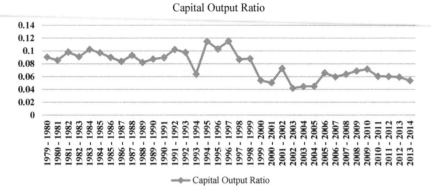

Fig. 2.6   Trend of Capital–Output Ratio (*Source* Author's own representation based on NAS data)

2.5   A Sum Up

The journey of India from being a regulated centrally planned economy to a liberalized economy altered the growth trajectory of the industrial sector as a whole, and the manufacturing sector in particular. A dream of 'democratic socialism' since independence shaped the policy of industrial development by setting up CPSEs (so-called 'temples of modern India'). Still, the excessive control and regulation of industries as well as imposition of industrial licensing yielded a very low rate of growth in the economy. In response, the reform measures were initiated first in the late 1980s and then major set of 'pro-market reforms' were undertaken first in 1991 and secondly during 1998–2005. The analysis of sectoral contribution to the GDP revealed a momentum of growth experience in the industrial sector and especially in the service sector. The manufacturing sector is no exception in exploiting the advantages of liberalization measures. The productivity of the manufacturing sector and the capital formation also improved in the post-liberalization era as compared to the pre-reform period. However, the economic crisis has far-reaching implications on the growth of the manufacturing sector especially in the wake of the East Asian Crisis of 1997 and the Economic Meltdown of 2008.

CHAPTER 3

Factors Affecting Financial Performance of Firms: An Exploration of the Existing Research Works

Abstract This chapter highlights the existing research works carried out in India and abroad by the scholars exploring the microeconomic, macroeconomic and industry-specific factors affecting the firm-level performance. Comprehensive review of the existing literature on the effect of these factors on the efficiency, profitability and stock prices was accomplished. The research gap in the existing literature was identified in this chapter by using Evidence Gap Map. The chapter also outlines the objectives of the study in the perspective of such research gap.

Keywords Manufacturing · Microeconomic factors · Macroeconomic factors · Industry-specific factors · Efficiency · Profitability · Stock price · Evidence gap map

3.1 Introduction

Many empirical research studies have been conducted in India and abroad to assess the impact of the different factors on the financial performance of the firms belonging to the manufacturing sector. By a careful inspection of the extant literature, we have chosen some significant foreign as well as Indian studies for review and subsequently examined these studies in order to ascertain the research gap and also to determine the scope of

S. K. Maji et al., *Indian Manufacturing Sector in Post-Reform Period*, https://doi.org/10.1007/978-981-19-2666-2_3

the present study. While selecting the research studies for review purpose, the issues associated with the effects of the important factors such as macroeconomic factors (like money supply, inflation, exchange rate, index of industrial production), microeconomic factors (like leverage, intellectual capital, size, age, growth, openness of the firm) and other factors (like political risk, Government policy, economic crisis) on the firm efficiency, firm profitability and stock market performance have been taken into account. Evidence gap map technique has been applied at the time of reviewing the selected research studies in India.

3.2   Research Studies in Foreign Countries

3.2.1   Financial Performance Analysis

Measurement of financial performance of a firm is not an easy task. It requires consideration of different factors which are instrumental in determining the financial performance of the firm (Kaplan, 1983). In the existing literature, it is found that there are three most important factors that affect the earning capability of the firm, such as company-specific factors, industry-specific factors and macroeconomic factors. The combined effect of all these three kinds of factors determines the profitability vis-à-vis the value of the firm in a business environment (Gatsi et al., 2016; Hansen & Wernerfelt, 1989).

3.2.1.1   Macroeconomic Factors

It is observed that various important macroeconomic factors, such as growth rate of GDP, real interest rate, inflation, size of the economy, economic openness, economic, political and social globalization, fiscal deficit, growth rate of money supply, financial sector growth, etc., have notable effect on the efficiency and profitability of the firms belonging to the banking sector (Ali et al., 2011; Mongid & Tahir, 2011; Sufian & Habibullah, 2009a, 2009b; Vejzagic & Zarafat, 2014; Vong & Chan, 2009; Zhang & Daly, 2013). A number of studies have attempted to identify the different factors within and beyond the control of the enterprises affecting the earning capability and value of the firms belonging to other industries. Some of the significant studies made on this issue are the studies conducted by Rumelt (1982), Selling and Stickney (1989), Siddharthan et al. (1994), Wagner (1995), Geroski et al. (1997), Peng and Luo (2000), Kakani et al. (2001), Goddard et al. (2005), Bhattacharjee and Han (2010), Burange and Ranadive (2014), Lee (2014), and Gatsi et al. (2016).

3.2.1.2   Microeconomic Factors

The existing literature has identified some microeconomic factors having discernible impact on the financial performance of the firms belonging to different industries especially the manufacturing sector, significant of which are size, age, human resource management, foreign control, openness, firm growth, financial leverage, import cost, short-term liquidity, long-term solvency, efficiency, parent company affiliation, competitive positioning, intensity of technology and capital, efficiency in controlling cost, past profitability, market share, fixed asset turnover ratio, marketing cost to sale ratio, research and development cost to sales ratio, liberalization, export to revenue ratio, import to turnover ratio, deviation of average cost of the firms, managerial remuneration to sales ratio, capital–output ratio, proportion of fixed assets to total assets, efficiency of the management, business risk, employee size, level of competition, separation of the owners from the management, cash flow, tangibility, underwriting risk, reinsurance usage, input cost, profitability of the holding company, operating cost ratio, family ownership, intellectual capital, etc. (Afza & Nazir, 2007; Ahmad et al., 2014; Ahmed et al., 2011; Asimakopoulos et al., 2009; Bhattacharjee & Han, 2010; Deloof, 2003; Eljelly, 2004; Gatsi et al., 2016; Geroski et al., 1997; Goddard et al., 2005; Hansen & Wernerfelt, 1989; Hussain et al., 2012; Kambhampati & Parikh, 2005; Lee, 2014; Lyroudi & Lazaridis, 2000; Majumdar, 1997; McGahan & Porter, 2002; Mehralian et al., 2012; Padachi, 2006; Papadogonas, 2006; Pratheepan, 2014; Pucci et al., 2015; Purohit & Tandon; 2015; Riahi-Belkaoui, 2003; Serrasqueiro & Nunes, 2008; Shin & Soenen, 1998; Spanos et al., 2004; Sur et al., 2014; Voulgaris et al., 2000).

3.2.1.3   Other Factors

There is no doubt that political scenario of a country influences its economic growth to a large extent. In fact, the prosperity or misery of a country's economic fate is largely dependent on its political situation (Bilson et al., 2002). Different political parties belong to different ideological schools and the ideology that the ruling party follows indeed influences the policy decisions taken by the Government. The success and failure of the firms to a considerable degree is dependent on the different industrial policy decisions adopted by the Government (Hillman & Hitt, 1999). An investment involves different risk factors, such as market risk stemming from the fluctuation of the input and output prices, business cycles, financial risk emanating from the volatility in the exchange rate, inflation rate, share price return, interest rate, etc., and the political risk arising out of political instability and other related factors mentioned above (Click & Weiner, 2007). The notable studies in the context of evaluating the effect of policy-related factors on the financial performance of the firms were carried out by Sufian and Habibullah (2010b), Mongid and Tahir (2011), Aburime (2009), Hillman et al. (2009), Rodriguez et al. (2006), Hillman et al. (2004), etc.

3.2.2   Efficiency Analysis

In the present age of exorbitant competition, it is inevitable to manage the business with the highest degree of efficiency to survive in the long run and such productive efficiency of the firms gets largely affected by the different firm-specific factors and macroeconomic factors (Sufian, 2009). For a long period of time the researchers have sought to evaluate the efficiency of the firms operating across the world because the productive efficiency of the firms is a good indicator of financial performance. It is argued that the higher the efficiency, the higher is the ability to cope with macroeconomic volatility, the greater is the sustainability; the greater is the profitability vis-à-vis firm value.

3.2.2.1   Macroeconomic Factors
The efficiency of the firms always gets magnified due to the openness of an economy because of the increased competition in the market which ensures optimum utilization of available resources (Driffield & Kambhampati, 2003). Reduction of industrial tariffs, withdrawal of industrial licensing and product licensing, deregulation, removal of restriction on import and export due to the economic reforms measures have made the manufacturing firms more efficient in the post-reform regime.

3.2.2.2   Microeconomic Factors
The existing literature has also identified different microeconomic factors having significant impact on the efficiency of the firms. Some of the important factors identified by the earlier research studies are size of the firm, age of the firms, ownership structure, number of employees, profitability, prevalence of competition, liberalization, exports, labour cost, foreign ownership, subsidies, management costs, education of the owners, quality of human capital, liberalization, R&D, existence of crimes

and political risk, infrastructure, product diversification and international diversification, use of technology, managerial efficiency, remuneration to the top management and workers, market to book value ratio, financial leverage, Government quality, taxes, foreign investment and training cost of the employees (Ahmed & Ahmed, 2013; Alvarez & Crespi, 2003; Baek & Neymotin, 2016; Blomström, 1986; Burki & Terrell, 1998; Castiglione & Infante, 2014; Chapelle & Plane, 2005; Chuang & Lin, 1999; Doaei et al., 2015; Fernandes, 2006; Firth et al., 2015; Forlani, 2012; Giokas et al., 2015; Halkos & Tzeremes, 2007; Hall et al., 2009; Hanousek et al., 2015; Hill & Kalirajan, 1993; Ismail & Sulaiman, 2007; Jain et al., 2015; Kalaitzandonakes et al., 1992; Kumbhakar et al., 1991; Le & Harvie, 2010; Lundvall & Battese, 2000; McConaughy et al., 1998; Pelham, 2000; Piesse & Thirtle, 2000; Pitt & Lee, 1981; Söderbom & Teal, 2004; Thatcher & Oliver, 2001; Van Biesebroeck, 2005; Vining & Boardman, 1992; Won & Ryu, 2015; Yang, 2006; Yang & Chen, 2009; Yu et al., 2012; Zhang et al., 2003).

3.2.2.3   Other Factors

The research studies which have attempted to explore the effect of policy-related variables on the level of efficiency of the firms are in fact very scanty.

3.2.3   Stock Market Analysis

The contribution of the stock market in the economic development of a country can never be undermined (Ali et al., 2010). Stock market development has a positive influence on the growth for high levels of per capita GDP (Durham, 2002). Stock markets of different countries enable the corporate houses to acquire their required capital with ease which has a significant impact on the overall macroeconomic situation of the countries (Adjasi & Biekpe, 2006). On the other hand, the different firm-specific (Fama & French, 2008), industry-specific (Hou & Robinson, 2006) and economy-specific factors affect the prices of the stocks of different companies in the stock markets. The impact of macroeconomic variables on the economic growth and stock market of different countries is well archived by the researchers in the field of finance. The correspondence between the macroeconomic variables and the stock market can be traced back in the Arbitrage Pricing Theory where the risk factors as indicated by the factor-specific beta coefficient could assumed to be used to determine the returns on assets (Ross, 1976). Under the Arbitrage Pricing Theory it is reckoned that return on an asset is dependent on various macroeconomic variables. Chen et al. (1986) even postulated that there cannot be a unidirectional relationship between the financial economy and macroeconomic factors. On the contrary, a bidirectional association is obvious between the two.

3.2.3.1   Macroeconomic Factors

The inflation has been recognized in the existing literature as one of the crucial macroeconomic variables having negative effect on stock return (Al-Sharkas, 2004; Ammer, 1994; Fama, 1981; Fama & Schwert, 1977; Omran & Pointon, 2001). Other major macroeconomic variables influencing the economic growth indicators and thereby the stock market of various countries including India are money supply (Al-Sharkas, 2004; Kraft & Kraft, 1977; Leigh, 1997), Government consumption (Grier & Tullock, 1989), political repression, fiscal policy (Easterly & Rebelo, 1993), economic growth (Ali et al., 2010; Barro, 1996; Hasanzadeh & Kianvand, 2012), foreign investment (Borensztein et al., 1998; Clark & Berko, 1997; Froot et al., 2001), exchange rate (Cenedese et al., 2015; Chkili & Nguyen, 2014; Granger et al., 2000; Hatemi-J & Roca, 2005; Mukherjee & Naka, 1995; Pan et al., 2007; Phylaktis & Ravazzolo, 2005), gold price, investment in housing sector, interest rate (Al-Sharkas, 2004; Malkiel, 1982), international crude oil price (Cunado & DeGracia, 2014; Gay Jr., 2011; Hondroyiannis & Papapetrou, 2001; Hosseini et al., 2011; Naifar & Al Dohaiman, 2013; Wang et al., 2013), foreign exchange reserve (Chen et al., 1986; Nishat et al., 2004), and integration with other stock markets (Grubel, 1968; John, 1993; Lessard, 1976; Mukherjee & Mishra, 2010; Ripley, 1973; Sheng & Tu, 2000). Other important studies in the direction of exploring the effect important macroeconomic variables on the stock market were carried out by Bilson et al. (2002), Gay Jr. (2011), Schumpeter (1912), Fama (1981, 1990), Hamao (1988), Poterba and Summers (1988), Bulmash and Trivoli (1991), Campbell (1987), Cochrane (1991), Chen (1991), Gan et al. (2006), Macdonald and Power (1991), Thornton (1993), Kaneko and Lee (1995), Cheung and Ng (1998), Darrat and Dichens (1999), Fama and French (1989), Abdalla and Murinde (1997), Muradoglu et al. (2000), Pallegedara (2012), Kwon and Shin (1999) Herve et al. (2011), Attari and Safdar (2013), Issahaku et al. (2013), Pilinkus (2015), etc.

3.2.3.2   Microeconomic Factors

There is also another stream of research studies intended to investigate into the factors affecting the share prices of different companies rather than evaluating the overall impact of different macroeconomic variables on the aggregate stock market return. These research studies directly looked into the different microeconomic and macroeconomic factors responsible for the changes in the share prices of the corporate houses belonging to different industries across the globe. Some of the pioneering works in this domain include the empirical studies on Capital Asset Pricing Model conducted by famous researchers such as Sharpe (1964), Linter (1969) and Black (1972) where they propagated that the cross-sectional expected stock return is linearly associated with the systematic risk as indicated by beta. Historically the market capitalization of a firm, an indicator of firm size and the price to book value of the firms were used by the financial economists to predict stock return (Jensen et al., 1997). With the passage of time the scholars have identified many other factors affecting the stock return in the literature. Some of the other noteworthy explanatory variables having direct influence on the stock market return of different companies were R & D expenditure to market value of equity ratio, debt ratio, growth opportunities, price–earnings ratio, leverage indicated by debt–equity ratio, monetary policy developments, earning yield, stake of FIIs, cash flow to price ratio (Chan et al., 2001; Drew et al., 2003; Fama & French, 1992, 1995; Jaffe et al., 1989; Jensen & Mercer, 2002; Lev, 1989; Szewczyk et al., 1996; Zantout, 1997). Chiek and Akpan (2016) suggested that the dividend declared by an enterprise has a significant positive impact on the share prices. However, there are a number of studies which contradicted that Tobin's Q, firm size, price–earnings ratio, age of the firm could not explain the stock return in a number of situations (Barbee et al., 1996; Kothari et al., 1995; Reinganum, 1981).

3.2.3.3   Other Factors

In an endeavour to explore the role of policy-related factors on the stock market, Antonakakis et al. (2013), Wu et al. (2016) and Schuler (1996) showed that policy uncertainty and volatility of the stock market are adversely associated with the stock market return. Similarly, the outcome study carried out by Arouri and Roubaud (2016) revealed that the policy uncertainty exacerbated significant negative implications towards the Indian and U.S. stock markets by augmenting the market volatility whereas the stock market of China was less sensitive and resilient towards any change in the policy uncertainty. That is why probably the cost of investing in the sensitive stock markets may become very high in the context of policy uncertainly. In addition, stock return can also be closely linked with the Government policies, Government spending and political cycle (Belo et al., 2013; Bilson et al., 2002; Croce et al., 2012; Diamonte et al., 1996; Erb et al., 1996; Günay, 2016; Pastor & Veronesi, 2012; Mensi et al., 2016).

3.3   Evidence Gap Map (EGM): Evidence on the Existing Empirical Literature in India

In Table 3.1 the relevant studies on the implications of microeconomic and macroeconomic factors on the efficiency, profitability and stock market carried out in the context of India are presented through EGM. It is one of the most contemporary methods to explore the gap in the existing literature in which the different cells represent the research works in different directions. For example, the first cell contained in Table 3.1 represents the works relating to the effect of macroeconomic variables on the profitability of the firms. In each cell the different research works are mentioned. The cell in an EGM which is crowded with a number of works indicates no research gap in that domain whereas if any cell contains no reference or a few, it signifies that there is scope of further research in that direction. From the analysis of Table 3.1, it is discovered that four of the cells are overcrowded whereas the rest of the cells hardly contains any reference and these cells represent the research gap in the existing literature in the context of India and especially the Indian manufacturing industry. Although a number of research gaps have been identified in the EGM, the book primarily focuses on three important domains of research gaps and efforts are made to address them in the subsequent chapters of the book.

3.4   Research Gap

First, the review of the existing literature points out several important factors influencing the earning capability of the firms which can be categorized into three factors: company-specific factors, industry-specific factors and macroeconomic factors. Out of these three, company-specific factors were the prime source of concern to the scholars in this field of research

Table 3.1 Evidence gap map of important works in the context of India

Determining factors	Outcome to the firm performance		Stock market	
	Profitability	Efficiency	Market index	Sectoral index
Macroeconomic factors	Mishra (2013)		Rao and Bhole (1990), Sultana and Pardhasaradhi (2012), Agrawalla and Tuteja (2008), Hassan and Sangmi (2013), Mukhopadhyay and Sarkar (2003), Naik and Padhi (2012), Patel (2012), Pethe and Karnik (2000), Srinivasan (2011), Azarmi et al. (2011), Chkili and Nguyen (2014), Ferdows and Roy (2012), and Bhattacharya and Mukherjee (2002)	

(continued)

Table 3.1 (continued)

Determining factors	Outcome to the firm performance		Stock market	
	Profitability	Efficiency	Market index	Sectoral index
Firm-specific factors	Majumdar and Bhattacharjee (2010), Majumdar (1997), Siddharthan et al. (1994), Kakani et al. (2001), Burange and Ranadive (2014), Batra and Kalia (2016), Banerjee (2015), Mistry (2012), Chander and Agarwal (2008), Basu and Das (2015), Aggarwal and Sato (2011), Kambhampati and Parikh (2005), and Iyer et al. (2011)	Kundi and Sharma (2015, 2016), Gambhir and Sharma (2015), Bhandari and Maiti (2007), Sharma and Sehgal (2015), Bhavani (1991), Neogi and Ghosh (1994), Kumar (2006), Madheswaran et al. (2007), Pattnayak and Thangavelu (2005), Mitra (1999), Mukherjee and Ray (2005), Ferrantino (1992), Mitra et al. (2011, 2012), Goldar et al. (2004), Dwivedi and Ghosh (2014), Sharma and Sehgal (2015), Hasan (2002), Basu and Das (2015), Majumdar (1997), and Baliyan and Baliyan (2015)		
Both Macro and Microeconomic Factors	Bhayani (2010) and Nandi et al. (2015)			

Determining factors	Outcome to the firm performance		Stock market	
	Profitability	Efficiency	Market index	Sectoral index
Other Policy-Related Factors	Majumdar and Bhattacharjee (2010), Golder and Kumari (2003), Driffield and Kambhampati (2003), Iyer et al. (2011), Kathuria et al. (2013), Gupta et al. (2008), and Siggel and Agrawal (2009)		Basu et al. (2011)	

Source Author's own presentation

for a long period of time. However, with the opening up of the economy and increasing cross-border transaction, the influence of industry-specific and macroeconomic factors has gained considerable attention. Yet, most of the efforts in this direction have been concentrated in exploring the determinants of profitability of the banking sector only. The earning capability of the banks gets influenced by a host of company-specific factors, such as capital adequacy, bank size, net interest margin, market share, etc. (Williams, 2003). Apart from this, it is also observed that various important macroeconomic factors such as growth rate of GDP, real interest rate, inflation, size of the economy, economic freedom, money supply growth, economic, political and social globalization and Government deficit were the major determinants of the profitability and efficiency of the banking sectors (Zhang & Daly, 2013). In the present age of heavy competition, it is inevitable to manage the business with the highest degree of efficiency to survive in the long run and the productive efficiency of the firms gets largely affected by the firm-specific factors and major macroeconomic factors (Sufian, 2009). Therefore, the present study considers a holistic framework in which firm-specific factors, industry-specific factors and macroeconomic factors act as the antecedents of the level of efficiency, profitability and stock price of the firms belonging to the Indian manufacturing sector.

In the context of intensely competitive business environment, a firm has to ensure efficiency to sustain in the long run. In India several research studies were carried out to evaluate the firm-level efficiency and its determinants (Bhandari & Maiti, 2007; Bhavani, 1991; Driffield & Kambhampati, 2003; Dwivedi & Ghosh, 2014; Ferrantino, 1992; Gambhir & Sharma, 2015; Goldar et al., 2004; Kumar, 2006; Kundi & Sharma, 2015, 2016; Madheswaran et al., 2007; Mitra, 1999; Mitra et al., 2002, 2011, 2012; Neogi & Ghosh, 1994; Pattnayak & Thangavelu, 2005; Sharma & Sehgal, 2010). The EGM (as shown in Table 3.1) discloses that the research studies so far conducted to evaluate the effect of both microeconomic and macroeconomic factors on the firms belonging to diverse industries within the broad manufacturing sector in India are very scanty.

Likewise, in the Indian scenario, Bhat (2014) conducted a study on the analysis of the financial performance of the Indian manufacturing sector in aggregate. Apart from this, some other studies were carried out to identify the factors affecting profitability of some specific sectors within the Indian manufacturing industry (Bhayani, 2010; Mistry, 2012;

Siddharthan et al., 1994). However, the EGM as depicted in Table 3.1 clearly reflects that the existing literature suffers from the dearth of studies[1] on the issue associated with the assessment of the effect of both microeconomic and macroeconomic factors at once on the profitability of the firms of different industries within the Indian manufacturing sector. In addition, there is also a paucity of literature pertaining to the exploration of the effect of macroeconomic variables on the real sector growth (such as manufacturing, service quarrying, mining, etc.).

Moreover, it is observed in the existing literature on corporate finance that the researchers have been concentrating on the impact of macroeconomic factors on the stock price[2] only. Most of the studies in India so far carried out have only considered the market indices for instance Sensex or Nifty as the dependent variable as these indices represent the pulse of the overall stock market. However, these market indices are comprised of market capitalization of various companies across different sectors. The different sectors are expected to respond differently in the context of dynamic macroeconomic environment in terms of their ingrained traits. Table 3.1 shows that there is a serious inadequacy of works in the literature which have tried to capture the effect of important macroeconomic factors on the stock index of a particular sector. Moreover, the effect of policy-related uncertainty on the sectoral stock indices belonging to the Indian manufacturing industry has remained an untouched domain as revealed through EGM.

---

[1] Banking sector is a notable exception in this regard. As a matter of fact, there are many empirical studies on the banking sector where the researchers have attempted to explain the profitability of banks of different countries on the basis of the various company-specific, industry-specific and macroeconomic factors (Ali et al., 2011; Goddard et al., 2004; Kosmidou et al., 2007; Ramya & Mahesha, 2012; Sufian & Habibullah, 2010a; Vejzagic & Zarafat, 2014; Vong & Chan, 2009; Williams, 2003; Zang & Daly, 2013). It has been observed that the profitability of banks and other firms is not only influenced by internal factors but also by the macroeconomic factors (Raza et al., 2013).

[2] Some of these notable studies in this context are the studies carried out by Schumpeter (1912), Fama (1981, 1990), Chen (1986), Hamao (1988), Poterba and Summers (1988), Macdonald and Power (1991), Thornton (1993), Kaneko and Lee (1995), Cheung and Ng (1998), Darrat and Dickens (1999), Mukhopadhyay and Sarkar (2003), Maysami et al. (2004), Vikramasinghe (2006), Agrawalla and Tuteja (2008), Asaolu and Ogunmuyiwa (2011), Sultana and Pardhasaradhi (2012), Hassan and Sangmi (2013), Chkili and Nguyen (2014), Pradhan et al. (2015), and Wu et al. (2016).

In this backdrop, the book endeavours a significant contribution to the existing literature by appraising the impact of microeconomic, industry-specific and macroeconomic factors together on the firm-level efficiency, financial performance and the share price of the firms in the Indian manufacturing sector. Further, the book attempts to measure the effect of the economic policy uncertainty on the sectoral stock indices of the Indian manufacturing industry.

3.5   Objectives of the Study

In the prelude of the research gap in the existing literature, it is important to assess the growth of the Indian manufacturing sector under different policy eras and the crisis situations. It is also of great significance to appraise how the different microeconomic and macroeconomic factors influence the level of efficiency and financial performance of the firms operating in the manufacturing sector. Additionally, the reaction of the different sectoral manufacturing stock indices to the dynamism of the macroeconomic situation is also expected to be assessed exhaustively. By virtue of the inherent unique characteristics of the different sectors across the Indian manufacturing industry, the level of efficiency, financial performances as well as sectoral stock index reactions are bound to be different. In this backdrop, the discrete objectives of the present study are as follows:

1. To evaluate the performance of the different industries in the manufacturing sector under alternative policy regimes in India and explore the impact of the economic crisis and the liberalization measures on the growth of the Indian manufacturing industry.
2. To measure the efficiency of the selected Indian manufacturing firms and their firm-specific and macroeconomic determinants.
3. To examine the sectoral variation in the financial performance (in particular profitability) of the manufacturing firms and to unearth the implications of various macroeconomic and firm-specific factors on the financial performance of the selected Indian manufacturing firms.
4. To assess the interrelationship between macroeconomic fundamentals and sector-specific stock indices belonging to the Indian manufacturing sector and to ascertain the effect of the financial crisis of 2008–2009 and economic policy-related uncertainty on the sector-specific stock indices belonging to the Indian manufacturing sector.

REFERENCES

Abdalla I. S. A., & Murinde V. (1997). Exchange rate and stock price interactions in emerging financial markets: Evidence on India, Korea, Pakistan and Philippines. *Applied Financial Economics, 7*, 25–35.

Aburime, T. U. (2009). Impact of corruption on bank profitability in Nigeria. *Euro Economica, 2*, 50–57.

Adjasi, C. K., & Biekpe, N. B. (2006). Stock market development and economic growth: The case of selected African countries. *African Development Review, 18*(1), 144–161.

Afza, T., & Nazir, M. S. (2007). Is it better to be aggressive or conservative in managing working capital. *Journal of Quality and Technology Management, 3*(2), 11–21.

Aggarwal, A., & Sato, T. (2011). *Firm dynamics and productivity growth in Indian manufacturing: Evidence from plant level panel dataset* (Research Institute for Economics and Business Administration, Discussion Paper Series DP2011–07). Kobe University.

Agrawalla, R. K., & Tuteja, S. K. (2008). Share prices and macroeconomic variables in India. *Journal of Management Research, 8*(3), 1–12.

Ahmad, N., Nadeem, M., Ahmad, R., & Hamad, N. (2014). Impact of family ownership on firm's financial performance a comparison study between manufacturing firms and financial firms in Pakistan. *Journal of Business and Management Review, 2*(8), 51–56.

Ahmed, M. S., & Ahmed, M. D. (2013). Efficiency variation of manufacturing firms: A case study of seafood processing firms in Bangladesh. *Review of Economics and Finance, 3*(2), 45–56.

Ahmed, N., Ahmed, Z., & Usman, A. (2011). Determinants of performance: A case of life insurance sector of Pakistan. *International Research Journal of Finance and Economics, 61*(1), 123–128.

Ali, I., Rehman, K. U., Yilmaz, A. K., Khan, M. A., & Afzal, H. (2010). Causal relationship between macro-economic indicators and stock exchange prices in Pakistan. *African Journal of Business Management, 4*(3), 312–319.

Ali, K., Akhtar, M. F., & Ahmed, H. Z. (2011). Bank-specific and macroeconomic indicators of profitability-empirical evidence from the commercial banks of Pakistan. *International Journal of Business and Social Science, 2*(6), 235–242.

Al-Sharkas, A. (2004). The dynamic relationship between macroeconomic factors and the Jordanian stock market. *International Journal of Applied Econometrics and Quantitative Studies, 1*, 97–114.

Alvarez, R., & Crespi, G. (2003). Determinants of technical efficiency in small firms. *Small Business Economics, 20*(3), 233–244.

Ammer, J. (1994). *Inflation, inflation risk, and stock returns* (International Finance Discussion Paper Number 464 of Board of Governors of the Federal

Reserve System). https://www.federalreserve.gov/pubs/ifdp/1994/464/ifd
p464.pdf
Antonakakis, N., Chatziantoniou, I., & Filis, G. (2013). Dynamic co-movements
of stock market returns, implied volatility and policy uncertainty. *Economics
Letters, 120*(1), 87–92.
Arouri, M., & Roubaud, D. (2016). On the determinants of stock market
dynamics in emerging countries: The role of economic policy uncertainty in
China and India. *Economics Bulletin, 36*(2), 760–770.
Asaolu, T. O., & Ogunmuyiwa, M. S. (2011). An econometric analysis of the
impact of macroecomomic variables on stock market movement in Nigeria.
Asian Journal of Business Management, 3(1), 72–78.
Asimakopoulos, I., Samitas, A., & Papadogonas, T. (2009). Firm-specific and
economy wide determinants of firm profitability: Greek evidence using panel
data. *Managerial Finance, 35*(11), 930–939.
Attari, M. I. J., & Safdar, L. (2013). The relationship between macroeconomic
volatility and the stock market volatility: Empirical evidence from Pakistan.
Pakistan Journal of Commerce and Social Sciences, 7(2), 309–320.
Azarmi, T., Lazar, D., & Jeyapaul, J. (2011). Is The Indian stock market a
casino? *Journal of Business & Economics Research, 3*(4), 63–72.
Baek, H. Y., & Neymotin, F. (2016). International involvement and production
efficiency among startup firms. *Global Economic Review, 45*(1), 42–62.
Baliyan, S. K., & Baliyan, K. (2015). Determinants of firm-level performance:
A study of Indian manufacturing and service sectors. *Indian Journal of
Economics and Development, 11*(3), 701–713.
Banerjee, S. (2015). An analysis of profitability trend in Indian cement industry.
Economic Affairs, 60(1), 171–179.
Barbee, W. C., Jr., Mukherji, S., & Raines, G. A. (1996). Do sales–price and
debt–equity explain stock returns better than book–market and firm size?
Financial Analysts Journal, 52(2), 56–60.
Barro, R. J. (1996). *Determinants of economic growth: A cross-country empirical
study* (National Bureau of Economic Research Working Paper No. w5698).
https://www.nber.org/papers/w5698.pdf
Basu, D., & Das, D. (2015). *Profitability in India's organized manufacturing
sector: The role of technology, distribution, and demand* (Working Paper, No.
2015-04). University of Massachusetts, Department of Economics. https://
www.econstor.eu/bitstream/10419/145413/1/821606948.pdf
Basu, S., Deepthi, D., & Reddy, J. (2011). *Country risk analysis in emerging
markets: The Indian example* (Working Paper No. 326, IIM Bangalore
Research Paper). http://research.iimb.ernet.in/bitstream/123456789/482/
1/wp.iimb.326.pdf
Batra, R., & Kalia, A. (2016). Rethinking and redefining the determinants of
corporate profitability. *Global Business Review, 17*(4), 921–933.

Belo, F., Gala, V. D., & Li, J. (2013). Government spending, political cycles, and the cross section of stock returns. *Journal of Financial Economics, 107*(2), 305–324.

Bhandari, A. K., & Maiti, P. (2007). Efficiency of Indian manufacturing firms: Textile industry as a case study. *International Journal of Business and Economics, 6*(1), 71–88.

Bhat, T. P. (2014). *Manufacturing sector and growth prospect* (Working Paper Number 173). Institute for Studies in Industrial Development. http://111. 93.232.162/pdf/WP173.pdf

Bhattacharjee, A., & Han, J. (2010). *Financial distress in chinese industry: Microeconomic, macroeconomic and institutional influences* (SIRE Discussion Paper Number SIRE-DP-2010–53). http://repo.sire.ac.uk/bitstream/ handle/10943/190/SIRE_DP_2010_53.pdf?sequence=1

Bhattacharya, B., & Mukherjee, J. (2002). *The nature of the causal relationship between stock market and macroeconomic aggregates in India: An empirical analysis.* Conference Paper Presented at 4th annual conference on money and finance, Mumbai. http://citeseerx.ist.psu.edu/viewdoc/download?doi=10.1. 1.467.4248&rep=rep1&type=pdf

Bhavani, T. A. (1991). Technical efficiency in Indian modern small scale sector: An application of frontier production function. *Indian Economic Review, 26*(2), 149–166.

Bhayani, S. J. (2010). Determinant of profitability in Indian cement industry: An economic analysis. *South Asian Journal of Management, 17*(4), 6–20.

Bilson, C. M., Brailsford, T. J., & Hooper, V. C. (2002). The explanatory power of political risk in emerging markets. *International Review of Financial Analysis, 11*(1), 1–27.

Black, F. (1972). Capital market equilibrium with restricted borrowing. *The Journal of Business, 45*(3), 444–455.

Blomström, M. (1986). Foreign investment and productive efficiency: The case of Mexico. *The Journal of Industrial Economics, 35*(1), 97–110.

Borensztein, E., De Gregorio, J., & Lee, J. W. (1998). How does foreign direct investment affect economic growth? *Journal of International Economics, 45*(1), 115–135.

Bulmash, S. B., & Trivoli, G. W. (1991). Time-lagged interactions between stocks prices and selected economic variables. *The Journal of Portfolio Management, 17*(4), 61–67.

Burange, L. G., & Ranadive, R. R. (2014). Inter-state analysis of the organised manufacturing sector in India. *Journal of Indian School of Political Economy, 26*(1–4), 1–83.

Burki, A. A., & Terrell, D. (1998). Measuring production efficiency of small firms in Pakistan. *World Development, 26*(1), 155–169.

Campbell, J. Y. (1987). Stock returns and the term structure. *Journal of Financial Economics, 18*(2), 373–399.

Castiglione, C., & Infante, D. (2014). ICTs and time-span in technical efficiency gains. A stochastic frontier approach over a panel of Italian manufacturing firms. *Economic Modelling, 41,* 55–65.

Cenedese, G., Payne, R., Sarno, L., & Valente, G. (2015). What do stock markets tell us about exchange rates? *Review of Finance, 20*(3), 1045–1080.

Chan, L. K., Lakonishok, J., & Sougiannis, T. (2001). The stock market valuation of research and development expenditures. *The Journal of Finance, 56*(6), 2431–2456.

Chander, S., & Aggarwal, P. (2008). Determinants of corporate profitability: An empirical study of Indian drugs and pharmaceutical industry. *Paradigm, 12*(2), 51–61.

Chapelle, K., & Plane, P. (2005). Technical efficiency measurement within the manufacturing sector in Côte d'Ivoire: A stochastic frontier approach. *Journal of Development Studies, 41*(7), 1303–1324.

Chen, N. F. (1991). Financial investment opportunities and the macroeconomy. *The Journal of Finance, 46*(2), 529–554.

Chen, N. F., Roll, R., & Ross, S. A. (1986). Economic forces and the stock market. *Journal of Business, 59*(3), 383–403.

Cheung, Y. W., & Ng, L. K. (1998). International evidence on the stock exchange and aggregate economic activity. *Journal of Empirical Finance, 5*(3), 281–296.

Chiek, A. N., & Akpan, M. N. (2016). Determinants of stock prices during dividend announcements: An evaluation of firms' variable effects in Nigeria's oil and gas sector. *OPEC Energy Review, 40*(1), 69–90.

Chkili, W., & Nguyen, D. K. (2014). Exchange rate movements and stock market returns in a regime-switching environment: Evidence for BRICS countries. *Research in International Business and Finance, 31,* 46–56.

Chuang, Y. C., & Lin, C. M. (1999). Foreign direct investment, R&D and spillover efficiency: Evidence from Taiwan's manufacturing firms. *The Journal of Development Studies, 35*(4), 117–137.

Clark J. & Berko E. (1997). *Foreign investment fluctuations and emerging market stock returns: The case of Mexico* (Federal Reserve Bank of New York, NY Staff Report Number 24). https://papers.ssrn.com/sol3/papers.cfm?abstract_id=993813

Click, R. W., & Weiner, R. J. (2007). *Does the shadow of political risk fall on asset prices?* https://business.gwu.edu/sites/g/files/zaxdzs1611/f/downloads/Does-the-Shadow-of-Risk-Fall-on-Asset-Prices.pdf

Cochrane, J. H. (1991). Production based asset pricing and the link between stock returns and economic fluctuations. *The Journal of Finance, 46*(1), 209–237.

Croce, M. M., Kung, H., Nguyen, T. T., & Schmid, L. (2012). Fiscal policies and asset prices. *Review of Financial Studies, 25*(9), 2635–2672.

Cunado, J., & DeGracia, F. P. (2014). Oil price shocks and stock market returns: Evidence for some European countries. *Energy Economics, 42*, 365–377.

Darrat, A. F., & Dichens, R. N. (1999). On the inter-relationship among real monetary and financial indicators. *Applied Financial Economics, 9*(3), 289–293.

Deloof, M. (2003). Does working capital management affect profitability of Belgian firms? *Journal of Business Finance & Accounting, 30*(3–4), 573–588.

Diamonte, R. L., Liew, J. M., & Stevens, R. L. (1996). Political risk in emerging and developed markets. *Financial Analysts Journal, 52*(3), 71–76.

Doaei, M., Anuar, M. A., & Ismail, Z. (2015). Corporate diversification and efficiency of manufacturing firms listed in Bursa Malaysia. *Iranian Journal of Management Studies, 8*(4), 523–543.

Drew, M. E., Naughton, T., & Veeraraghavan, M. (2003). Firm size, book-to-market equity and security returns: Evidence from the Shanghai stock exchange. *Australian Journal of Management, 28*(2), 119–139.

Driffield, N. L., & Kambhampati, U. S. (2003). Trade liberalization and the efficiency of firms in Indian manufacturing. *Review of Development Economics, 7*(3), 419–430.

Durham, J. B. (2002). The effects of stock market development on growth and private investment in lower-income countries. *Emerging Markets Review, 3*(3), 211–232.

Dwivedi, A. K., & Ghosh, P. (2014). *Efficiency measurement of Indian sugar manufacturing firms: A DEA approach* (Centre for Research in Entrepreneurship Education and Development, Entrepreneurship Development Institute of India, Ahmedabad Working Paper Number [CREED/2014/01]). http://library.ediindia.ac.in:8181/xmlui/bitstream/handle/123456789/1834/Efficiency%20Measurement%20of%20Indian%20Sugar%20Manufacturing%20Firms%20A%20DEA%20Approach.pdf?sequence=1&isAllowed=y

Easterly, W., & Rebelo, S. (1993). Fiscal policy and economic growth. *Journal of Monetary Economics, 32*(3), 417–458.

Eljelly, A. M. (2004). Liquidity profitability tradeoff: An empirical investigation in an emerging market. *International Journal of Commerce and Management, 14*(2), 48–61.

Erb, C. B., Harvey, C. R., & Viskanta, T. E. (1996). Political risk, economic risk, and financial risk. *Financial Analysts Journal, 52*(6), 29–46.

Fama, E. F. (1981). Stock returns, real activity, inflation, and money. *The American Economic Review, 71*(4), 545–565.

Fama, E. F. (1990). Stock returns, expected returns, and real activity. *The Journal of Finance, 45*(4), 1089–1108.

Fama, E. F., & French, K. R. (1989). Business conditions and expected returns on stocks and bonds. *Journal of Financial Economics, 25*(1), 23–49.

Fama, E. F., & French, K. R. (1992). The cross-section of expected stock returns. *The Journal of Finance, 47*(2), 427–465.

Fama, E. F., & French, K. R. (1995). Size and book-to-market factors in earnings and returns. *The Journal of Finance, 50*(1), 131–155.

Fama, E. F., & French, K. R. (2008). Dissecting anomalies. *The Journal of Finance, 63*(4), 1653–1678.

Fama, E. F., & Schwert, W. G. (1977). Asset returns and inflation. *Journal of Financial Economics, 5*(2), 115–146.

Ferdows, S. S., & Roy, A. (2012). A study on the international diversification in the emerging equity market and its effect on the Indian capital market. *International Journal of Contemporary Business Studies, 3*(4), 79–96.

Fernandes, A. M. (2006). *Firm productivity in Bangladesh manufacturing industries* (World Bank Policy Research Working Paper Number 3988). https://openknowledge.worldbank.org/bitstream/handle/10986/8363/wps3988.pdf;sequence=1

Ferrantino, M. J. (1992). Technology expenditures, factor intensity, and efficiency in Indian manufacturing. *The Review of Economics and Statistics, 74*(4), 689–700.

Firth, M., Leung, T. Y., Rui, O. M., & Na, C. (2015). Relative pay and its effects on firm efficiency in a transitional economy. *Journal of Economic Behavior & Organization, 110*, 59–77.

Forlani, E. (2012). *Competition in services and efficiency of manufacturing firms: does' liberalization' matter?* (Katholieke Universiteit Leuven, LICOS Discussion Paper Number 311). https://www.econstor.eu/bitstream/10419/74898/1/dp311.pdf

Froot, K. A., O'Connel, P. G., & Seasholes, M. S. (2001). The portfolio flows of international investors. *Journal of Financial Economics, 59*(2), 151–194.

Gambhir, D., & Sharma, S. (2015). Productivity in Indian manufacturing: Evidence from the textile industry. *Journal of Economic and Administrative Sciences, 31*(2), 71–85.

Gan, C., Lee, M., Yong, H. H. A., & Zhang, J. (2006). Macroeconomic variables and stock market interactions: New Zealand evidence. *Investment Management and Financial Innovations, 3*(4), 89–101.

Gatsi, J. G., Okpoti, C. A., Gadzo, S. G., & Anipa, C. A. A. (2016). Determinants of market and book based performance of manufacturing companies in Ghana: An empirical study. *International Journal of Economics, Commerce and Management, 4*(1), 393–411.

Gay, R. D., Jr. (2011). Effect of macroeconomic variables on stock market returns for four emerging economies: Brazil, Russia, India, and China. *International Business & Economics Research Journal, 7*(3), 1–8.

Geroski, P. A., Machin, S. J., & Walters, C. F. (1997). Corporate growth and profitability. *The Journal of Industrial Economics, 45*(2), 171–189.

Giokas, D., Eriotis, N., & Dokas, I. (2015). Efficiency and productivity of the food and beverage listed firms in the pre-recession and recessionary periods in Greece. *Applied Economics, 47*(19), 1927–1941.

Goddard, J., Molyneux, P., & Wilson, J. O. (2004). The profitability of European banks: A cross sectional and dynamic panel analysis. *The Manchester School, 72*(3), 363–381.

Goddard, J., Tavakoli, M., & Wilson, J. O. (2005). Determinants of profitability in European manufacturing and services: Evidence from a dynamic panel model. *Applied Financial Economics, 15*(18), 1269–1282.

Goldar, B., Renganathan, V. S., & Banga, R. (2004). Ownership and efficiency in engineering firms: 1990–91 to 1999–2000. *Economic and Political Weekly, 39*(5), 441–447.

Golder, B., & Kumari, A. (2003). Import liberalisation and productivity growth in Indian manufacturing in the 1990s. *Developing Economies, 41*(4), 436–460.

Granger, C. W. J., Huang, B. N., & Yang, C. W. (2000). A bivariate causality between stock prices and exchange rate: Evidence from recent Asian Flu. *Quarterly Review of Economics and Finance, 40*(3), 337–354.

Grier, K. B., & Tullock, G. (1989). An empirical analysis of cross-national economies 1951–1980. *Journal of Monetary Economics, 24*(2), 259–276.

Grubel, H. G. (1968). Internationally diversified portfolios: Welfare gains and capital flows. *The American Economic Review, 58*(5), 1299–1314.

Günay, S. (2016). Is political risk still an issue for Turkish stock market? *Borsa Istanbul Review, 16*(1), 21–31.

Gupta, P., Hasan, R., & Kumar, U. (2008). *What constrains Indian manufacturing?* https://www.econstor.eu/bitstream/10419/176229/1/icr ier-wp-211.pdf

Halkos, G. E., & Tzeremes, N. G. (2007). Productivity efficiency and firm size: An empirical analysis of foreign owned companies. *International Business Review, 16*(6), 713–731.

Hall, B. H., Lotti, F., & Mairesse, J. (2009). Innovation and productivity in SMEs: Empirical evidence for Italy. *Small Business Economics, 33*(1), 13–33.

Hamao, Y. (1988). An empirical examination of the arbitrage pricing theory: Using Japanese data. *Japan and the World Economy, 1*(1), 45–61.

Hanousek, J., Kočenda, E., & Shamshur, A. (2015). Corporate efficiency in Europe. *Journal of Corporate Finance, 32*, 24–40.

Hansen, G. S., & Wernerfelt, B. (1989). Determinants of firm performance: The relative importance of economic and organizational factors. *Strategic Management Journal, 10*(5), 399–411.

Hasan, R. (2002). The impact of imported and domestic technologies on the productivity of firms: Panel data evidence from Indian manufacturing firms. *Journal of Development Economics, 69*(1), 23–49.

Hasanzadeh, A., & Kianvand, M. (2012). The impact of macroeconomic variables on stock prices: The case of Tehran stock exchange. *Money and Economy, 6*(2), 171–190.

Hassan, M. M. S., & Sangmi, M. U. D. G. (2013). *Macro-economic variables and stock prices in India* [Doctoral dissertation].

Hatemi-J, A., & Roca, E. (2005). Exchange rates and stock prices interaction during good and bad times: Evidence from the ASEAN 4 countries. *Applied Financial Economics, 15*(8), 539–546.

Herve, D. B. G., Chanmalai, B., & Shen, Y. (2011). The study of causal relationship between stock market indices and macroeconomic variables in Cote d'Ivoire: Evidence from error-correction models and granger causality test. *International Journal of Business & Management, 6*(12), 146–167.

Hill, H., & Kalirajan, K. P. (1993). Small enterprise and firm-level technical efficiency in the Indonesian garment industry. *Applied Economics, 25*(9), 1137–1144.

Hillman, A. J., & Hitt, M. A. (1999). Corporate political strategy formulation: A model of approach, participation, and strategy decisions. *Academy of Management Review, 24*(4), 825–842.

Hillman, A. J., Keim, G. D., & Schuler, D. (2004). Corporate political activity: A review and research agenda. *Journal of Management, 30*(6), 837–857.

Hillman, A. J., Withers, M. C., & Collins, B. J. (2009). Resource dependence theory: A review. *Journal of Management, 35*(6), 1404–1427.

Hondroyiannis, G., & Papapetrou, E. (2001). Macroeconomic influences on the stock market. *Journal of Economics and Finance, 25*(1), 33–49.

Hosseini, S. M., Ahmad, Z., & Lai, Y. W. (2011). The role of macroeconomic variables on stock market index in China and India. *International Journal of Economics and Finance, 3*(6), 233–243.

Hou, K., & Robinson, D. T. (2006). Industry concentration and average stock returns. *The Journal of Finance, 61*(4), 1927–1956.

Hussain, A., Farooq, S. U., & Khan, K. U. (2012). Aggressiveness and conservativeness of working capital: A case of Pakistani manufacturing sector. *European Journal of Scientific Research, 73*(2), 171–182.

Ismail, R., & Sulaiman, N. (2007). Technical efficiency in Malay manufacturing firms. *International Journal of Business and Society, 8*(2), 47–62.

Issahaku, H., Ustarz, Y., & Domanban, P. B. (2013). Macroeconomic variables and stock market returns in Ghana: Any causal link? *Asian Economic and Financial Review, 3*(8), 1044–1062.

Iyer, A. V., Koudal, P., Saranga, H., & Seshadri, S. (2011). *Indian manufacturing–strategic and operational decisions and business performance* (IIM

Bangalore Working Paper No. Number 338). https://s3.amazonaws.com/academia.edu.documents/30720563/Indian_Manufacturing-_Strategic_and_Operational_Decisions_and_Business_Performance1_WP_338.pdf?AWSAcc essKeyId=AKIAIWOWYYGZ2Y53UL3A&Expires=1551869392&Signature=88fkpmJLcZJEyO%2BFcQMPlTdj0vU%3D&response-content-disposition=inline%3B%20filename%3DIndian_Manufacturing_Strategic_and_Opera.pdf

Jaffe, J., Keim, D. B., & Westerfield, R. (1989). Earnings yields, market values, and stock returns. *The Journal of Finance, 44*(1), 135–148.

Jain, N. K., Kundu, S. K., & Newburry, W. (2015). Efficiency seeking emerging market firms: Resources and location choices. *Thunderbird International Business Review, 57*(1), 33–50.

Jensen, G. R., & Mercer, J. M. (2002). Monetary policy and the cross-section of expected stock returns. *Journal of Financial Research, 25*(1), 125–139.

Jensen, G. R., Johnson, R. R., & Mercer, J. M. (1997). New evidence on size and price-to-book effects in stock returns. *Financial Analysts Journal, 53*(6), 34–42.

John, M. (1993). Emerging equity markets in the global economy. *Quarterly Review-Federal Reserve Bank of New York, 18*(2), 54–83.

Kakani, R. K., Saha, B., & Reddy, V. N. (2001). *Determinants of financial performance of Indian corporate sector in the post-liberalization era: An exploratory study* (National Stock Exchange of India Limited Research Initiative Paper Number 5). https://www.nseindia.com/content/research/Paper18.pdf

Kalaitzandonakes, N. G., Wu, S., & Ma, J. C. (1992). The relationship between technical efficiency and firm size revisited. *Canadian Journal of Agricultural Economics/revue Canadienne D'agroeconomie, 40*(3), 427–442.

Kambhampati, U. S., & Parikh, A. (2005). Has liberalization affected profit margins in Indian industry? *Bulletin of Economic Research, 57*(3), 273–304.

Kaneko, T., & Lee, B. S. (1995). Relative importance of economic factors in the US and Japanese stock markets. *Journal of the Japanese and International Economies, 9*(3), 290–307.

Kaplan, R. S. (1983). Measuring manufacturing performance: A new challenge for managerial accounting research. *The Accounting Review, 58*(4), 686–705.

Kathuria, V., Raj, S. R., & Sen, K. (2013). The effects of economic reforms on manufacturing dualism: Evidence from India. *Journal of Comparative Economics, 41*(4), 1240–1262.

Kosmidou, K., Pasiouras, F., & Tsaklanganos, A. (2007). Domestic and multinational determinants of foreign bank profits: The case of Greek banks operating abroad. *Journal of Multinational Financial Management, 17*(1), 1–15.

Kothari, S. P., Shanken, J., & Sloan, R. G. (1995). Another look at the cross-section of expected stock returns. *The Journal of Finance, 50*(1), 185–224.

Kraft, J., & Kraft, A. (1977). Determinants of common stock prices: A time series analysis. *Journal of Finance, 32*(2), 417–425.

Kumar, S. (2006). A decomposition of total productivity growth. *International Journal of Productivity and Performance Management, 55*(3–4), 311–331.

Kumbhakar, S. C., Ghosh, S., & McGuckin, J. T. (1991). A generalized production frontier approach for estimating determinants of inefficiency in US dairy farms. *Journal of Business & Economic Statistics, 9*(3), 279–286.

Kundi, M., & Sharma, S. (2015). Efficiency analysis and flexibility: A case study of cement firms in India. *Global Journal of Flexible Systems Management, 16*(3), 221–234.

Kundi, M., & Sharma, S. (2016). Efficiency of glass firms in India: An application of data envelopment analysis. *Journal of Advances in Management Research, 13*(1), 59–74.

Kwon, C. S., & Shin, T. S. (1999). Cointegration and causality between macroeconomic variables and stock market returns. *Global Finance Journal, 10*(1), 71–81.

Le, V., & Harvie, C. (2010). *Firm performance in Vietnam: Evidence from manufacturing small and medium enterprises* (Economics Working Paper Number 4-10). University of Wollongong Faculty of Business. https://ro.uow.edu.au/cgi/viewcontent.cgi?article=1223&context=commwkpapers

Lee, C. Y. (2014). The effects of firm specific factors and macroeconomics on profitability of property-liability insurance industry in Taiwan. *Asian Economic and Financial Review, 4*(5), 681–691.

Leigh, M. L. (1997). *Stock market equilibrium and macroeconomic fundamentals.* https://www.elibrary.imf.org/abstract/IMF001/06510-9781451843224/06510-9781451843224/06510-9781451843224_A001.xml?redirect=true&redirect=true

Lessard, D. R. (1976). World, country, and industry relationships in equity returns: Implications for risk reduction through international diversification. *Financial Analysts Journal, 32*(1), 32–38.

Lev, B. (1989). On the usefulness of earnings and earnings research: Lessons and directions from two decades of empirical research. *Journal of Accounting Research, 27*, 153–192.

Linter, J. (1969). The valuation of risky assets and the selection of risky investments in stock portfolios and budget constraints. *Review of Economics and Statistics, 51*(2), 222–224.

Lundvall, K., & Battese, G. E. (2000). Firm size, age and efficiency: Evidence from Kenyan manufacturing firms. *The Journal of Development Studies, 36*(3), 146–163.

Lyroudi, K., & Lazaridis, Y. (2000). *The cash conversion cycle and liquidity analysis of the food industry in Greece.* https://papers.ssrn.com/sol3/papers.cfm?abstract_id=236175

MacDonald, R., & Power, D. (1991). Persistence in UK stock market returns: Aggregated and disaggregated perspectives. In M. P. Taylor (Ed.), *Money and financial markets* (pp. 277–296). Basil Blackwell.

Madheswaran, S., Liao, H., & Rath, B. N. (2007). Productivity growth of Indian manufacturing sector: Panel estimation of stochastic production frontier and technical inefficiency. *The Journal of Developing Areas, 40*(2), 35–50.

Majumdar, S. K. (1997). The impact of size and age on firm-level performance: Some evidence from India. *Review of Industrial Organization, 12*(2), 231–241.

Majumdar, S. K., & Bhattacharjee, A. (2010). *The profitability dynamics of Indian firms.* https://www.isid.ac.in/~pu/conference/dec_10_conf/Papers/SumitK Majumdar.pdf

Malkiel, B. G. (1982). *Risk and return: A new look* (National Bureau of Economic Research Working Paper number 700). https://www.nber.org/pap ers/w0700.pdf

Maysami, R. C., Howe, L. C., & Hamzah, M. A. (2004). Relationship between macroeconomic variables and stock market indices: Cointegration evidence from stock exchange of Singapore's All-S sector indices. *Jurnal Pengurusan, 24*, 47–77.

McConaughy, D. L., Walker, M. C., Henderson, G. V., & Mishra, C. S. (1998). Founding family controlled firms: Efficiency and value. *Review of Financial Economics, 7*(1), 1–19.

McGahan, A. M., & Porter, M. E. (2002). What do we know about variance in accounting profitability? *Management Science, 48*(7), 834–851.

Mehralian, G., Rajabzadeh, A., Reza Sadeh, M., & Reza Rasekh, H. (2012). Intellectual capital and corporate performance in Iranian pharmaceutical industry. *Journal of Intellectual Capital, 13*(1), 138–158.

Mensi, W., Hammoudeh, S., Yoon, S. M., & Nguyen, D. K. (2016). Asymmetric linkages between BRICS stock returns and country risk ratings: Evidence from dynamic panel threshold models. *Review of International Economics, 24*(1), 1–19.

Mishra, S. (2013). Relationship between macroeconomic variables and corporate health of manufacturing firms in India. *Journal of Quantitative Economics, 11*(1&2), 230–249.

Mistry, D. S. (2012). Determinants of profitability in Indian automotive industry. *Tecnia Journal of Management Studies, 7*(1), 20–23.

Mitra, A. (1999). Total factor productivity growth and technical efficiency in Indian industries. *Economic and Political Weekly, 34*(31), M98–M105.

Mitra, A., Sharma, C., & Veganzones, M. A. (2011). *Total factor productivity and technical efficiency of Indian manufacturing: The role of infrastructure*

and information & communication technology. https://www.researchgate.
net/profile/Marie_Ange_Veganzones/publication/228433873_Total_Fac
tor_Productivity_and_Technical_Efficiency_of_Indian_Manufacturing_The_
Role_of_Infrastructure_and_Information_Communication_Technology/
links/02bfe50d1fc204595f000000.pdf

Mitra, A., Sharma, C., & Véganzonès, M. A. (2012). Estimating impact of
infrastructure on productivity and efficiency of Indian manufacturing. *Applied
Economics Letters, 19*(8), 779–783.

Mitra, A., Varoudakis, A., & Veganzones-Varoudakis, M. A. (2002). Productivity and technical efficiency in Indian states' manufacturing: The role of
infrastructure. *Economic Development and Cultural Change, 50*(2), 395–426.

Mongid, A., & Tahir, I. M. (2011). Impact of corruption on banking profitability
in ASEAN countries: An empirical analysis. *Banks and Bank Systems, 6*(1),
41–48.

Mukherjee, K., & Mishra, R. K. (2010). Stock market integration and volatility
spillover: India and its major Asian counterparts. *Research in International
Business and Finance, 24*(2), 235–251.

Mukherjee, K., & Ray, S. C. (2005). Technical efficiency and its dynamics in
Indian manufacturing: An inter-state analysis. *Indian Economic Review*, 101–
125.

Mukherjee, T. K., & Naka, A. (1995). Dynamic relations between macroeconomic variables and the Japanese stock market: An application of a vector
error correction model. *Journal of Financial Research, 18*(2), 223–237.

Mukhopadhyay, D., & Sarkar, N. (2003). *Stock return and macroeconomic fundamentals in model specification framework: Evidence from Indian stock market*.
https://www.isical.ac.in/~eru/erudp/2003-05.pdf

Muradoglu, G., Taskin, F., & Bigan, I. (2000). Causality between stock returns
and macroeconomic variables in emerging markets. *Russian & East European
Finance and Trade, 36*(6), 33–53.

Naifar, N., & Al Dohaiman, M. S. (2013). Nonlinear analysis among crude
oil prices, stock markets' return and macroeconomic variables. *International
Review of Economics & Finance, 27*, 416–431.

Naik, P. K., & Padhi, P. (2012). The impact of macroeconomic fundamentals on
stock prices revisited: Evidence from Indian data. *Eurasian Journal of Business
and Economics, 5*(10), 25–44.

Nandi, S., Majumder, D., & Mitra, A. (2015). *Is exchange rate the dominant factor influencing corporate profitability in India* (RBI Working
Paper 04/2015). http://rbidocs.rbi.org.in/rdocs/Publications/PDFs/WP0
49A3B62D596234C97B8CD1B2CC9CBC1CE.PDF

Neogi, C., & Ghosh, B. (1994). Intertemporal efficiency variations in Indian
manufacturing industries. *Journal of Productivity Analysis, 5*(3), 301–324.

Nishat, M., Shaheen, R., & Hijazi, S. T. (2004). Macroeconomic factors and the Pakistani equity market. *The Pakistan Development Review, 43*(4), 619–637.

Omran, M., & Pointon, J. (2001). Does the inflation rate affect the performance of the stock market? The case of Egypt. *Emerging Markets Review, 2*(3), 263–279.

Padachi, K. (2006). Trends in working capital management and its impact on firms' performance: An analysis of Mauritian small manufacturing firms. *International Review of Business Research Papers, 2*(2), 45–58.

Pallegedara, A. (2012). *Dynamic relationships between stock market performance and short term interest rate-empirical evidence from Sri Lanka.* https://mpra.ub.uni-muenchen.de/40773/1/MPRA_paper_40773.pdf

Pan, M. S., Fok, R. C. W., & Liu, Y. A. (2007). Dynamic linkages between exchange rates and stock prices: Evidence from East Asian markets. *International Review of Economics & Finance, 16*(4), 503–520.

Papadogonas, T. A. (2006). The financial performance of large and small firms: Evidence from Greece. *International Journal of Financial Services Management, 2*(1–2), 14–20.

Pastor, L., & Veronesi, P. (2012). Uncertainty about government policy and stock prices. *The Journal of Finance, 67*(4), 1219–1264.

Patel, S. (2012). The effect of macroeconomic determinants on the performance of the Indian stock market. *NMIMS Management Review, 22*(1), 117–127.

Pattnayak, S. S., & Thangavelu, S. M. (2005). Economic reform and productivity growth in Indian manufacturing industries: An interaction of technical change and scale economies. *Economic Modelling, 22*(4), 601–615.

Pelham, A. M. (2000). Market orientation and other potential influences on performance in small and medium-sized manufacturing firms. *Journal of Small Business Management, 38*(1), 48.

Peng, M. W., & Luo, Y. (2000). Managerial ties and firm performance in a transition economy: The nature of a micro-macro link. *Academy of Management Journal, 43*(3), 486–501.

Pethe, A., & Karnik, A. (2000). Do Indian stock markets matter? Stock market indices and macro-economic variables. *Economic and Political Weekly, 35*(5), 349–356.

Phylaktis, K., & Ravazzolo, F. (2005). Stock prices and exchange rate dynamics. *Journal of International Money and Finance, 24*(7), 1031–1053.

Piesse, J., & Thirtle, C. (2000). A stochastic frontier approach to firm level efficiency, technological change, and productivity during the early transition in Hungary. *Journal of Comparative Economics, 28*(3), 473–501.

Pilinkus, D. (2015). Stock market and macroeconomic variables: Evidences from Lithuania. *Economics and Management, 14*, 884–891.

Pitt, M. M., & Lee, L. F. (1981). The measurement and sources of technical inefficiency in the Indonesian weaving industry. *Journal of Development Economics,* *9*(1), 43–64.

Poterba, J. M., & Summers, L. H. (1988). Mean reversion in stock prices: Evidence and implications. *Journal of Financial Economics, 22*(1), 27–59.

Pradhan, R. P., Arvin, M. B., & Ghoshray, A. (2015). The dynamics of economic growth, oil prices, stock market depth, and other macroeconomic variables: Evidence from the G-20 countries. *International Review of Financial Analysis, 39*, 84–95.

Pratheepan, T. (2014). A Panel data analysis of profitability determinants: Empirical results from Sri Lankan manufacturing companies. *International Journal of Economics, Commerce and Management, 2*(12).

Pucci, T., Simoni, C., & Zanni, L. (2015). Measuring the relationship between marketing assets, intellectual capital and firm performance. *Journal of Management & Governance, 19*(3), 589–616.

Purohit, H., & Tandon, K. (2015). Intellectual capital, financial performance and market valuation: A study on IT and pharmaceutical companies in India. *IUP Journal of Knowledge Management, 13*(2), 7.

Ramya, M., & Mahesha, M. (2012). Impact of financial crisis on profitability of Indian banking sector-panel evidence in bank-specific and macroeconomic determinants. *Asian Journal of Research in Banking and Finance, 2*(12), 27–43.

Rao, K. N., & Bhole, L. M. (1990). Inflation and equity returns. *Economic and Political Weekly, 25*(21), 91–96.

Raza, S. A., Jawaid, S. T., & Shafqat, J. (2013). *Profitability of the banking sector of Pakistan: Panel evidence from bank-specific, industry-specific and macroeconomic determinants.* https://mpra.ub.uni-muenchen.de/48485/1/MPRA_paper_48485.pdf

Reinganum, M. R. (1981). Misspecification of capital asset pricing: Empirical anomalies based on earnings' yields and market values. *Journal of Financial Economics, 9*(1), 19–46.

Riahi-Belkaoui, A. (2003). Intellectual capital and firm performance of US multinational firms: A study of the resource-based and stakeholder views. *Journal of Intellectual Capital, 4*(2), 215–226.

Ripley, D. M. (1973). Systematic elements in the linkage of national stock market indices. *The Review of Economics and Statistics, 55*(3), 356–361.

Rodriguez, P., Siegel, D. S., Hillman, A., & Eden, L. (2006). Three lenses on the multinational enterprise: Politics, corruption, and corporate social responsibility. *Journal of International Business Studies, 37*(6), 733–746.

Ross, S. A. (1976). The arbitrage theory of capital asset pricing. *Journal of Economic Theory, 13*(3), 341–360.

Rumelt, R. P. (1982). Diversification strategy and profitability. *Strategic Management Journal, 3*(4), 359–369.

Schuler, D. A. (1996). Corporate political strategy and foreign competition: The case of the steel industry. *Academy of Management Journal, 39*(3), 720–737.

Schumpeter, J. A. (1912). 1934. *The theory of economic development: An inquiry into profits, capital, credit, interest and the business cycle.* Harvard University Press.

Selling, T. I., & Stickney, C. P. (1989). The effects of business environment and strategy on a firm's rate of return on assets. *Financial Analysts Journal, 45*(1), 43–52.

Serrasqueiro, Z. S., & Nunes, P. M. (2008). Performance and size: Empirical evidence from Portuguese SMEs. *Small Business Economics, 31*(2), 195–217.

Sharma, C., & Sehgal, S. (2010). Impact of infrastructure on output, productivity and efficiency: Evidence from the Indian manufacturing industry. *Indian Growth and Development Review, 3*(2), 100–121.

Sharma, S. K., & Sehgal, S. (2015). Productivity, innovations and profitability of manufacturing industries in India: A regional study of Haryana state. *International Journal of Business Excellence, 8*(6), 700–723.

Sharpe, W. F. (1964). Capital asset prices: A theory of market equilibrium under conditions of risk. *The Journal of Finance, 19*(3), 425–442.

Sheng, H. C., & Tu, A. H. (2000). A study of cointegration and variance decomposition among national equity indices before and during the period of the Asian financial crisis. *Journal of Multinational Financial Management, 10*(3), 345–365.

Shin, H. H., & Soenen, L. (1998). Efficiency of working capital management and corporate profitability. *Financial Practice and Education., 8*(2), 37–45.

Siddharthan, N. S., Pandit, B. L., & Agarwal, R. N. (1994). Growth and profit behavior of largescale Indian firms. *The Developing Economies, 32*(2), 188–209.

Siggel, E., & Agrawal, P. (2009). *The impact of economic reforms on Indian manufacturers: Evidence from a small sample survey* (Institute of Economic Growth, University of Delhi Working Paper Series No. E/300/2009). http://iegindia.org/upload/pdf/wp300.pdf

Söderbom, M., & Teal, F. (2004). Size and efficiency in African manufacturing firms: Evidence from firm-level panel data. *Journal of Development Economics, 73*(1), 369–394.

Spanos, Y. E., Zaralis, G., & Lioukas, S. (2004). Strategy and industry effects on profitability: Evidence from Greece. *Strategic Management Journal, 25*(2), 139–165.

Srinivasan, P. (2011). Causal nexus between stock market return and selected macroeconomic variables in India: Evidence from the National Stock Exchange (NSE). *IUP Journal of Financial Risk Management, 8*(4), 7.

Sufian, F. (2009). Determinants of bank efficiency during unstable macroeconomic environment: Empirical evidence from Malaysia. *Research in International Business and Finance, 23*(1), 54–77.

Sufian, F., & Habibullah, M. S. (2009a). Bank specific and macroeconomic determinants of bank profitability: Empirical evidence from the China banking sector. *Frontiers of Economics in China, 4*(2), 274–291.

Sufian, F., & Habibullah, M. S. (2009b). Determinants of bank profitability in a developing economy: Empirical evidence from Bangladesh. *Journal of Business Economics and Management, 10*(3), 207–217.

Sufian, F., & Habibullah, M. S. (2010a). Assessing the impact of financial crisis on bank performance: Empirical evidence from Indonesia. *ASEAN Economic Bulletin, 27*(3), 245–262.

Sufian, F., & Habibullah, M. S. (2010b). Does economic freedom fosters banks' performance? Panel evidence from Malaysia. *Journal of Contemporary Accounting & Economics, 6*(2), 77–91.

Sultana, S. T., & Pardhasaradhi, S. (2012). Impact of flow of FDI & FII on Indian stock market. *Finance Research, 1*(3), 4–10.

Sur, D., Maji, S. K., & Banerjee, D. (2014). Working capital management in Select Indian pharmaceutical companies: A Cross-sectional analysis. In N. Ray & K. Chakraborty (Eds.), *Handbook of research on strategic business infrastructure development and contemporary issues in finance* (pp. 1–11). IGI Global.

Szewczyk, S. H., Tsetsekos, G. P., & Zantout, Z. (1996). The valuation of corporate R&D expenditures: Evidence from investment opportunities and free cash flow. *Financial Management, 25*(1), 105–110.

Thatcher, M. E., & Oliver, J. R. (2001). The impact of technology investments on a firm's production efficiency, product quality, and productivity. *Journal of Management Information Systems, 18*(2), 17–45.

Thornton, J. (1993). Money, output and stock prices in the UK: Evidence on some (non) relationships. *Applied Financial Economics, 3*(4), 335–338.

Van Biesebroeck, J. (2005). Exporting raises productivity in sub-Saharan African manufacturing firms. *Journal of International Economics, 67*(2), 373–391.

Vejzagic, M., & Zarafat, H. (2014). An analysis of macroeconomic determinants of commercial banks profitability in Malaysia for the period 1995–2011. *Asian Economic and Financial Review, 4*(1), 41–57.

Vikramasinghe, B. G. (2006). *Macro economic forces and stock prices: Some empirical evidence from an emerging market* (Working Paper Series 06/14). University of Wollongong. https://ro.uow.edu.au/cgi/viewcontent.cgi?ref erer=https://scholar.google.co.in/&httpsredir=1&article=1029&context=acc finwp

Vining, A. R., & Boardman, A. E. (1992). Ownership versus competition: Efficiency in public enterprise. *Public Choice, 73*(2), 205–239.

Vong, P. I., & Chan, H. S. (2009). Determinants of bank profitability in Macao. *Macau Monetary Research Bulletin, 12*(6), 93–113.

Voulgaris, F., Doumpos, M., & Zopounidis, C. (2000). On the evaluation of Greek industrial SME's performance via multicriteria analysis of financial ratios. *Small Business Economics, 15*(2), 127–136.

Wagner, J. (1995). Exports, firm size, and firm dynamics. *Small Business Economics, 7*(1), 29–39.

Wang, Y., Wu, C., & Yang, L. (2013). Oil price shocks and stock market activities: Evidence from oil-importing and oil-exporting countries. *Journal of Comparative Economics, 41*(4), 1220–1239.

Williams, B. (2003). Domestic and international determinants of bank profits: Foreign banks in Australia. *Journal of Banking & Finance, 27*(6), 1185–1210.

Won, J., & Ryu, S. L. (2015). Determinants of operating efficiency in Korean construction firms: Panel data analysis. *International Information Institute (Tokyo). Information, 18*(5B), 1885–1892.

Wu, T. P., Liu, S. B., & Hsueh, S. J. (2016). The causal relationship between economic policy uncertainty and stock market: A panel data analysis. *International Economic Journal, 30*(1), 109–122.

Yang, C. H., & Chen, K. H. (2009). Are small firms less efficient? *Small Business Economics, 32*(4), 375–395.

Yang, J. C. (2006). The efficiency of SMEs in the global market: Measuring the Korean performance. *Journal of Policy Modelling, 28*(8), 861–876.

Yu, Y. S., Barros, A., Yeh, M. L., Lu, M. J., & Tsai, C. H. (2012). A study of estimating the technical efficiency of optoelectronic firms: An application of data envelopment analysis and tobit analysis. *International Journal of Academic Research in Business and Social Sciences, 2*(7), 192.

Zantout, Z. Z. (1997). A test of the debt monitoring hypothesis: The case of corporate R&D expenditures. *Financial Review, 32*(1), 21–48.

Zhang, A., Zhang, Y., & Zhao, R. (2003). A study of the R&D efficiency and productivity of Chinese firms. *Journal of Comparative Economics, 31*(3), 444–464.

Zhang, X., & Daly, K. (2013). The Impact of bank specific and macroeconomic factors on China's bank performance. *Global Economy and Finance Journal, 6*(2), 1–25.

CHAPTER 4

Measurement of Efficiency of the Select Indian Manufacturing Firms and Its Determinants: Implications of Firm-Specific and Macroeconomic Factors

Abstract Firm-level efficiency is at the centre of competitive strength and financial resilience of any business firm. Operational efficiency directly contributes towards amplifying the profitability and subsequently value maximization of a firm. This chapter makes an effort to measure the level of technical efficiency of the firms in the Indian manufacturing sector by using stochastic frontier analysis. The various microeconomic and macroeconomic factors affecting such technical efficiency were also investigated in this chapter. Sector-wise variation in the level of efficiency was very much evident from the outcome of the study. The effect and significance of different microeconomic and macroeconomic factors were not uniform across different sub-sectors within the Indian manufacturing industry during the period of study.

Keywords Efficiency · Stochastic frontier analysis · Value maximization · Financial resilience · Microeconomic factors · Macroeconomic factors

© The Author(s), under exclusive license to Springer Nature
Singapore Pte Ltd. 2022
S. K. Maji et al., *Indian Manufacturing Sector in Post-Reform Period*,
https://doi.org/10.1007/978-981-19-2666-2_4

4.1   INTRODUCTION

Traditionally it is believed that the prime objective of a firm is to maximize its value, which in turn depends on the firm's efficiency at large. Efficiency analysis is of utmost priority to the managers of the corporate firms in making appropriate managerial decisions and strategies so as to attain the objective of wealth maximization and optimum utilization of the available resources (Kundi & Sharma, 2016). The efficient firms are expected to be sustainable in the milieu of current dynamic macroeconomic environment.

The journey of the Indian industries has gone through the phases of ups and downs till 1980 (Bhandari & Maiti, 2007). Only after the introduction of the pro-market economic policies in late 1980s and early 1990s, a favourable business environment was created where the industries could grow (Kochhar et al., 2006). It has been empirically established that the reduction of tariffs, withdrawal of industrial licensing, deregulation, removal of restriction on import and export promoted the efficiency of Indian industries. As a matter of fact, it is inevitable to manage the business firm with the highest degree of efficiency to sustain in the emergence of a tremendously competitive business environment (Driffield & Kambhampati, 2003).

With the unfolding of the liberalization measures in India in 1991, such competition has become more intensified. As a result, effective utilization of the available scarce resources is utmost important for achieving corporate excellence in the forms of cost effectiveness, profitability and ultimately the market value of the firm. Possibly, this is one of the principal reasons for which many research scholars have delved into the estimation of the level of efficiency of the firms and its determinants. The determinants of productive efficiency can be broadly segregated into firm-specific factors and macroeconomic factors (Sufian, 2009). The important firm-specific factors identified in the literature are size of the firm age of the firms, technological upgradation, geographical location, Government assistance, innovation capability, R&D intensity, experience of the workforce, foreign collaboration, female participation in the workforce, export orientation, education of the owner, subcontracting possibility, conglomeration strategy and financial integration (Ahmed & Ahmed, 2013; Alvarez & Crespi, 2003; Burki & Terrell, 1998; Firth et al., 2015; Halkos & Tzeremes, 2007; Hall et al., 2009; Hanousek et al., 2015; Hill & Kalirajan, 1993; Kalaitzandonakes et al., 1992;

Kambhampati & Parikh, 2005; Le & Harvie, 2010; Lundvall & Battese, 2000; Maji et al., 2020; Pelham, 2000; Pitt & Lee, 1981; Söderbom & Teal, 2004; Yang, 2006; Yang & Chen, 2009). Some other important economic factors influencing the efficiency of the manufacturing firms as identified in the literature are innovation (Sharma & Sehgal, 2015), technology (Basu & Das, 2015; Hasan, 2002), ownership structure of the firm (Blomström, 1986; Goldar et al., 2004; McConaughy et al., 1998; Vining & Boardman, 1992) and corporate governance (Gill & Biger, 2013).

The research studies on Indian manufacturing sector have been conducted by making either a cross-industry analysis (Driffield & Kambhampati, 2003; Kumar, 2006; Madheswaran et al., 2007; Mitra et al., 2011, 2012; Pattnayak & Thangavelu, 2005; Sharma & Sehgal, 2010) or an analysis of specific industry. Some specific industry-level studies have been carried out on metal industry (Bhavani, 1991), engineering industry (Goldar et al., 2004), sugar industry (Dwivedi & Ghosh, 2014), glass industry (Kundi & Sharma, 2016), cement industry (Kundi & Sharma, 2015), textile industry (Bhandari & Maiti, 2007; Gambhir & Sharma, 2015), etc.

4.2 Measurement of Efficiency and Its Determinants

There are two distinct approaches to measuring efficiency: Data Envelopment Analysis (based on mathematical programming estimation) and Stochastic Frontier Analysis (SFA) (based on Econometric estimation). In this study, SFA was employed to measure the efficiency of the firms. A two-stage approach has been adopted to attain the objectives of the study. In the first stage, the estimation of a stochastic frontier production function has been made and the predicted values of firm-level technical efficiency scores have been ascertained while in the second stage, these predicted technical efficiency scores have been regressed upon firm-specific and macroeconomic factors in order to identify the sensitive factors influencing the efficiency. The specification of the inputs and outputs in the first stage of measuring technical efficiency presented in Table 4.1.

Table 4.1 Input and output variables for estimating production function

Variables	Description
Raw Material Cost (RMC)	Natural logarithm of Raw Material
Employee Cost (EC)	Natural logarithm of Employee Cost
Power and Fuel Cost (PFC)	Natural logarithm of Power and Fuel Cost
Gross block of Asset (GBA)	Natural logarithm of Gross block of Asset
Value of Output (O)	Natural logarithm of Value of Output

Source Maji et al. (2020)

In the first stage, the following specification of the stochastic frontier production function has been estimated under the panel data framework:

$$Ln(O_{it}) = \beta_0 + \beta_1 ln(GBA_{it}) + \beta_2 ln(RMC_{it}) + \beta_3 ln(PFC_{it})$$
$$+ \beta_1 ln(EC_{it}) + (V_{it} - U_{it})$$

where V represents random error which is associated with random factors beyond the control of the firm, U represents the one sided inefficiency component, Maximum likelihood Estimates of the parameters of the model have been obtained together with the variance parameters $\sigma^2 = \sigma_u^2 + \sigma_v^2$. The parameter, γ, has been derived from variance parameters such as $\gamma = \frac{\sigma_u^2}{\sigma_u^2 + \sigma_v^2}$ and thereby it lies between zero and one. The estimation output also provides the values of Mu (a measure of inefficiency in the model) and eta (representing the change of inefficiency of the firms over the time).

Technical efficiency of a firm at a given period of time is defined as the ratio of the observed output to the frontier output which could be produced by a fully efficient firm, i.e. $T.E_i = \frac{Y_i}{f(x;\beta)} = \frac{f(x;\beta)e^{-u_i}}{f(x;\beta)} = e^{-u_i}$.

In the second stage, Panel Censored Tobit regression model has been used to examine the determinants of such efficiency (firm-specific and macroeconomic factors). Since the efficiency scores lie between 0 and 1, the following econometric specification of a censored regression model has been used.

$$Efficiency_{it} = \lambda_0 + \lambda_1(Leverage)_{it} + \lambda_2(Growth)_{it} + \lambda_3(Size)_{it}$$
$$+ \lambda_4(Age)_{it} + \lambda_5(Openness)_{it} + \lambda_6(Exchange\ Rate)_{it}$$
$$+ \lambda_7(Inflation)_{it} + \varepsilon_{it}$$

where λ_is are the parameters to be estimated, Firm and time are denoted by 'i' and 't' respectively, $i = 1, 2, ... N$ and time $t = 1, 2, ... T$.

The expected signs for variables determining the sources of technical efficiency are summarized in Table 4.2.

Following the insights of the existing literature, underlying hypotheses have been formulated (shown by the expected signs in Table 4.2). In the empirical estimation on the different sub-sectors of the manufacturing industry, it is of great interest to examine whether the results corroborate with the hypnotized sign of the parameter or not. It is contemplated that the effects of the different variables on the firm-level technical efficiency are different across manufacturing sub-sectors due to their inherent nature.

Table 4.2 Expected sign of the determinants in technical efficiency model

Variables	Description	Parameter	Expected sign
Leverage	Debt/Equity	λ_1	+
Growth	Natural logarithm of (current relevant year – year of inception)	λ_2	+
Size	Natural logarithm of total assets of the firm	λ_3	+
Age	[(Current year Net Sales – Previous year Net Sales) / Previous year Net Sales] * 100	λ_4	+
Openness	(Export + Import) / Total Sales	λ_5	±
Exchange Rate	Real Effective Exchange Rate	λ_6	±
Inflation	Whole Sale Price Index[1]	λ_7	±

Source Maji et al. (2020)

[1] WPI is the better measure of inflation in the industrial performance evaluation context as compared to Consumer Price Index (CPI). WPI basically reflects the level of price at which goods and services are exchanged between firms within and between different industries (Mishra, 2013).

4.3   Results and Discussion

4.3.1   Estimation of Stochastic Production Function:

Manufacturing sub-sector-wise production functions have been estimated in Table 4.3. It is apparent that all the coefficients (β_1 to β_4) were positive and found to be statistically significant across all the manufacturing sub-sectors. It signifies that the raw material, employees, energy and assets of the firm made a notable contribution towards augmenting the value of the output. Few exceptional situations have also been noticed where statistically insignificant coefficients such as power and fuel cost coefficient, coefficient of gross block of assets and coefficient of employee cost have appeared in the Construction and Engineering, Food product and cement sub-sectors respectively.

The variance parameter 'gamma' (a measure of the extent of inefficiency) reflects the distance to the efficient frontier. A higher value of gamma also signifies that the majority of the error was due to variation in inefficiency. The estimated gamma values in different sub-sectors were also found to be statistically significant and they range between 31.4% (Chemicals sub-sector) and 84.1% (Pharmaceutical and Biotechnology sub-sector). It insinuates that the variance of the inefficiency effect was a significant component of the total error term variance and thus, the firms' deviations from the optimal behaviour were not only due to random factors. A significant variation in the efficiency levels among the firms belonging to the different sub-sectors in the manufacturing industry has also been established from the statistically significant values of Sigma Squared.

Positive and significant values of 'Mu' in different sub-sectors (except Electrical Equipment) underscore the presence of inefficiency among the firms operating in the different manufacturing sub-sectors. However, a negative and significant value of Mu in the Electrical Equipment sub-sector reflects that the firms belonging to the Electrical Equipment sub-sector were efficient in production and no inefficiency in the Electrical Equipment sub-sector was noticed. It is also supported by sub-sector specific individual technical efficiency scores. In fact, the Electrical Equipment sub-sector was found to be the most efficient sub-sector among the ten selected sectors.

'Eta' represents the change in inefficiency among the firms operating during the period under study. A significant heterogeneity in the estimated values of eta was observed in the empirical results. Positive values

Table 4.3 Estimate of Stochastic production function of different manufacturing sectors

Variables	Auto parts and equipment	Cement	Chemicals	Construction and engineering	Electrical equipment	Food products	Industrial machinery	Pharmaceutical and biotechnology	Steel	Textile
Constant (β_0)	2.174[a]	0.524[a]	0.160[a]	2.470[a]	0.912[b]	3.347[a]	1.378[a]	1.184[a]	3.494[a]	3.232[a]
GBA (β_1)	0.058[a]	0.584[a]	0.415[a]	0.877[a]	0.007	−0.934[a]	0.420[a]	0.600[a]	0.015	0.389[a]
RM (β_2)	0.726[a]	0.439[a]	0.336[a]	0.012[b]	0.841[a]	0.060[c]	0.103[a]	0.019[b]	0.353[a]	0.220[a]
PFC (β_3)	0.038[a]	0.039[a]	0.041[a]	−0.001[b]	0.001	0.978[a]	0.003	0.017[b]	0.318[a]	0.061[a]
EC (β_4)	0.134[a]	−0.032[b]	0.228[a]	0.077[a]	0.086[b]	1.110[a]	0.535[a]	0.370[a]	0.384[a]	0.292[a]
γ	0.748[a]	0.487[a]	0.314[a]	0.322[a]	0.830[a]	0.437[a]	0.733[a]	0.841[a]	0.563[a]	0.534[a]
σ^2	0.021[a]	0.098[a]	0.516[a]	1.628[a]	2.578[a]	2.261[a]	0.438[a]	1.396[b]	1.963[a]	0.509[a]
μ	0.254[a]	0.437[a]	0.805[a]	0.621[a]	−2.926[a]	1.988[a]	1.133[a]	0.432	2.103[a]	1.042[a]
η	0.001	0.004	0.006	0.008	−0.297[a]	−0.022[b]	−0.010[b]	−0.025[a]	0.000	0.000
N	720	330	1200	705	494	375	645	1020	675	1485

Source Author's own compilation

Notes a, b and c represents statistical significance at 1, 5 and 10% levels respectively

(increasing efficiency) of eta in Auto Parts and Equipment, Cement, Chemicals, Construction and Engineering, Steel and Textile sub-sectors were found while negative values (decreasing inefficiency) of eta were noticed in the rest of the sub-sectors.

4.4   MEASUREMENT OF EFFICIENCY

The mean efficiency scores of the different sub-sectors of the manufacturing industry are presented in Fig. 4.1. A wide variation in the mean efficiency is noticed during the period of study. It was observed to be the highest (0.90) in Electrical Equipment while it was the least (0.13) in the Steel sub-sector. The mean efficiency scores of all other sub-sectors were placed in between these two extremes. Variation in efficiency scores also followed the same pattern: high in Pharmaceutical and Biotechnology, Steel, Textile, Chemicals sub-sector and low in Electrical Equipment sub-sector.

Interestingly, the pattern of mean efficiency score is in sync with the predicted value of gamma (estimated earlier in production function). Auto Parts and Equipment, Pharmaceutical and Biotechnology and Electrical Equipment sub-sectors revealed relatively high-efficiency score (above

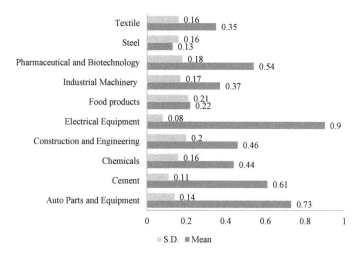

Fig. 4.1 Mean and Standard Deviation (S.D.) of efficiency estimates for various sub-sectors (*Source* Author's own compilation)

0.50) and high estimated gamma value (above 0.50). On the other hand, Chemicals, Construction and Engineering and Food sub-sectors exhibited lower efficiency score and gamma value (below 0.50). It confirms that the variation in the error term among the firms was due to the difference in technical efficiency.

The descriptive statistics of the microeconomic factors are presented in Table 4.4. The analysis made in Table 4.4 reveals that the Steel sub-sector was found to be the most levered one followed by Textiles, Chemicals, Cement, Food products, Construction and Engineering, Electrical Equipment, Auto Parts and Equipment, Pharmaceutical and Biotechnology and Industrial Machinery sub-sectors respectively. The inter-sub-sector range of leverage was noticed to be 0.60 (Industrial Machinery) to 2.54 (Steel) which signifies the presence of a wide variation among the various manufacturing sub-sectors in terms of leverage during the period under study. The intra-sub-sector variation in leverage was found to be very prominent in Chemicals, Food products, Pharmaceutical and Biotechnology, Steel and Auto Parts and Equipment sub-sectors whereas the same was observed to be very low in Cement and Construction and Engineering sub-sectors. The inter-sub-sector variation in growth is also very much evident from the range of growth which was observed to be lying between 13.91% (Industrial Machinery) and 104.86% (Construction and Engineering). The intra-sub-sector C.V. values with respect to growth were found to be much higher in most of the manufacturing sub-sectors which also signifies the existence of notable variation among the firms within various sub-sectors (particularly Construction and Engineering, Chemicals, Food products, Steel and Textiles). As far as the size of the firms is concerned, the analysis made in Table 4.4 clearly shows that Cement and Industrial Machinery sub-sectors were found to be at the top and bottom respectively.

The intra- sub-sector and inter-sub-sector variations in size of the firms operating in various sub-sectors were not found to be markedly different from each other. Similarly, the range of the firm age was also found to be lying within 3.16 (Steel) to 3.54 (Industrial Machinery) which along with low intra-sub-sector C.V. values rejected the presence of significant inter- and intra-sub-sector variation in firm age during the study period. However, unlike size and age of the firms, a significant difference between the openness of the firms among the various sub-sectors was observed.

Table 4.4 Descriptive statistics of the determinants of the efficiency

Variables	Statistics	Auto parts and equipment	Cement	Chemicals	Construction and engineering	Electrical equipment	Food products	Industrial machinery	Pharmaceutical and biotechnology	Steel	Textile
Leverage	Mean	0.85	1.46	1.63	1.21	1.01	1.26	0.60	0.77	2.54	2.17
	CV	98.74	62.08	175.81	64.28	90.48	100.79	92.53	101.44	105.25	86.32
	Range	0.02–5.85	0.49–4.38	0.01–15.39	0.08–3.48	0.01–4.23	0.00–4.94	0.00–2.26	0.01–3.79	0.03–13.70	0.06–12.31
Growth	Mean	15.50	21.68	20.24	104.86	21.17	24.24	13.91	21.23	56.24	15.79
	CV	42.25	75.78	140.16	469.68	69.02	167.91	106.20	87.42	347.40	155.61
	Range	4.51–34.02	9.10–84.36	–10.30–187.68	1.87–3214.41	1.62–84.87	–0.31–213.96	–6.64–94.93	–15.11–104.79	–3.65–1256.59	–6.85–214.31
Size	Mean	5.12	6.40	4.75	6.22	5.61	4.81	4.68	5.16	5.97	5.17
	CV	29.25	22.43	30.70	23.65	32.37	34.54	33.48	34.41	37.39	28.32
	Range	0.71–8.16	3.88–9.23	1.33–8.78	2.62–10.20	2.15–10.46	0.14–7.64	0.56–7.47	1.49–8.57	2.02–10.72	1.99–9.20
Age	Mean	3.37	3.37	3.39	3.31	3.39	3.16	3.54	3.27	3.16	3.33
	CV	18.44	19.65	13.03	17.64	15.66	16.37	15.22	15.26	17.51	16.02
	Range	0.17–4.26	2.18–4.30	2.66–4.49	2.39–4.60	2.09–4.30	4.30–4.46	1.86–4.62	2.31–4.62	1.67–4.61	2.37–4.86
Openness	Mean	0.23	0.09	0.32	0.13	0.30	0.15	0.23	0.43	0.22	0.35
	CV	106.99	97.03	71.80	169.03	103.66	168.19	74.04	74.58	95.76	96.67
	Range	0.00–1.54	0.00–0.28	0.00–0.88	0.00–0.96	0.01–1.65	0.00–0.83	0.00–0.66	0.00–1.11	0.00–0.77	0.00–2.38

Source Author's own calculation

4.5   DESCRIPTIVE STATISTICS
OF THE FIRM-SPECIFIC FACTORS

The highest mean value of openness was observed in Pharmaceutical and Biotechnology sub-sector (0.43) followed by Textile, Chemicals, Electrical Equipment, Auto Parts and Equipment, Industrial Machinery, Steel, Food products, Construction and Engineering and Cement (0.09) sub-sectors respectively. The intra-sub-sector variation was found to be higher in Auto Parts and Equipment, Cement, Construction and Engineering, Electrical Equipment, Food products, Steel and textile sub-sectors.

4.6   DETERMINANTS OF EFFICIENCY

The implications of firm-specific and macroeconomic variables on technical efficiency scores in the different manufacturing sectors are presented in Table 4.5.

4.6.1   *Leverage*

Generally it is expected that firms which employ more debt will be more efficient because the managers engage themselves to monitor the operating and functional activities cautiously (Majumdar, 1997). So, the use of more external funds in the capital structure not only induces greater discipline among the managers (Grossman & Hart, 1982; Opler & Titman, 1993) but also encourages them to act for the benefit of the investors (Jensen, 1986). The empirical results indicate that the coefficients associated with the firm leverage were positive and found to be statistically significant in the Construction and Engineering and Industrial Machinery sub-sectors. However, highly leveraged firms in the Auto Parts and Equipment, Electrical Equipment and Food products sub-sector were found to be less efficient. Intuitively, it can be explained by the *Agency Theory*, which stipulates that the managers are often concerned with attaining the personal objective as compared to firm objectives (Doaei et al., 2015; Ouattara, 2010). No significant relationship was established in the remaining sub-sectors (Cement, Chemicals, Pharmaceutical and Biotechnology, Steel and Textile).

Table 4.5   Sector-wise determinants of efficiency scores

Variables	Auto parts and equipment	Cement	Chemicals	Construction and engineering	Electrical equipment	Food products	Industrial machinery	Pharmaceutical and biotechnology	Steel	Textile
Constant	0.7198487^a	0.8668502^a	0.3194033^a	0.2703879^a	2.36638^a	0.5834567^a	0.6172149^a	1.184904^a	0.1209774^a	0.3795832^b
Leverage	-0.0000666^a	-0.0000363	-6.10e-06	0.0001914^b	-0.0071448^a	-0.0001645^b	0.0006611^a	0.0002579	3.58e-06	0.0002472
Growth	1.41e-06^c	-2.56e-06^b	7.75e-07	-7.47e-09	0.0000425	-9.16e-07	7.94e-07	8.36e-06	-1.69e-07	0.0000153
Size	0.003894^a	-0.0012058^a	0.0002715^a	0.0001827^c	0.0036337	0.0002959	-0.0005399^a	-0.0045007^a	-0.0001888^a	0.0101042^a
Age	0.0070183^a	-0.001338^a	-0.0050664^a	0.0023202^a	0.00324	-0.0371372^a	-0.0019573^a	0.0118199^a	-0.0017654^a	-0.0224655
Openness	0.0002286^a	0.0031735^a	-0.0002095	-0.0061971^a	0.0621156^a	0.0077798^b	0.0011847^b	0.0060215^a	-0.0009291^a	0.0161105^c
Exchange Rate	-0.0000918	0.0047265	-0.0043301^a	-0.0046218	0.0492045	0.00648	0.0056286	0.0175812	-0.0008687	-0.0015333
Inflation	-0.0003643^a	-0.0451914^a	0.0367098^a	0.0397014^a	-0.3574884^a	-0.0579176^a	-0.0556463^a	-0.1513798^a	0.003845^a	-0.0017015
Wald Chi square	26,318.74^a	87,483.24^a	25,087.12^a	7235.82^a	1010.29^a	6104.88^a	17,309.87^a	5663.13^a	562.10^a	18.11^a
Log-likelihood	4156.9403	1454.645	5355.7576	2418.9667	641.11793	1174.3794	2604.7484	2406.3661	3118.6574	1820.4024
N	720	314	1194	603	468	345	640	995	643	1452

Source Author's own computation

Notes a, b and c represents statistical significance at 1, 5 and 10% levels respectively

4.6.2 Openness

Greater openness (i.e. participation in international market) of the firms is generally considered as a major driving factor in ensuring efficiency in firm behaviour (Baliyan & Baliyan, 2015; Bigsten et al., 2004; Chang & Wang, 2007; Doaei et al., 2015; Gambhir & Sharma, 2015; Van Biesebroeck, 2005). The empirical results show that the relatively open firms (belonging to the Auto Parts and Equipment, Cement, Electrical Equipment, Food products, Industrial Machinery, Pharmaceutical and Biotechnology and Textile sub-sectors) were more efficient. However, the coefficients associated with the openness were negative and found to be statistically significant in the Steel[2] and Construction and Engineering[3] sub-sectors. The coefficients of exchange rate in these two sectors were also observed to be negative (but not found to be significant) which to some extent intuitively justifies that the importing firms in these sub-sectors were relatively inefficient as compared to their competitors.

4.6.3 Size

Large size firms are generally found to be efficient in operation due to the advantages emanating from the economies of scale and diversification in operation (Firth et al., 2015; Halkos & Tzeremes, 2007; Kalaitzandonakes et al., 1992; Lundvall & Battese, 2000; Pitt & Lee, 1981; Söderbom & Teal, 2004). Larger firms were noticed to be relatively more efficient in the Auto Parts and Equipment, Chemicals, Construction and Engineering and Textile sub-sectors. The results with respect to the Textile sub-sector were in conformity with the study carried out by Bhandari and Maiti (2007) where they have noticed positive effect of the size of the Textile firms on the technical efficiency during 2000–2001. However, larger firms operating in Cement, Industrial Machinery, Pharmaceutical and Biotechnology and Steel sub-sectors were found to be relatively inefficient during the study period. In fact, the inefficiency of the large size Indian Cement firms corroborates the outcome derived

---

[2] The average import expenditure of firms belonging to Steel Sector stepped up from Rs. 97.74 crore in 2000–2001 to Rs. 1307.16 crore during 2014–2015.

[3] The average import expenditure of firms belonging to Construction and Engineering Sector was Rs. 32.02 crore in 2000–2001 whereas same was found to be Rs. 421.51 crore in 2014–2015.

from the study conducted by Kundi and Sharma (2015). Such inefficiency of the large firms can be explained by the demerits of excessive concentration of market power (Leibenstein, 1976). Further, Majumdar (1997) advocated that large size Indian firm were very much happy with their prevailing situation and thereby there was no initiative in improving the efficiency or reducing the cost which eventually led to inefficiency.

4.6.4   Growth

Size of the firm can determine the possibility of growth of the firm. Like size of the firm, the prospects of growth induced efficiency in the Auto Parts and Equipment sub-sector while the growth in the Cement sub-sector was not reflected in efficiency in operation. The coefficients of growth in all other sub-sectors were not found to be statistically significant.

4.6.5   Age

Following the *Learning Curve Effect* proposition, it can be conjectured that the experienced firms are better able to utilize their available resources in more productive manner (Pelham, 2000; Weston & Mansinghka, 1971). In Auto Parts and Equipment, Construction and Engineering and Pharmaceutical and Biotechnology sub-sectors, learning curve enabled the firms to become efficient whereas the same was not observed to be true in case of firms belonging to the Cement, Chemicals, Food products, Industrial Machinery and Steel sub-sectors. Older firms may suffer from inertia in making adjustment with the changing in the business environment and thereby they gradually become inefficient (Marshall, 1920). On the other hand, newer firms enter into the market with new technology, innovative ideas, and greater flexibility in adapting the dynamic business environment and thus they are more efficient (Le & Harvie, 2010).

4.6.6   Exchange Rate

Rate of exchange was an insignificant determinant of the efficiency of the firms in all the sub-sectors except Chemicals. As a matter of fact, the firms in Chemical sub-sector reaped the advantages of engaging in international market (as mentioned in the coefficient of openness of the

Chemicals firms). The efficiency of the Chemical firms is reflected in increasing exports in the face of devaluation of exchange rate. However, firms in other sub-sectors were noticed to be excessively dependent on international trade for importing raw materials and thereby vulnerable to the devaluation of the exchange rate[4] Exchange rate fluctuations exerted a significant negative impact on the technical efficiency of the Chemical manufacturing firms in Malaysia (Doaei et al., 2015).

4.6.7   Inflation

Inflationary shocks affect the efficiency of firms adversely in the Auto Parts and Equipment, Cement, electrical equipment, Industrial Machinery, Pharmaceutical and Biotechnology and Textile sub-sectors. In fact, cost pull inflationary situation restricted the firms in ensuring optimum level of efficiency. However, other sub-sectors (such as Chemicals, Construction and Engineering and Steel) were found to be resilient in absorbing inflationary shock and thereby performed efficiently even in times of inflation.

4.7   A SUM UP

Achieving efficiency in operation is conceived as the prerequisite in the present competitive environment in the global business. This Chapter measures technical efficiency of the manufacturing firms belonging to the different sub-sectors by using Stochastic Frontier Analysis and explores its determinants. The empirical evidences suggest that firms belonging to the Electrical equipment sub-sector were the most efficient followed by the firms operating the Auto Parts and Equipment, Cement, Pharmaceutical and Biotechnology, Construction and Engineering, Chemicals, Industrial Machinery, Textile, Food products and Steel sub-sectors. A significant variation of efficiency among the firms of the different sub-sectors was also present during the study period.

---

[4] The analysis of the data of the chemical sector as a whole revealed that average import expenditure for this sector has increased from Rs. 26.901 crore in 2000–2001 to Rs. 253.03 crore in 2014–2015 due to devaluation. RBI statistics suggest that Real Effective Exchange Rate has increased from Rs. 99.43 in 2000–2001 to Rs. 104.50 in 2014–2015.

The study also identified the instrumental firm-specific and macroeconomic factors explaining the efficiency variation of different sub-sectors within the broad manufacturing industry. The study showed that firm-specific factors were not equally affecting the efficiency of the firms belonging to the different sub-sectors. The relatively efficient firms in the Auto Parts and Equipment sector were primarily driven by leverage, age, growth, size, openness and inflation. Firms in the Cement, Industrial Machinery and Construction and Engineering sub-sectors were also influenced by all these factors (except leverage). Exposure to international market significantly influenced firm-level efficiency in the Auto Parts and Equipment, Cement, Electrical Equipment, Food products, Industrial Machinery Sector, Pharmaceutical and Biotechnology and Textile sub-sectors. Firms in the Chemical sector were only insulated from the shocks of exchange rate in achieving higher efficiency level. Inflation was observed to be impacting the efficiency of Steel and Pharmaceutical and Biotechnology firms during the period of study.

REFERENCES

Ahmed, M. S., & Ahmed, M. D. (2013). Efficiency variation of manufacturing firms: A case study of seafood processing firms in Bangladesh. *Review of Economics and Finance, 3*(2), 45–56.

Alvarez, R., & Crespi, G. (2003). Determinants of technical efficiency in small firms. *Small Business Economics, 20*(3), 233–244.

Baliyan, S. K., & Baliyan, K. (2015). Determinants of firm-level performance: A study of Indian manufacturing and service sectors. *Indian Journal of Economics and Development, 11*(3), 701–713.

Basu, D., & Das, D. (2015). *Profitability in India's organized manufacturing sector: The role of technology, distribution, and demand* (Working Paper, No. 2015-04). University of Massachusetts, Department of Economics. https://www.econstor.eu/bitstream/10419/145413/1/821606948.pdf

Bhandari, A. K., & Maiti, P. (2007). Efficiency of Indian manufacturing firms: Textile industry as a case study. *International Journal of Business and Economics, 6*(1), 71–88.

Bhavani, T. A. (1991). Technical efficiency in Indian modern small scale sector: An application of frontier production function. *Indian Economic Review, 26*(2), 149–166.

Bigsten, A., Collier, P., Dercon, S., Fafchamps, M., Gauthier, B., Willem Gunning, J., Oduro, A., Pattillo, C., Söderbom, M., & Teal, F. (2004). Do

African manufacturing firms learn from exporting? *Journal of Development studies*, *40*(3), 115–141.

Blomström, M. (1986). Foreign investment and productive efficiency: The case of Mexico. *The Journal of Industrial Economics*, *35*(1), 97–110.

Burki, A. A., & Terrell, D. (1998). Measuring production efficiency of small firms in Pakistan. *World Development*, *26*(1), 155–169.

Chang, S. C., & Wang, C. F. (2007). The effect of product diversification strategies on the relationship between international diversification and firm performance. *Journal of World Business*, *42*(1), 61–79.

Doaei, M., Anuar, M. A., & Ismail, Z. (2015). Corporate diversification and efficiency of manufacturing firms listed in Bursa Malaysia. *Iranian Journal of Management Studies*, *8*(4), 523–543.

Driffield, N. L., & Kambhampati, U. S. (2003). Trade liberalization and the efficiency of firms in Indian manufacturing. *Review of Development Economics*, *7*(3), 419–430.

Dwivedi, A. K., & Ghosh, P. (2014). *Efficiency measurement of Indian sugar manufacturing firms: A DEA approach* (Centre for Research in Entrepreneurship Education and Development, Entrepreneurship Development Institute of India, Ahmedabad Working Paper Number [CREED/2014/01]). http://library.ediindia.ac.in:8181/xmlui/bitstream/handle/123456789/1834/Efficiency%20Measurement%20of%20Indian%20Sugar%20Manufacturing%20Firms%20A%20DEA%20Approach.pdf?sequence=1&isAllowed=y

Firth, M., Leung, T. Y., Rui, O. M., & Na, C. (2015). Relative pay and its effects on firm efficiency in a transitional economy. *Journal of Economic Behavior & Organization*, *110*, 59–77.

Gambhir, D., & Sharma, S. (2015). Productivity in Indian manufacturing: Evidence from the textile industry. *Journal of Economic and Administrative Sciences*, *31*(2), 71–85.

Gill, A. S., & Biger, N. (2013). The impact of corporate governance on working capital management efficiency of American manufacturing firms. *Managerial Finance*, *39*(2), 116–132.

Goldar, B., Renganathan, V. S., & Banga, R. (2004). Ownership and efficiency in engineering firms: 1990–91 to 1999–2000. *Economic and Political Weekly*, *39*(5), 441–447.

Grossman, S. J., & Hart, O. D. (1982). Corporate financial structure and managerial incentives. In *The economics of information and uncertainty*. https://www.nber.org/chapters/c4434.pdf

Halkos, G. E., & Tzeremes, N. G. (2007). Productivity efficiency and firm size: An empirical analysis of foreign owned companies. *International Business Review*, *16*(6), 713–731.

Hall, B. H., Lotti, F., & Mairesse, J. (2009). Innovation and productivity in SMEs: Empirical evidence for Italy. *Small Business Economics*, *33*(1), 13–33.

Hanousek, J., Kočenda, E., & Shamshur, A. (2015). Corporate efficiency in Europe. *Journal of Corporate Finance, 32,* 24–40.

Hasan, R. (2002). The impact of imported and domestic technologies on the productivity of firms: Panel data evidence from Indian manufacturing firms. *Journal of Development Economics, 69*(1), 23–49.

Hill, H., & Kalirajan, K. P. (1993). Small enterprise and firm-level technical efficiency in the Indonesian garment industry. *Applied Economics, 25*(9), 1137–1144.

Jensen, M. C. (1986). Agency costs of free cash flow, corporate finance, and takeovers. *The American Economic Review, 76*(2), 323–329.

Kalaitzandonakes, N. G., Wu, S., & Ma, J. C. (1992). The relationship between technical efficiency and firm size revisited. *Canadian Journal of Agricultural Economics/revue Canadienne D'agroeconomie, 40*(3), 427–442.

Kambhampati, U. S., & Parikh, A. (2005). Has liberalization affected profit margins in Indian industry? *Bulletin of Economic Research, 57*(3), 273–304.

Kochhar, K., Kumar, U., Rajan, R., Subramanian, A., & Tokatlidis, I. (2006). India's pattern of development: What happened, what follows? *Journal of Monetary Economics, 53*(5), 981–1019.

Kumar, S. (2006). A decomposition of total productivity growth. *International Journal of Productivity and Performance Management, 55*(3–4), 311–331.

Kundi, M., & Sharma, S. (2015). Efficiency analysis and flexibility: A case study of cement firms in India. *Global Journal of Flexible Systems Management, 16*(3), 221–234.

Kundi, M., & Sharma, S. (2016). Efficiency of glass firms in India: An application of data envelopment analysis. *Journal of Advances in Management Research, 13*(1), 59–74.

Le, V., & Harvie, C. (2010). *Firm performance in Vietnam: Evidence from manufacturing small and medium enterprises* (Economics Working Paper Number 4-10). University of Wollongong Faculty of Business. https://ro.uow.edu.au/cgi/viewcontent.cgi?article=1223&context=commwkpapers

Leibenstein, H. (1976). *Beyond economic man.* Harvard University Press.

Lundvall, K., & Battese, G. E. (2000). Firm size, age and efficiency: Evidence from Kenyan manufacturing firms. *The Journal of Development Studies, 36*(3), 146–163.

Madheswaran, S., Liao, H., & Rath, B. N. (2007). Productivity growth of Indian manufacturing sector: Panel estimation of stochastic production frontier and technical inefficiency. *The Journal of Developing Areas, 40*(2), 35–50.

Maji, S. K., Laha, A., & Sur, D. (2020b). Macroeconomic and microeconomic determinants of efficiency of Indian construction & engineering firms: An investigation. *Ramanujan International Journal of Business and Research, 5,* 105–121.

Majumdar, S. K. (1997). The impact of size and age on firm-level performance: Some evidence from India. *Review of Industrial Organization, 12*(2), 231–241.

Marshall, A. (1920). *Industry and trade.* McMaster University Archive for the History of Economic Thought. https://socialsciences.mcmaster.ca/~econ/ugcm/3ll3/marshall/Industry&Trade.pdf

McConaughy, D. L., Walker, M. C., Henderson, G. V., & Mishra, C. S. (1998). Founding family controlled firms: Efficiency and value. *Review of Financial Economics, 7*(1), 1–19.

Mishra, S. (2013). Relationship between macroeconomic variables and corporate health of manufacturing firms in India. *Journal of Quantitative Economics, 11*(1&2), 230–249.

Mitra, A., Sharma, C., & Veganzones, M. A. (2011). *Total factor productivity and technical efficiency of Indian manufacturing: The role of infrastructure and information & communication technology.* https://www.researchgate.net/profile/Marie_Ange_Veganzones/publication/228433873_Total_Factor_Productivity_and_Technical_Efficiency_of_Indian_Manufacturing_The_Role_of_Infrastructure_and_Information_Communication_Technology/links/02bfe50d1fc204595f000000.pdf

Mitra, A., Sharma, C., & Véganzonès, M. A. (2012). Estimating impact of infrastructure on productivity and efficiency of Indian manufacturing. *Applied Economics Letters, 19*(8), 779–783.

Opler, T., & Titman, S. (1993). The determinants of leveraged buyout activity: Free cash flow vs. financial distress costs. *The Journal of Finance, 48*(5), 1985–1999.

Ouattara, W. (2010). Economic efficiency analysis in Cte dIvoire. *Journal of Development and Agricultural Economics, 2*(9), 316–325.

Pattnayak, S. S., & Thangavelu, S. M. (2005). Economic reform and productivity growth in Indian manufacturing industries: An interaction of technical change and scale economies. *Economic Modelling, 22*(4), 601–615.

Pelham, A. M. (2000). Market orientation and other potential influences on performance in small and medium-sized manufacturing firms. *Journal of Small Business Management, 38*(1), 48.

Pitt, M. M., & Lee, L. F. (1981). The measurement and sources of technical inefficiency in the Indonesian weaving industry. *Journal of Development Economics, 9*(1), 43–64.

Sharma, C., & Sehgal, S. (2010). Impact of infrastructure on output, productivity and efficiency: Evidence from the Indian manufacturing industry. *Indian Growth and Development Review, 3*(2), 100–121.

Sharma, S. K., & Sehgal, S. (2015). Productivity, innovations and profitability of manufacturing industries in India: A regional study of Haryana state. *International Journal of Business Excellence, 8*(6), 700–723.

Söderbom, M., & Teal, F. (2004). Size and efficiency in African manufacturing firms: Evidence from firm-level panel data. *Journal of Development Economics*, *73*(1), 369–394.

Sufian, F. (2009). Determinants of bank efficiency during unstable macroeconomic environment: Empirical evidence from Malaysia. *Research in International Business and Finance*, *23*(1), 54–77.

Van Biesebroeck, J. (2005). Exporting raises productivity in sub-Saharan African manufacturing firms. *Journal of International Economics*, *67*(2), 373–391.

Vining, A. R., & Boardman, A. E. (1992). Ownership versus competition: Efficiency in public enterprise. *Public Choice*, *73*(2), 205–239.

Weston, J. F., & Mansinghka, S. K. (1971). Tests of the efficiency performance of conglomerate firms. *The Journal of Finance*, *26*(4), 919–936.

Yang, C. H., & Chen, K. H. (2009). Are small firms less efficient? *Small Business Economics*, *32*(4), 375–395.

Yang, J. C. (2006). The efficiency of SMEs in the global market: Measuring the Korean performance. *Journal of Policy Modelling*, *28*(8), 861–876.

CHAPTER 5

Implications of Various Macroeconomic and Firm-Specific Factors on the Financial Performance of the Select Indian Manufacturing Firms

Abstract Profitability of the firm is considered as a prerequisite for value maximization and long-run survival. This chapter examines the profitability of the various firms across ten different sectors in the Indian manufacturing industry. Attempt was also made in this chapter to explore the various microeconomic and macroeconomic factors affecting firm-level profitability. Variation in the level of profitability among the different manufacturing sub-sectors was very much reflected from the outcome of the study. The analysis of the results of the study suggested that neither all the microeconomic and macroeconomic factors were significant nor the effect of such factors were uniform across the diverse sectors within the broad manufacturing industry. In aggregate, an all-embracing implication of inflation, leverage and intellectual capital efficiency in determining the profitability of the various manufacturing sub-sectors was noticed during the period of study.

Keywords Manufacturing · Profitability · Intellectual capital · Leverage · Inflation

5.1   INTRODUCTION

The primary functional areas of corporate financial management are the procurement of funds from different sources considering their associated risk, cost, control and flexibility and effective deployment of the funds in different short-term and long-term assets to maximize the shareholders' wealth. The value maximization objective of a corporate firm substantially depends on its financial performance which is influenced by firm-specific factors, industry-specific factors and macroeconomic factors (Hansen & Wernerfelt, 1989). Profitability of the firm is of perennial significance in shareholders' value maximization. A profitable firm is proficient to make more investments to expand its business operations which also enables it to promote output growth (Basu & Das, 2015). The issue associated with the determinants of the firm performance is a debatable one as revealed in the existing literature. Some researchers opine that the industry-specific and macroeconomic factors make significant contribution towards determining the financial performance of the firms while the others posit that the contribution of the firm-specific factors is the most important. In this regard, the study carried out by Majumdar and Bhattacharjee (2010) advocates that the predominance of either industry-specific and macroeconomic factors or microeconomic ones is closely interlinked to the nature of the economic system. The existing literature shows that in India the firm-specific factors were found to be instrumental during both the pre- and post-liberalization eras. However, industry-specific and macroeconomic factors were observed to be more important during the post-liberalization regime (Majumdar & Bhattacharjee, 2010).

The review of the related literature reveals that size of the firm (Goddard et al., 2005; Pratheepan, 2014), advertising intensity (Spanos et al., 2004), age of the firms (Agiomirgianakis et al., 2006; Majumdar, 1997), leverage (Batra & Kalia, 2016; Ghosh, 2008), growth (Geroski et al., 1997), tangibility (Asimakopoulos et al., 2009; Nanda & Panda, 2018), working capital management (Voulgaris et al., 2000), international diversification (Hitt et al., 1997), research and development (Kambhampati & Parikh, 2005), intellectual capital (Bontis et al., 2000), operating efficiency (Gatsi et al., 2016), ownership structure, diversification strategy (Rumelt, 1982), human capital (Hansen & Wernerfelt, 1989), etc., are the significant firm-specific factors influencing the financial performance of the firms while economic growth (Mishra, 2013; Nugent, 1999), price level (Bhutta & Hasan, 2013; Tahir & Anuar, 2015), exchange rate

(Asimakopoulos et al., 2009; Bhattacharjee & Han, 2010), interest rate
(Bhattacharjee & Han, 2010; Gatsi et al., 2016; Nugent, 1999), etc.,
are considered as the important macroeconomic factors having notable
influence on the firms' financial performance.

In the context of India, size and age of the firms, growth of the firms,
the firms' marketing intensity and intellectual capital possessed by the
firms (Bhayani, 2010; Kakani et al., 2001; Majumdar, 1997; Purohit &
Tandon, 2015; Riahi-Belkaoui, 2003; Siddharthan et al., 1994) are recognized as the significant determinants of the firms' profitability. In addition
to these factors, the long-term debt paying capability (Bhayani, 2010;
Mistry, 2012) as well as short-term debt paying capacity have also tremendous potential to influence the profitability of the firms. The profitability
of the firms also gets implicated by the efficiency in managing their
assets (Chander & Aggarwal, 2008). In the liberalized economy, firm can
benefit from diversifying its business activities into the other economies.
Participation in such international trade enables the firms to magnify profitability (Majumdar, 1997). Moreover, it is also interesting to note that
not only the sources of finance but also ownership patterns have also
bearing on the overall financial performance of the firms (Siddharthan
et al., 1994). The role of infrastructure can also never be undermined
in explaining the growth of Indian manufacturing sector (Gupta et al.,
2008). In addition to these microeconomic variables, a very limited
number of studies have identified some macroeconomic factors such as
inflation, rate of interest, economic growth and openness exacerbating
noticeable influence on the financial performance of the firms belonging
to different sectors in Indian economy (Bhayani, 2010; Mishra, 2013).

It is of utmost significance to evaluate whether the empirical results
of the estimation conform to the expected signs of the parameters or
not especially in the context of different sub-sectors under the broad
Indian manufacturing industry. It is anticipated that the implications of
the different microeconomic and macroeconomic variables on the firm-
level profitability are not uniform across the different sub-sectors. In Table
5.1 the relationship of the various microeconomic and macroeconomic
variables with the ROA is presented.

5.2 SECTOR-WISE MEASUREMENT OF PROFITABILITY

The objective of the present chapter is to measure the effect of the
different microeconomic and macroeconomic factors on the financial

Table 5.1   List of independent variables and their expected relationship with ROA

Micro/Macro variables	Descriptions	Data sources	Expected relationship
Microeconomic variables			
Leverage	Debt/Equity	Capitaline Database published by Capital Market Publishers Private Ltd. Mumbai, India	+/−
Liquidity	Current Assets/Current Liabilities		−
Intellectual Capital Efficiency	VAIC™		+
Growth	[(Current year Net Sales − Previous year Net Sales)/Previous year Net Sales] × 100		+
Size	Natural logarithm of total assets of the firm		+
Age	Natural logarithm of (current relevant year − year of inception)		+
Openness[b]	(Export + Import)/Total Sales		−/+
Microeconomic variables			
Economic Growth	Index of Industrial Production (IIP)	Database on Indian Economy, RBI	+
Exchange Rate	Real Effective Exchange Rate (REER)		−/+
Inflation	Whole Sale Price Index (WPI)		−

Source Author's own compilation

Value Added Intellectual Coefficient (VAIC™) as suggested by Pulic (1998) can be calculated by adding the Capital Employed Efficiency (CEE), Human Capital Efficiency (HCE) and Structural Capital Efficiency (SCE), i.e.,

VAIC™ = CEE + HCE + SCE

where, CEE = VA/CE, HCE = VA/HC, SCE = SC/VA, Value Added (VA) = Profit Before Tax + Depreciation + Interest + Employee Cost

Human Capital (HC) is represented by the employee cost

Structural Capital (SC) = VA − HC

[b]Hitt et al. (1997)

performance of the firms operating in distinct sub-sectors of the Indian manufacturing industry. Return on Assets (ROA), a very popular and robust measure of profitability of the firm, has been considered as the financial performance indicator in this study. The ratio of operating profit reflecting the operating performance of a firm as indicated by its Earnings before Interest and Taxes (EBIT) to total assets has been adopted as the ROA. Thus, while ascertaining the ROA, the following formula has been used:

$$ROA = \frac{EBIT}{Total\ Assets} \times 100$$

The mean and standard deviation (SD) of the financial performance as measured by ROA of the different manufacturing sub-sectors are presented in Fig. 5.1. Based on the analysis of the mean values as shown in Fig. 5.1, it can be deduced that the Food Products sector (19.87%) was the most profitable sector, followed by Auto Parts and Equipment sector (17.50%), Electric Equipment sector (17.27%), Pharmaceutical and Biotechnology sector (16.32%), Industrial Machinery sector (15.67%),

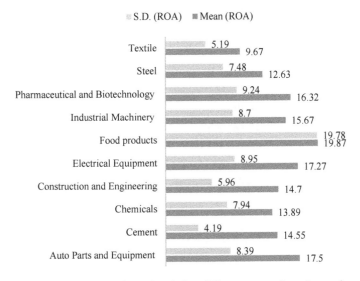

Fig. 5.1 Mean and SD of ROA of the different manufacturing sub-sectors (*Source* Author's own compilation)

Construction and Engineering sector (14.70%), Cement sector (14.55%), Chemicals sector (13.89%), Steel sector (12.63%) and Textile sector (9.67%) respectively during the period under study.

Figure 5.1 also depicts that the variation of profitability among the firms in the Cement sub-sector was the least (SD 4.19) while it was the highest in the Food products sub-sector (SD 19.78). In the remaining sub-sectors under study, the SD varied between 5.96 and 7.48 signifying that the inter-firm variation within these manufacturing sub-sectors was not at all significant during the period of study. However, a considerable amount of variation in respect of the profitability among the firms in the different sub-sectors under the manufacturing industry was noticed during the study period.

The descriptive statistics of the various microeconomic factors (leverage, size, age, growth, openness) have already been elaborately discussed in Chapter 4. In addition to these variables, two new additional microeconomic variables such as Intellectual Capital and Liquidity were also considered while explaining the level of profitability of the firms in the various sub-sectors. Therefore, the descriptive statistics of these two microeconomic variables are exhibited here in this chapter.

The descriptive statistics of VAIC and liquidity in the different manufacturing sub-sectors are presented in Fig. 5.2. The analysis of Fig. 5.2

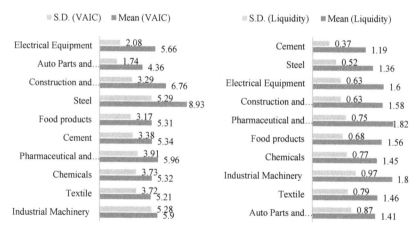

Fig. 5.2 Descriptive statistics of VAIC and liquidity (*Source* Author's own compilation)

reveals that the IC efficiency as measured by the VAIC was found to be the highest in the Steel sub-sector followed by Construction and Engineering, Pharmaceutical and Biotechnology, Industrial Machinery, Electrical Equipment, Cement, Chemicals, Food products, Textile and Auto Parts and Equipment sub-sectors respectively.

The inter-firm variation (as represented by the coefficient of variation) in respect of VAIC was found to be the highest in the Industrial Machinery sub-sector while it was the lowest in the Electrical Equipment sub-sector and the values of VAIC in the remaining sub-sectors ranged between 1.74 (Auto Parts and Equipment) and 3.91 (Pharmaceutical and Biotechnology). The mean values of the liquidity ratio among the various sub-sectors fluctuated between 1.19 (Cement) and 1.82 (Pharmaceutical and Biotechnology) indicating that the inter-sub-sector variation in mean liquidity was not at all noticeable across the various sub-sectors. The inter-firm variation in respect to liquidity was very much evident in the Auto Parts and Equipment, Chemicals and Industrial Machinery sub-sectors.

5.3 DETERMINANTS OF PROFITABILITY: IMPLICATIONS OF FIRM-SPECIFIC AND MACROECONOMIC FACTORS

In order to explore the microeconomic and macroeconomic determinants of profitability, the panel data regression method has been used with the following empirical model specification.

$$\text{ROA}_{it} = \alpha + \beta_1 \text{Leverage}_{it} + \beta_2 \text{Liquidity}_{it} + \beta_3 \text{VAIC}^{\text{TM}}_{it}$$
$$+ \beta_4 \text{Growth}_{it} + \beta_5 \text{Size}_{it} + \beta_6 \text{Age}_{it}$$
$$+ \beta_7 \text{Openness}_{it} + \beta_8 \text{IIP}_{it} + \beta_9 \text{ExchangeRate}_{it} + \beta_{10} \text{Inflation}_{it} + u_{it} \quad (5.1)$$

where $t = 1, 2, 3, \ldots\ldots\ldots T$ and $i = 1, 2, 3, \ldots\ldots\ldots n$

In model (5.1), the ROA is the dependent variable, α is the intercept term, β values are the $k \times 1$ vectors of parameters to be estimated, leverage, liquidity, VAIC™, growth, size, age, openness, IIP, exchange rate and inflation are the $1 \times k$ number of observations of the independent variables and u_{it} represents the error term.

Three empirical models such as Constant Coefficient Model (CCM), Random Effects Model (REM) and Fixed Effect Model (FEM) exist under the panel data regression theoretical framework. While using the panel data regression method, at first the applicability of CCM or FEM/REM is determined using Breusch-Pagan (BP) test. Once, CCM method is rejected then either FEM or REM is selected based on the outcome of Hausman Test. The outcome of the BP test clearly suggested that in case of all the estimations with respect to the various manufacturing sub-sectors the CCM was not applicable at all. Consequently, the result of the Hausman Test revealed that REM was found to be appropriate in the Cement, Electrical Equipment, Industrial Machinery, Pharmaceutical and Biotechnology, Steel and Textile sub-sectors. In the remaining sectors (such as Auto Parts and Equipment, Chemicals, Construction and Engineering and Food Products sub-sectors) the FEM was found to be suitable. Table 5.2 illustrates the result of the panel data regression reflecting the implications of the different factors on the financial performance of the firms belonging to diversified sub-sectors within the Indian manufacturing industry.

5.3.1   Leverage

Capital structure as delineated by the leverage ratio is one of the most important facets in financial management. The selection of the sources of funds to finance a project depends on the risk associated with the sources of fund, cost of the fund, control of the owners and flexibility. Financial risk is associated with the selection of the source of finance. It is a theoretically established proposition that if a firm employs more debt in its capital structure, its financial risk also augments on account of the possibility of failure in mitigating its fixed financial obligations (Goddard et al., 2005). In addition to that, in the event of bankruptcy the claim of the debenture holders will have to be settled prior to the owners' capital. But the cost of debt fund is lower as compared to that of equity. As per the Income Tax Act, 1961, the interest burden is a charge against profit and therefore, the effective cost of debt is lower than the face value of interest on debt. On the contrary, the dividend is not at all allowed as a charge against profit unlike cost of debt. Moreover, the expectations of the equity shareholders are higher if the firm is highly geared on account of high financial risk associated with its debt fund which enhances the bankruptcy cost of the firm. Obtaining fund by the way of issuing equity is a time taking process as compared to debt financing. Thus, if a firm is inordinately debt dependent then the flexibility also reduces.

The evidences available in the existing literature clearly imply that the effect of leverage on the profitability of the firms can be either positive or

Table 5.2 Sector-wise determinants of profitability in manufacturing industry

Variables	Auto parts & equipment	Cement	Chemicals	Construction & engineering	Electric equipment	Food products	Industrial machinery	Pharmaceutical & biotechnology	Steel	Textile
Leverage	-1.002^a	-0.733^a	-0.162^a	-0.528	-1.217^a	-0.036	-3.700^a	-0.510^a	-0.147^c	-0.132^a
Liquidity	0.110	-0.040	-0.153	-1.129^a	-3.044^a	-1.950^b	-1.561^a	-0.010	-3.763^a	-0.120
VAIC^{TM}	0.832^a	0.018^a	1.275^a	1.080^a	0.073	1.206^a	0.255^a	0.102^a	0.505^a	0.130^a
Growth	0.107^a	0.050^a	-0.005	0.000	-0.003	0.007	0.024^a	0.015^a	-0.000	0.013^a
Size	-1.409	0.391	-0.062	1.057	1.152^a	-0.705	1.876^a	0.171	-0.195	0.072
Age	4.138	-1.814^c	1.077^a	9.483^c	-0.460	14.425	-0.042	6.772^a	4.838^a	-1.037
Openness	8.545^a	15.074^a	-0.028	0.946	-4.552	-7.066	5.047^c	5.724^a	-2.105	1.129
IIP	3.888	51.114^a	-0.369	15.219^a	45.094^a	11.300	36.441^a	4.297	9.898	-4.556
REER	-5.865	-31.591^c	0.295	-1.762	-34.611^a	7.953	-17.277	9.064	6.906	18.474^a
WPI	-9.290^b	-62.212^a	0.087	-43.734^a	-58.845^a	-10.263	-55.410^a	-17.845^a	-26.724^a	51.114^a
Constant	57.08	210.837^a	-2.617	115.487^b	242.359^a	-13.389^a	176.801^a	12.839	47.661	-71.536^a
$\bar{\chi}^2$(BP Test)	617.24^a	1.86^c	59.61^a	101.48^a	272.85^a	631.13^a	457.65^a	695.33^a	20.14^a	1207.78^a
χ^2(Hausman Test)	22.05^a	9.11	38.92^a	114.43^a	15.08	23.65^a	6.49	8.71	4.17	9.87
Model	FEM	REM	FEM	FEM	REM	FEM	REM	REM	REM	REM
Wald χ^2/(F-value)	(17.61^a)	227.77^a	(24.45^a)	(33.01^a)	219.99^a	(1.72^a)	279.90^a	79.43^a	165.22^a	123.91^a
N	720	314	1194	603	468	345	640	995	643	1452

Source Author's own calculation

Notes a, b and c represents statistical significance at 1, 5 and 10% levels respectively

negative. In line with the findings of the studies carried out by Agiomirgianakis et al. (2006), Ghosh (2008), Majumdar (1997), Goddard et al. (2005) and Nanda and Panda (2018), the analysis made in Table 5.2 also exhibits that the effect of leverage was negative and found to be statistically significant in the Auto Parts and Equipment, Cement, Chemicals, Industrial machinery, Pharmaceutical and Biotechnology, Steel, Textile and Electrical Equipment sub-sectors. First of all, the cost associated with the debt is normally higher and therefore will adversely affect the profitability of the firms. Such a negative effect can also be elucidated using 'Pecking Order Hypothesis' in which Myers (1984) propagates that managers in the firms favour employing internal funds as compared to the external funds. Naturally, a profitable firm will have more internal funds at its disposal and will prefer to make use of its internal funds rather than borrowing from market (Kakani et al., 2001). Further, the failure of financial institutions including scheduled commercial banks in India resulting in the introduction of strong monitoring mechanism for ensuring profitable use of the funds by the Indian corporate houses led to the negative effect of leverage on profitability during the period of the study (Majumdar, 1997).

5.3.2   Liquidity

The negative relationship between liquidity and profitability is well established in the literature (Carpenter & Johnson, 1983; Eljelly, 2004; Padachi, 2006). Efficient working capital management is of paramount significance so as to ensure uninterrupted running of the operating activities of the firm. It not only enables the firms to tackle any unprecedented contingent situation but also minimizes the risk exposure of the creditors (Bhayani, 2010; Chander & Aggarwal, 2008; Goddard et al., 2005). In tune with the findings of the studies carried out by Agiomirgianakis et al. (2006), Afza and Nazir (2007), Mathuva (2009) and Hussain et al. (2012), the outcome of the study revealed negative and statistically significant relationship between liquidity and profitability in the Construction and Engineering, Electrical Equipment, Food Products, Industrial Machinery and Steel sub-sectors during the study period. However, such relationship was not found to be statistically significant in the remaining sub-sectors under study.

5.3.3   Intellectual Capital

The success of the firms in the present-day highly competitive market place is conditioned upon its innovation ability to a large extent and that in turn rests on its Intellectual Capital (IC). The significance of the IC can be established from the fact that effective use of the other resources is largely influenced by the IC of the organization (Maji & Goswami, 2016). Therefore, theoretically it can be deduced that a firm with greater IC is also expected to be more profitable. The effect of IC as measured by VAIC was positive and found to be statistically notable in the Auto Parts and Equipment, Cement, Chemicals, Food products, Pharmaceutical and Biotechnology, Steel, Textile, Construction and Engineering and Industrial machinery sub-sectors which is consistent with the findings of the studies carried out by Riahi-Belkaoui (2003), Mehralian et al. (2012), Maji and Goswami (2016), Singh and Narwal (2018). However, the positive effect of VAIC on ROA in the Electrical Equipment sub-sector was found to be statistically insignificant during the period of study.

5.3.4   Size of the Firm

The effect of firm size was positive and found to be statistically significant in the Electrical Equipment and Industrial Machinery sub-sectors during the period under study which corroborates the similar kind of findings obtained in the studies carried out by Majumdar (1997), Kakani et al. (2001), Ghosh (2008) and Pratheepan (2014). Such positive effect may have been derived from the large firms enjoying economies of scale, diversification, greater bargaining power in accessing cheaper financial resources and formalization of procedure. It is interesting to note that the effect of size on the firm-level efficiency was found to be negative in the Electrical Equipment and Industrial Machinery sub-sectors (Chapter 4). It denotes that size exerted negative impact on the productivity but exerted positive impact on the profitability which is similar to the findings of the study accomplished by Majumdar (1997). However, only in two out of the ten sub-sectors under consideration the firm size was found to be a significant explanatory factor of profitability. It suggests that size of the firms did not play a pivotal role in determining the profitability of the firms operating within broad manufacturing sector in general. Such outcome was consistent with the results revealed in the studies carried out by Chander and Aggarwal (2008) and Gatsi et al. (2016).

5.3.5   Age of the Firm

Age of the firm is often correlated with the experience. With an increase in age, the operating process becomes more formalized which empowers the firms to improve its efficiency vis-à-vis profitability by exploiting learning curve effect (Bhayani, 2010). The analysis made in Table 5.2 illustrates that firms operating in the Chemicals, Construction and Engineering, Food, Steel and Textile sub-sectors could utilize the learning curve effect in augmenting the profitability during the period of study. If the effect of age on efficiency is considered (Chapter 4) in these sub-sectors, then it is observed that the effect of age on productivity was also found to be positive in the Construction and Engineering sector and Pharmaceutical and Biotechnology sector. However, the existing literature indicates that such effect may also be negative if the older firms fail to adapt themselves to the changing business environment due to inertia (Chander & Aggarwal, 2008). The analysis shown in Table 5.2 suggests that new firms were more profitable as compared to the older ones in the Cement sub-sector which is consistent with the outcome of the studies carried out by Majumdar (1997), Agiomirgianakis et al. (2006) and Kakani et al. (2001). The old cement firms were also found to be less efficient (please see Chapter 4). Therefore, it can be concluded that the inertia of old cement firms to cope up with the dynamic business environment exerted negative effect on the level of efficiency and such negative impact trickled down to profitability. The effect of age on ROA in the remaining sub-sectors was not found to be statistically significant.

5.3.6   Growth of the Firm

The effect of growth of the firm was positive and found to be statistically notable in the firms operating in Auto Parts and Equipment, Cement, Industrial machinery, Pharmaceutical and Biotechnology and Textile sub-sectors during the period under study (Table 5.2). The positive effect of growth of firms in these sub-sectors underscored the availability of profitable investment opportunities existent in these sub-sectors. The coefficients associated with growth in the remaining sub-sectors were not found to be statistically significant.

5.3.7   Openness of a Firm

The study revealed that the coefficient of openness was positive and found to be statistically significant in the firms belonging to the Auto Parts and Equipment,[1] Cement,[2] Industrial Machinery[3] and Pharmaceutical and Biotechnology[4] sub-sectors during the study period. An internationally diversified firm enjoys economies of scale (due to large customer base), economies of learning, innovation, enhanced bargaining power in the factor market, exploitation of market imperfections, profitable use of the intangibles, resource endowment in different geographies, organizational learning and risk mitigation by the way of geographical diversification, import of technology embedded in inputs etc. (Hitt et al., 1997; Lu & Beamish, 2004; Thomas, 2006). The effect of international diversification on firm-level technical efficiency in these sectors was also found to be positive (refer to Chapter 4). Thus it can be deduced that the positive effect of openness on the productivity of the firms also got transmitted on the profitability which is congruous with the findings of the studies conducted by Hitt et al. (1997) and Kakani et al. (2001).

5.3.8   Index of Industrial Production

IIP being the proxy of real economic activities will surge with growing demand in the economy (Srinivasan, 2011). If the state of the demand in the economy is good (as reflected by increasing IIP) automatically the

---

[1] Auto Parts & Equipment sector have grown from $4.2 billion in 2009–2010 to $11.2 billion in 2014–2015, which is Compounded Annual Growth Rate of approximately 29% whereas the imports for this sector grew at a Compounded Annual Growth Rate of 11% (Capitaline Corporate Database).

[2] India is the second largest consumer as well as producer of cement in the world after China. The export of Indian cement industry was $240.05 million in 2011–2012 which increased to $378.31million during 2014–2015. However the import during the same period declined by $0.59 million (Directorate General of Commercial Intelligence and Statistics, Ministry of Commerce and Industry, Government of India).

[3] India has remained a net importer for this sector. The volume of export and import in 2015–2016 amounted to $19.4 billion and $34.0 billion respectively. Import of industrial machinery signifies import of latest technology embedded in such industrial machines (Export Import Bank of India, 2017).

[4] The global market share of the Indian Pharmaceutical sector has augmented to 21.3% in 2016–2017 which is pegged at $28 billion from 8.3% in 2012–2013 (Capitaline Corporate Database).

various sub-sectors will become more profitable by augmenting output to match the supply with growing demand. Therefore, it is quite natural that if IIP steps up, the profits of the corporate houses especially in the manufacturing sector will also increase. In line with the findings of the study carried out by Ghosh (2008), Table 5.2 also reflects that the effect of IIP was found to be favorable and statistically notable in nine out of the ten sub-sectors during the study period (Auto Parts and Equipment, Cement, Construction and Engineering, Food products, Industrial machinery, Steel, Pharmaceutical and Biotechnology and Electrical Equipment sub-sector).

5.3.9   Exchange Rate

The issue relating to the impact of exchange rate on the level of profitability is inconclusive in nature in the existing literature and primarily it depends on the level of import and export of the individual firm vis-à-vis sub-sectors (Nanda & Panda, 2018; Nandi et al., 2015). The outcome of the study exhibits that the textile being a net exporter[5] sub-sector got benefited due to the increasing exchange rate. However, the profitability of the net importer sub-sectors such as Electrical Equipment[6] and Cement[7] got adversely affected due to such surging exchange rate during the period of study. Such adverse effect of exchange rate on profitability is also evident in the studies carried out by Gatsi et al. (2016) and Nanda and Panda (2018).

5.3.10   Inflation

The analysis made in Table 5.2 depicted that the level of inflation had significant negative effect on the profitability of the firms operating in

---

[5] The cumulative revenue in forex and expenditure in forex for all the 99 companies under Textile sector were Rs. 5795.88 crore and Rs. 2519.55 crore during 2000–2001 respectively whereas the same figures were Rs. 27,131.58 crore and Rs. 11,311.33 crore during 2014–2015 respectively.

[6] The aggregate net import of the selected firms under Electrical equipment sector was found to be Rs. 335.22 crore that increased to Rs. 3252.51 crore in 2014–2015.

[7] The cumulative revenue in forex and expenditure in forex for all the selected 22 cement companies were found to be Rs. 556.85 crore and Rs.628.08 crore during 2000–2001 respectively whereas the same figures were Rs. 1895.45 crore and Rs. 5602.85 crore during 2014–2015 respectively.

the Auto Parts and Equipment, Cement, Construction and Engineering, Electrical Equipment, Pharmaceutical and Biotechnology and Steel sub-sectors which corroborates the findings of the studies carried out by Tahir and Anuar (2015), Bhayani (2010) and Nandi et al. (2015). The underlying reason may be that with inflation, purchasing power of the people vis-à-vis overall demand reduces. Moreover, the rate of increase in consumer output prices is slower than the rate of growth of input cost which adversely affects the level of profitability of the firms during inflation (Defina, 1991). The textile sector being a part of essential commodity class with elasticity of one or less (Haraguchi et al., 2017) was a notable exception in this regard where the effect of inflation was found to be positive during the period of study which is in line with the outcome of the studies carried out by Gatsi et al (2016), Mishra (2013) and Widyastuti et al. (2017).

5.4   A Sum Up

In the present age of stiff competition it is imperative for the firms to strive for sound financial performance for long run endurance. In the present chapter an attempt was made to unearth the different microeconomic as well as macroeconomic factors influencing the financial performance of the manufacturing firms in India. Among the various microeconomic factors, leverage and IC were found to be the two sensitive determinants of the profitability of the various manufacturing subsectors whereas inflation established itself as the major macroeconomic determinant of the profitability during the period of study.

The determination of sub-sector-specific sensitive microeconomic and macroeconomic factors was a special focal point of the chapter. The study revealed that leverage, growth, IC, openness and inflation were found to be the factors affecting profitability in the Auto Parts and Equipment sub-sector whereas in addition to these factors, age and economic growth were also identified as the major determinants of profitability in the Cement sub-sector. Leverage, IC and age of the firms established themselves as the major driving forces of the profitability in the Chemical firms during the period under study. Insulation from the effect of any of the macroeconomic factors reflects the strength of the Chemical sub-sector. Similarly, the Food Product sub-sector also remained unaffected with the volatility of macroeconomic variables although the profitability of the sector was influenced by liquidity and IC. Liquidity, IC, age and

IIP were found to be principal determinants of the profitability in the Construction and Engineering firms. Electrical Equipment sub-sector-specific important determinants were leverage, liquidity, size, IIP and inflation. The profitability of Industrial machinery sub-sector got affected by almost all the firm-specific and macroeconomic variables barring age and exchange rate. As far as the profitability of the firms operating in the Pharmaceutical and Biotechnology sector is concerned, all the microeconomic factors except liquidity and size of the firms proved themselves as the significant determinants whereas inflation was considered as the only important macroeconomic factor in this sector during the study period. The financial performance of the firms belonging to the Steel sector was primarily influenced by the VAIC, age, leverage, liquidity, and inflation whereas leverage, VAIC, growth of firms, exchange rate and inflation were observed to be the major microeconomic and macroeconomic determinants of the profitability of firms operating in the Textile sub-sector during the period under study.

REFERENCES

Afza, T., & Nazir, M. S. (2007). Is it better to be aggressive or conservative in managing working capital. *Journal of Quality and Technology Management, 3*(2), 11–21.

Agiomirgianakis, G., Voulgaris, F., & Papadogonas, T. (2006). Financial factors affecting profitability and employment growth: The case of Greek manufacturing. *International Journal of Financial Services Management, 1*(2–3), 232–242.

Asimakopoulos, I., Samitas, A., & Papadogonas, T. (2009). Firm-specific and economy wide determinants of firm profitability: Greek evidence using panel data. *Managerial Finance, 35*(11), 930–939.

Basu, D., & Das, D. (2015). *Profitability in India's organized manufacturing sector: The role of technology, distribution, and demand* (Working Paper, No. 2015-04). University of Massachusetts, Department of Economics. https://www.econstor.eu/bitstream/10419/145413/1/821606948.pdf

Batra, R., & Kalia, A. (2016). Rethinking and redefining the determinants of corporate profitability. *Global Business Review, 17*(4), 921–933.

Bhattacharjee, A., & Han, J. (2010). *Financial distress in chinese industry: Microeconomic, macroeconomic and institutional influences* (SIRE Discussion Paper Number SIRE-DP-2010-53). http://repo.sire.ac.uk/bitstream/handle/10943/190/SIRE_DP_2010_53.pdf?sequence=1

Bhayani, S. J. (2010). Determinant of profitability in Indian cement industry: An economic analysis. *South Asian Journal of Management, 17*(4), 6–20.

Bhutta, N. T., & Hasan, A. (2013). Impact of firm specific factors on profitability of firms in food sector. *Open Journal of Accounting, 2*(2), 19.

Bontis, N., Keow, W. C C., & Richardson, S. (2000). Intellectual capital and business performance in Malaysian industries. *Journal of Intellectual Capital, 1*(1), 85–100.

Carpenter, M. D., & Johnson, K. H. (1983). The association between working capital policy and operating risk. *The Financial Review, 18*(3), 106–126.

Chander, S., & Aggarwal, P. (2008). Determinants of corporate profitability: An empirical study of Indian drugs and pharmaceutical industry. *Paradigm, 12*(2), 51–61.

Defina, R. H. (1991). Does inflation depress the stock market. *Business Review, 3*, 3–12.

Eljelly, A. M. (2004). Liquidity profitability tradeoff: An empirical investigation in an emerging market. *International Journal of Commerce and Management, 14*(2), 48–61.

Gatsi, J. G., Okpoti, C. A., Gadzo, S. G., & Anipa, C. A. A. (2016). Determinants of market and book based performance of manufacturing companies in Ghana: An empirical study. *International Journal of Economics, Commerce and Management, 4*(1), 393–411.

Geroski, P. A., Machin, S. J., & Walters, C. F. (1997). Corporate growth and profitability. *The Journal of Industrial Economics, 45*(2), 171–189.

Ghosh, S. (2008). Leverage, foreign borrowing and corporate performance: Firm-level evidence for India. *Applied Economics Letters, 15*(8), 607–616.

Goddard, J., Tavakoli, M., & Wilson, J. O. (2005). Determinants of profitability in European manufacturing and services: Evidence from a dynamic panel model. *Applied Financial Economics, 15*(18), 1269–1282.

Gupta, P., Hasan, R., & Kumar, U. (2008). *What constrains Indian manufacturing?* https://www.econstor.eu/bitstream/10419/176229/1/icr ier-wp-211.pdf

Hansen, G. S., & Wernerfelt, B. (1989). Determinants of firm performance: The relative importance of economic and organizational factors. *Strategic Management Journal, 10*(5), 399–411.

Haraguchi, N., Cheng, C. F. C., & Smeets, E. (2017). The importance of manufacturing in economic development: Has this changed? *World Development, 93*, 293–315.

Hitt, M. A., Hoskisson, R. E., & Kim, H. (1997). International diversification: Effects on innovation and firm performance in product-diversified firms. *Academy of Management Journal, 40*(4), 767–798.

Hussain, A., Farooq, S. U., & Khan, K. U. (2012). Aggressiveness and conservativeness of working capital: A case of Pakistani manufacturing sector. *European Journal of Scientific Research, 73*(2), 171–182.

Kakani, R. K., Saha, B., & Reddy, V. N. (2001). *Determinants of financial performance of Indian corporate sector in the post-liberalization era: An exploratory study* (National Stock Exchange of India Limited Research Initiative Paper Number 5). https://www.nseindia.com/content/research/Paper18.pdf

Kambhampati, U. S., & Parikh, A. (2005). Has Liberalization affected profit margins in Indian Industry? *Bulletin of Economic Research, 57*(3), 273–304.

Lu, J. W., & Beamish, P. W. (2004). International diversification and firm performance: The S-curve hypothesis. *Academy of Management Journal, 47*(4), 598–609.

Maji, S. G., & Goswami, M. (2016). Intellectual capital and firm performance in emerging economies: The case of India. *Review of International Business and Strategy, 26*(3), 4–24.

Majumdar, S. K. (1997). The impact of size and age on firm-level performance: Some evidence from India. *Review of Industrial Organization, 12*(2), 231–241.

Majumdar, S. K., & Bhattacharjee, A. (2010). *The profitability dynamics of Indian firms.* https://www.isid.ac.in/~pu/conference/dec_10_conf/Papers/SumitK Majumdar.pdf

Mathuva, D. M. (2009). Capital adequacy, cost income ratio and the performance of commercial banks: The Kenyan Scenario. *The International Journal of Applied Economics and Finance, 3*(2), 35–47.

Mehralian, G., Rajabzadeh, A., Reza Sadeh, M., & Reza Rasekh, H. (2012). Intellectual capital and corporate performance in Iranian pharmaceutical industry. *Journal of Intellectual Capital, 13*(1), 138–158.

Mishra, S. (2013). Relationship between macroeconomic variables and corporate health of manufacturing firms in India. *Journal of Quantitative Economics, 11*(1&2), 230–249.

Mistry, D. S. (2012). Determinants of profitability in Indian automotive industry. *Tecnia Journal of Management Studies, 7*(1), 20–23.

Myers, S. C. (1984). The capital structure puzzle. *Journal of Finance, 39*(3), 575–592.

Nanda, S., & Panda, A. K. (2018). The determinants of corporate profitability: An investigation of Indian manufacturing firms. *International Journal of Emerging Markets, 13*(1), 66–86.

Nandi, S., Majumder, D., & Mitra, A. (2015). *Is exchange rate the dominant factor influencing corporate profitability in India* (RBI Working Paper 04/2015). http://rbidocs.rbi.org.in/rdocs/Publications/PDFs/WP0 49A3B62D596234C97B8CD1B2CC9CBC1CE.PDF

Nugent, J. (1999). Corporate profitability in Ireland: Overview and determinants: Discussion. *Journal of the Statistical and Social Inquiry Society of Ireland, 28*(1), 80–81.

Padachi, K. (2006). Trends in working capital management and its impact on firms' performance: An analysis of Mauritian small manufacturing firms. *International Review of Business Research Papers, 2*(2), 45–58.

Pratheepan, T. (2014). A Panel data analysis of profitability determinants: Empirical results from Sri Lankan manufacturing companies. *International Journal of Economics, Commerce and Management, 2*(12).

Pulic, A. (1998). *Measuring the performance of intellectual potential in knowledge economy.* http://www.academia.edu/download/35277685/pulic_1998.doc

Purohit, H., & Tandon, K. (2015). Intellectual capital, financial performance and market valuation: A study on IT and pharmaceutical companies in India. *IUP Journal of Knowledge Management, 13*(2), 7.

Riahi-Belkaoui, A. (2003). Intellectual capital and firm performance of US multinational firms: A study of the resource-based and stakeholder views. *Journal of Intellectual Capital, 4*(2), 215–226.

Rumelt, R. P. (1982). Diversification strategy and profitability. *Strategic Management Journal, 3*(4), 359–369.

Siddharthan, N. S., Pandit, B. L., & Agarwal, R. N. (1994). Growth and profit behavior of largescale Indian firms. *The Developing Economies, 32*(2), 188–209.

Singh, R. D., & Narwal, K. P. (2018). Examining the relationship between intellectual capital and financial performance: An empirical study of service and manufacturing sector of India. *International Journal of Learning and Intellectual Capital, 15*(4), 309–340.

Spanos, Y. E., Zaralis, G., & Lioukas, S. (2004). Strategy and industry effects on profitability: Evidence from Greece. *Strategic Management Journal, 25*(2), 139–165.

Srinivasan, P. (2011). Causal nexus between stock market return and selected macroeconomic variables in India: Evidence from the National Stock Exchange (NSE). *IUP Journal of Financial Risk Management, 8*(4), 7.

Tahir, M., & Anuar, M. B. A. (2015). The determinants of working capital management and firms performance of textile sector in Pakistan. *Quality & Quantity, 50*(2), 605–618.

Thomas, D. E. (2006). International diversification and firm performance in Mexican firms: A curvilinear relationship? *Journal of Business Research, 59*(4), 501–507.

Voulgaris, F., Doumpos, M., & Zopounidis, C. (2000). On the evaluation of Greek industrial SME's performance via multicriteria analysis of financial ratios. *Small Business Economics, 15*(2), 127–136.

Widyastuti, M., Oetomo, H. W., & Riduwan, A. (2017). Working capital and macroeconomic variables as value creation in Indonesian textile companies. *International Journal of Business and Finance Management Research, 5*, 7–16.

CHAPTER 6

Interrelationship Between Macroeconomic Fundamentals and Sector-Specific Stock Indices of the Indian Manufacturing Sector

Abstract This chapter focuses on the dynamic relationship between the select manufacturing sector-specific stock market indices and the various macroeconomic factors. The long-run and short-run interrelation between the indices and the macroeconomic variables was accomplished using Auto Regressive Distributed Lag framework. The outcome of the study showed the existence of both short-run and long-run relationships. The effect of all the macroeconomic variables was not found to be statistically significant for all the sector-specific indices. However, economic policy uncertainty, foreign portfolio investment ratio and price factor emerged as the most sensitive macroeconomic variables affecting the selected sector-specific indices during the period under study.

Keywords Manufacturing · Macroeconomic factors · Auto regressive distributed lag · Economic policy uncertainty · Foreign portfolio investment ratio and Price factor

© The Author(s), under exclusive license to Springer Nature Singapore Pte Ltd. 2022
S. K. Maji et al., *Indian Manufacturing Sector in Post-Reform Period*,
https://doi.org/10.1007/978-981-19-2666-2_6

6.1   INTRODUCTION

Stock market plays a very vital role in facilitating capital formation in a country by channelizing fund from the surplus sectors to the deficit sectors in an economy (Mohammad et al., 2009). As a matter of fact, capital formation is contemplated as the prerequisites of industrial growth vis-à-vis economic growth of a country (Sultana & Reddy, 2017). Development of stock market is conditioned upon microeconomic (i.e. firm-specific factors), industry-specific factors and the macroeconomic factors. In an atmosphere of financial globalization, macroeconomic environment of a country greatly influences stock market behaviour. In the existing literature, the issue associated with the interrelationship between macroeconomic fundamental (such as economic growth, inflation, money supply, interest rate, openness of the economy, political risk, foreign fund flow etc.) and the stock market movement has received considerable attention. Stock market indices are used as an indicator of the overall health of the stock market in most of the research studies carried out across the globe.

The theoretical framework on the linkages between macroeconomic factors and share price discovery rests on the earlier works of Random Walk Hypothesis (Malkiel & Fama, 1970) and *Arbitrage Price Theory* (Fama & Schwert, 1977; Ross, 1976). In the *Random Walk Hypothesis* which is consistent with the efficient market proposition, it is believed that the change in the macroeconomic factors is supposed to be absorbed in the stock prices and therefore making an abnormal profit is not possible. On the contrary, the *Arbitrage Price Theory* postulates that the expected return of financial assets can be modelled and therefore leaves a possibility of earning short-term profit. In the empirical testing of these hypotheses, many scholars investigated into the linkages between the movement of the stock market index and different macroeconomic variables (Al-Sharkas, 2004; Antonakakis et al., 2013; Chen et al., 1986; Cheung & Ng, 1998; Darrat & Dickens, 1999; Easterly & Rebelo, 1993; Fama & French, 1989; Herve et al., 2011; Kaneko & Lee, 1995; Maji et al., 2020; Mukherjee & Naka, 1995; Nishat et al., 2004; Sultana & Pardhasaradhi, 2012; Thornton, 1993). The genesis of the effect of the macroeconomic variables on the stock market can be comprehended from the simple dividend discounting model of Share Price Valuation.[1] Any kind of change or movement in the macroeconomic variables directly affects either the dividend expectation of the investors or the discounting rate and the consequent impact of such changes in the macroeconomic variables gets reflected on the current share prices.

In the context of the Indian economy, several studies have been carried out to evaluate the implications of macroeconomic fundamentals on the important stock indices in India, such as Nifty and Sensex (Agrawalla & Tuteja, 2008; Ferdows & Roy, 2012; Hassan & Sangmi, 2013; Mukhopadhyay & Sarkar, 2003; Naik & Padhi, 2012; Patel, 2012; Pethe & Karnik, 2000; Rao & Bhole, 1990; Srinivasan, 2011; Sultana & Pardhasaradhi, 2012). However, a comprehensive stock market index (such as Sensex or Nifty or S&P 500 or Nikkei) which is constituted of market capitalization of companies across various sectors represents the market sentiments in general and therefore it is not possible to comprehend the sector-specific differential effect of macroeconomic fundamentals in particular. In fact, industries are different in respect of their characteristics, customer base, demand situation, foreign market operational exposure, cost structure, and financing pattern and therefore it is pertinent to investigate into the long-run as well as short-run relationships between those sector-specific stock indices of the Indian manufacturing industry and the macroeconomic factors. While addressing this gap of knowledge in the existing literature, the present chapter made a modest effort to shed some light afresh on the interrelation between the different macroeconomic fundamentals and the sectoral stock indices especially belonging to the Indian manufacturing industry.

---

[1] The model can be expressed in the following form:

$$P_0 = \frac{D_1}{(1 + K_e)^1} + \frac{D_2}{(1 + K_e)^2} + \ldots + \frac{D_n + P_n}{(1 + K_e)^n}$$

where, P_0 is the price of the share at time t_0, D represents the expected dividends at different time period ranging from 1 to n, P_n is the terminal price at nth period and K_e is the appropriate discounting rate.

6.2   Trend of Sectoral
Manufacturing Stock Indices

Out of the indices of the different sectors belonging to the Indian manufacturing industry, five major manufacturing sector-specific indices, namely BSE-Basic Materials (BSE-BM), BSE-Consumer Discretionary Goods and Services (BSE-CDGS), BSE-Fast Moving Consumer Goods (BSE-FMCG), BSE-Health Care (BSE-HC) and BSE-Industrials (BSE-IND) were chosen. Following the earlier firm-level analysis, these five representative sectors were purposively selected. These selected sectors engulf all of the firms considered in the analysis made in Chapters 4 and 5.

The trends of the sectoral manufacturing stock indices are presented in Fig. 6.1. It is evident that the sectoral indices of FMCG and health care (BSE-FMCG and BSE-HC) followed a steady upward movement during the period of study, mainly due to huge domestic market demand for food products and pharmaceutical products. Support from domestic demand makes these two sectors resilient in comparison to other sectors in the manufacturing industry.

All other sectoral indices (such as BSE-BM, BSE-IND and BSE-CDGS) showed a similar co-movement during the period under study. The impact of global financial meltdown is distinctly visible in the sharp downward movement during 2008–2009. The Indian economy experienced a huge drain out of FPIs from the Indian stock market in the wake of global meltdown. A sign of recovery of the sectoral indices was noticed at the end of 2009. BSE-FMCG and BSE-HC also exhibited an early recovery from the financial crisis.

6.3   Relationships Between Sectoral
Stock Indices and Macroeconomic Factors

In this chapter, an attempt was made to undertake an aggregative time series analysis to ascertain the long-run and short-run implications of macroeconomic factors on sectoral stock indices. In accordance with the standard time series literature, if long-run relationship exists, then only there is a need to examine short-run relationship. However, the choice of methods in testing long-run relationship is reliant on the order of integration. Johansen's test of cointegration is one of the widely used popular

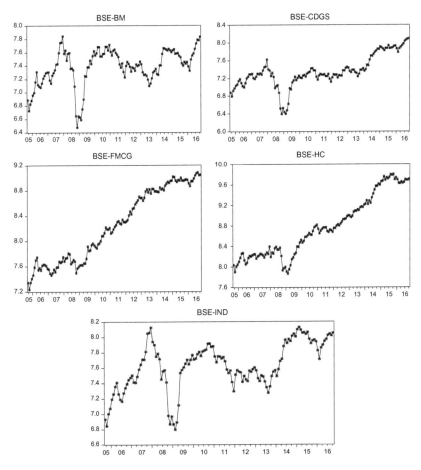

Fig. 6.1 Trend of the sectoral indices (*Source* Author's own representation)

techniques for testing long-run relationship. In this testing, the estimation procedure is based on the error-correction representation of the Vector Auto Regression (VAR) model with Gaussian errors. If a long-run relationship is established in this method, then the short-run adjustment process can be estimated in a Vector Error Correction Model. However, this testing procedure is appropriate only if all the variables are of same order (more specifically integrated of order one). Generally, time series data are expected to be non-stationary at level but stationary at first difference. However, most of the financial time series data do not follow this property (Nkoro & Uko, 2016) and they are integrated into different orders, i.e. I(0), I(1) or I(2). Under such circumstances, it is not advisable to apply cointegration test. As an alternative, the Auto Regressive Distributed Lag (ARDL) Model as advocated by Pesaran and Shin (1998) and Pesaran et al. (2001) can be employed. In this framework, it is practicable to estimate the long-run and short-run relationships among the time series variables which are either I(0) or I(1) but not I(2) (Bhattacharya et al., 2019; Gokmenoglu & Fazlollahi, 2015; Khan et al., 2017; Lima et al., 2016; Pesaran et al., 2001; Shahbaz et al., 2016; Tursoy, 2019; Wada, 2017).

In establishing the long-run relationship between macroeconomic fundamentals and sector-specific stock indices, the following steps were adopted.

6.3.1   Step 1—Selection of Macroeconomic Factors and Sector-Specific Stock Indices

In this study, five major manufacturing sector-specific stock indices such as BSE-Basic Materials, BSE-Consumer Discretionary Goods and Services, BSE- Fast Moving Consumer Goods, BSE-Health Care and BSE-Industrials were chosen. The selected macroeconomic variables encompass Gold Price, Index of Industrial Production, Wholesale Price Index, Money Supply as proxied by M3, i.e. broad money, Foreign Portfolio Investment Ratio,[2] Rate of Interest as indicated by 91 days Treasury Bill Rate, Real Effective Exchange Rate and Crude Oil Price. Policy related uncertainty was captured by the concept of Economic Policy Uncertainty Index. However, it was noticed that monthly data corresponding to the time frame used in Chapters 4 and 5 were not available. Therefore, the period of study considered in this chapter was restricted from September 2005 to October 2016 based on the availability of monthly data on the selected macroeconomic factors and sectoral indices.

---

[2] $FPIR = \frac{\text{Foreign Portfolio Purchase}}{\text{Foreign Portfolio Sales}}$ (Vardhan & Sinha, 2014).
FPIR > 1, it indicates the inflow and FPIR < 1, it implies outflow.

However, a new variable 'Price Factor' (PF) was estimated by synthesizing the influence of four macroeconomic variables such as WPI, IIP, Money Supply (MS) and Gold Price (GP). Intuitively, this could be feasible as the pairs of different combination of the four macroeconomic variables possessed high degree of correlation among themselves. Following Tripathi and Seth (2014), Principal Component Analysis (PCA) was employed to derive the new variable (PF): $\ln PF = \beta_{ij} \ln GP + \beta_{ij} \ln MS + \beta_{ij} \ln IIP + \beta_{ij} \ln WPI$ where, β_{ij} are the respective coefficients or factor loadings to be estimated for the 'jth' variable in the 'ith' principal component. Following the methodology proposed by the Joint Research Centre-European Commission (2008), weights of the respective variables were estimated. The time period and the sources of data are presented in brief in Table 6.1. All the selected variables were expressed in natural logarithmic so as to reduce the sharpness of the data and measurement of elasticities (Shahbaz et al., 2016).

6.3.2   Step 2—Testing Stationarity

Property of stationarity is viewed as the most desirable characteristics of macroeconomic and financial time series data.[3] Augmented Dickey-Fuller Test (ADF Test) and Philips and Perron Test (PP Test) were applied in this study to test stationarity. ADF test consists of a regression of the first difference of the series y_t against the series lagged k times as follows: $\Delta y_t = \alpha + \delta y_{t-1} + \sum \beta_s \Delta y_{t-k} + \varepsilon_t$ where Δy_t denotes the change in the value of y and ε_t is the white noise error term. Testable hypotheses in this framework can be written as: $H_0 : \delta = 0$(Unit root exists), $H_1 :$ $\delta < 0$(No Unit root exists). However, the ADF Test pre-supposes that the error term is serially independent with a constant variance, which may not be tenable in reality. PP test offers an innovative solution to the problem associated with serial correlation in the error terms (Gujarati, 2009). The empirical specification of PP test considers the following equation: $\Delta y_t = \varnothing_0 + \delta y_{t-1} + \alpha_t$. A similar hypothesis is also formulated in PP test.

In this study, ADF and PP tests of stationarity were employed both at level and first difference forms under the model specification of 'constant and no trend' and 'constant and linear trend'.

---

[3] A series is said to be stationary if the mean and covariance are constant overtime and the auto-covariance of the series depends only on the lag between two time periods-not the actual time at which the covariance is computed.

Table 6.1　Time period and data sources of the variables

Variables	Description	Data source
BSE-BM	BSE-Basic Materials	Website of Bombay Stock
BSE-CDGS	BSE-Consumer Discretionary Goods and Services	Exchange,[a] Mumbai
BSE-FMCG	BSE-Fast Moving Consumer Goods	
BSE-HC	BSE-Health Care	
BSE-IND	BSE-Industrials	
GP	Gold Price	Database of Indian Economy
IIP	Index of Industrial Production	website of Reserve Bank of India[b]
WPI	Wholesale Price Index	
MS	Money Supply	
FPIR	Foreign Portfolio Investment Ratio	
INT	Rate of Interest	
REER	Real Effective Exchange Rate	
COP	Crude Oil Price	Petroleum Planning and Analysis Cell of Ministry of Petroleum and Natural Gas, Government of India[c]
EPU	Economic policy uncertainty	Policy Uncertainty Database (Baker et al., 2016[d])

Source Author's own representation
[a] https://www.bseindia.com/indices/IndexArchiveData.aspx
[b] https://dbie.rbi.org.in/DBIE/dbie.rbi?site=publications
[c] http://ppac.org.in/content/149_1_PricesPetroleum.aspx
[d] http://www.policyuncertainty.com/india_monthly.html

The general conclusion from the results of the stationarity tests as revealed in Tables 6.2 and 6.3 suggests that the sectoral stock indices and macroeconomic variables were integrated of different forms: $I(0)$ or $I(1)$. In particular, BSE-BM, BSE-IND, EPU and PF were observed to be stationary at their level [i.e. $I(0)$], whereas all other sectoral stock indices (BSE-CDGS, BSE-FMCG and BSE-HC) and the rest of the macroeconomic variables (INT, COP, REER and FPIR) were observed to be stationary at first difference [i.e. $I(1)$].

Table 6.2 Result of ADF test

Variables	Constant and no trend		Order of integration	Constant and linear trend		Order of integration
	Level	First difference		Level	First difference	
lnBSE^{BM}	-3.06^b	-9.63^a	I(0)	-3.24^c	-9.60^a	I(0)
lnBSE^{CDGS}	-0.85	-9.93^a	I(1)	-1.83	-9.89^a	I(1)
lnBSE^{FMCG}	-0.78	-12.54^a	I(1)	-2.56	-12.51^a	I(1)
lnBSE^{HC}	-0.24	-11.71^a	I(1)	-2.25	-11.66^a	I(1)
lnBSE^{IND}	-3.02^b	-8.85^a	I(0)	-3.32^c	-8.83^a	I(0)
lnEPU	-2.28	-12.76^a	I(1)	-1.90	-12.92^a	I(1)
lnFPIR	-7.87^a	-9.16^a	I(0)	-7.84^a	-7.84^a	I(0)
lnINT	-1.98	-15.22^a	I(1)	-1.95	-15.18^a	I(1)
lnREER	-1.74	-10.05^a	I(1)	-2.27	-10.02^a	I(1)
lnPF	-3.54^c	-16.15^a	I(0)	-0.86	-17.15^a	I(1)
lnCOP	-2.42	-7.20^a	I(1)	-2.44	-7.23^a	I(1)

Source Author's own calculation
Note a, b and c indicates statistically significant at 1, 5 and 10% respectively

Table 6.3 Result of PP test

Variables	Constant and no trendl		Order of integration	Constant and linear trend		Order of integration
	Level	First difference		Level	First difference	
lnBSE^{BM}	-2.75^c	-9.72^a	I(0)	-3.05	-9.69^a	I(0)
lnBSE^{CDGS}	-1.25	-10.07^a	I(1)	-2.36	-10.04^a	I(1)
lnBSE^{FMCG}	-0.75	-12.54^a	I(1)	-2.50	-12.51^a	I(1)
lnBSE^{HC}	-0.24	-11.70^a	I(1)	-2.37	-11.65^a	I(1)
lnBSE^{IND}	-2.63^c	-8.82^a	I(0)	-2.96	-8.81^a	I(1)
lnEPU	-3.41	-18.03^a	I(0)	-3.22^c	-21.12^a	I(0)
lnFPIR	-7.83^a	-53.26^a	I(0)	-7.80^a	-70.15^a	I(0)
lnINT	-2.42	-15.21^a	I(1)	-2.50	-15.17^a	I(1)
lnREER	-1.92	-10.00^a	I(1)	-2.44	-9.96^a	I(1)
lnPF	-3.40^a	-15.56^a	I(0)	-1.30	-17.22^a	I(1)
lnCOP	-1.96	-7.19^a	I(1)	-1.93	-7.21^a	I(1)

Source Author's own calculation
Note a, b and c indicate statistically significant at 1, 5 and 10% respectively

6.3.3   Step 3—Choosing an Appropriate Model

As variables in the study were integrated of different orders, Johansen's test of cointegration could not be applied. As an alternative, the study employed ARDL model to estimate the long-run relationships among the sectoral indices and the different macroeconomic variables. To ascertain the presence of long-run relationship, Bound test for Cointegration was used (Nkoro & Uko, 2016). In this testing procedure, F-statistic was computed and thereafter compared with the critical values ranging within $I(0)$ and $I(1)$. Based on the analysis made in Table 6.4, it can be observed that, in all the estimated regressions, the computed values of F-statistic exceeded the upper bound, i.e. $I(1)$. Thus, the existence of a long-run relationship between the different sector-specific manufacturing stock indices and the macroeconomic variables was confirmed.

6.3.4   Step 4—Measurement of Long-Run Elasticity

After confirmation of the prevalence long-run relationship, the different stock indices were examined to ascertain their reaction to the dynamism in the different macroeconomic variables. The empirical specification in the ARDL framework can be expressed as:

$$\Delta \ln\text{BSE}_t^k = \alpha_0 + \sum_{i=1}^{n} \alpha_1 \Delta \ln\text{BSE}_{t-i}^k + \sum_{i=1}^{n} \alpha_2 \Delta \ln\text{EPU}_{t-i}$$
$$+ \sum_{i=1}^{n} \alpha_3 \Delta \ln\text{FPIR}_{t-i} + \sum_{i=1}^{n} \alpha_4 \Delta \ln\text{INT}_{t-i}$$
$$+ \sum_{i=1}^{n} \alpha_5 \Delta \ln\text{REER}_{t-i} + \sum_{i=1}^{n} \alpha_6 \Delta \ln\text{PF}_{t-i}$$
$$+ \sum_{i=1}^{n} \alpha_7 \Delta \ln\text{COP}_{t-i}$$
$$+ \delta_1 \ln\text{BSE}_{t-1}^i + \delta_2 \ln\text{EPU}_{t-1} + \delta_3 \ln\text{FPIR}_{t-1} + \delta_4 \ln\text{INT}_{t-1}$$
$$+ \delta_5 \ln\text{REER}_{t-1} + \delta_6 \ln\text{PF}_{t-1} + \delta_7 \ln\text{COP}_{t-1} + \varepsilon_t$$

where k = BM, FMCG, HC, IND and CDGS. Altogether five sector-specific equations are estimated. In this equation, Δ is the first difference operators $\alpha_1 to \alpha_7$ are the short-run dynamics and $\delta_1 to \delta_7$ are the long-run dynamics. In the ARDL approach, the selection of the appropriate lag length is very crucial. The optimum lag order was selected based

Table 6.4 Result of bound test for cointegration

Equation	F-statistics	Conclusion
$\left(\ln BSE^{BM}|\ln EPU, \ln FPIR, \ln INT, \ln REER, \ln PF, \ln COP\right)$	$F_{\ln BSE^{BM}} = 7.20$	Significant
$\left(\ln BSE^{CDGS}|\ln EPU, \ln FPIR, \ln INT, \ln REER, \ln PF, \ln COP\right)$	$F_{\ln BSE^{CDGS}} = 12.90$	Significant
$\left(\ln BSE^{FMCG}|\ln EPU, \ln FPIR, \ln INT, \ln REER, \ln PF, \ln COP\right)$	$F_{\ln BSE^{FMCG}} = 4.64$	Significant
$\left(\ln BSE^{HC}|\ln EPU, \ln FPIR, \ln INT, \ln REER, \ln PF, \ln COP\right)$	$F_{\ln BSE^{HC}} = 5.98$	Significant
$\left(\ln BSE^{IND}|\ln EPU, \ln FPIR, \ln INT, \ln REER, \ln PF, \ln COP\right)$	$F_{\ln BSE^{IND}} = 10.65$	Significant

Source Author's own calculation
Note ARDL Critical Bounds at 1% level of Significance at $I(0) = 2.88$; and at $I(1) = 3.99$

Table 6.5   Estimation of long-run elasticities

Independent variables	BSE^{BM}	BSE^{CDGS}	BSE^{FMCG}	BSE^{HC}	BSE^{IND}
lnEPU	−0.389[a]	−0.502[a]	−0.109	−0.463[c]	−0.4238[b]
lnFPIR	1.589[a]	2.073[a]	1.504[b]	2.472	2.814[a]
lnINT	−0.300[c]	0.135	0.106	−0.023	−0.114
lnREER	1.765[c]	0.558	0.676	−1.859	1.158
lnPF	0.532[b]	1.065[a]	1.515[a]	2.162[a]	0.554[c]
lnCOP	0.040	−0.444[b]	−0.213	−0.412	−0.366
Constant	−5.834	−5.302	−13.854[a]	−6.756	−1.370
ARDL (p,q) Model	(1,4,1,0,0,0,2)	(1,4,0,0,0,2,3)	(1,0,2,0,0,1,0)	(1,3,0,2,0,2,2)	(1,4,0,0,0,2,3)

Source Author's own calculation
Note a, b and c indicates statistically significant at 1, 5 and 10% respectively

on appropriate model selection yardsticks such as Akaike Information Criterion, and Schwarz Bayesian Criterion.[4]

Table 6.5 illustrates the estimates of the long-run elasticities with respect to the different macroeconomic factors in five ARDL specifications. The appropriate lag length of the ARDL model is shown in the last row of Table 6.5.

6.3.5   Economic Policy Uncertainty

Development of stock market of any economy is conditioned upon economic growth, good governance, strong rule of law and political steadiness. Governments of different countries pursue various types of industrial policies and these policies essentially shape the fate of the firms operating in different sectors in the economy. Pro-market industrial and economic policies serve as a boon to the stock market by affecting the investors' sentiment favourably whereas conservative industrial policies,

---

[4] The trial and error process was used in selection of maximum lag for the ARDL model. For example initially for both the dependent and independent variables the lag was specified as (1,1), then in the next instance lag of (1,2) then (1,3). In this way all the possible combinations up to (5,5) are considered. Optimum lag guided by the lowest possible of value of AIC. Thus different sector-specific ARDL model had different optimal lag length.

high rate of taxes, restrictions on import and export, unfavourable foreign investment and divestment policies, etc., affect the stock market adversely. In addition, the instability of the Government due to coalition, political coup, industrial unrest and corruption are the major impediments in the way of stock market development (Bilson et al., 2002; Cherian & Perotti, 2001; Hillman & Hitt, 1999; Hillman et al., 1999). EPU is a comprehensive and popular benchmark which appraises the prevalence of precariousness in the economic policy as suggested by Baker et al. (2016). Theoretically, it is expected that with an increase in economic policy uncertainty the sentiments of the investors' community vis-à-vis stock market will get adversely affected (Antonakakis et al., 2013). The evaluation made in Table 6.5 clearly indicates that all the selected sectoral manufacturing indices got negatively affected by the EPU during the period of study which corroborates the findings of the studies carried out by Arouri and Roubaud (2016), Ko and Lee (2015) and Liu and Zhang (2015). However, such negative impact was not found to be statistically significant in BSE-FMCG which may be on account of the strength of the FMCG sector driven by huge domestic market.

6.3.5.1   Foreign Investment

In any emerging economy, investment in the form of FPI plays a pivotal role in shaping the movement of the overall stock market. Due to lucrative high rates of returns, Indian stock markets were able to win over huge FPI (even during 2008–2009 crisis) from around the globe since the opening up of stock market to foreign investment in 1992 (Bhargava & Malhotra, 2015). In order to capture the effect of both inflow and outflow of foreign portfolio investment the ratio of purchase and sale by the foreign institutional investors as denoted by FPIR was considered (Vardhan & Sinha, 2014). Similar to the findings of the studies carried out by Suganthi and Dharshanaa (2014), Srivastava and Behl (2015), Acharya et al. (2016), Mukherjee and Roy (2016) and Sultana and Reddy (2017) the analysis made in Table 6.5 also underscores the statistically significant favourable impact of foreign portfolio investment on all the sectoral stock indices during the period under study. However, the positive effect of FPIR on BSE-HC was not found to be statistically notable during the study period.

6.3.5.2   Interest Rate

Based on the assessment made in Table 6.5, it is apparent that in almost all the selected indices except BSE-BM, the coefficients associated with the rate of interest were found to be statistically insignificant. Therefore, it may be deduced that the interest rate does not determine the movement of the manufacturing stock prices in India. Such irrelevance of rate of interest towards stock market was also noticed across different stock markets around the globe (Ibrahim & Musah, 2014; Msindo, 2016; Talla, 2013) and the Indian economy in particular (Naik & Padhi, 2012; Tripathi & Seth, 2014). However, the effect of the rate of interest on BSE-BM was negative and found to be statistically notable during the study period which is in line with the findings of the studies carried out by Mukherjee and Naka (1995), Liu and Shrestha (2008), Khan et al. (2017) and Shabbir (2018). The adverse impact of interest rate can be theoretically justified on the basis of couple of facts. Firstly, rising interest rate inflates the cost of capital of the firms and thereby reduces the profit margin and consequently declines dividend (Ibrahim & Musah, 2014) and secondly, hike in interest rate triggers draining funds from stock market to fixed income generating financial instruments (Mukherjee & Roy, 2016).

6.3.5.3   Exchange Rate

The existing literature remains inconclusive regarding the effect of rate of exchange on the stock prices (Cenedese et al., 2015). If the firms in an industry are export oriented, the rise in exchange rate is expected to exacerbate positive effect whereas the implication will prove to be negative if the firms depend excessively on imports. From the analysis of Table 6.5, it is observed that like the rate of interest, the exchange rate was also found to be an insignificant determinant of stock prices in majority of the manufacturing sectoral stock indices. More specifically, BSE-CDGS, BSE-FMCG, BSE-HC and BSE-IND remained protected from the fluctuations of rate of exchange during the period of study. However, the long-run elasticity associated with the REER in respect of BSE-BM was positive and found to be statistically significant which endorses the findings of the studies carried out by Mukherjee and Naka (1995), Naik and Padhi (2012) and Khan et al. (2017). Moreover, it is also seen in Chapter 5 that the effects of REER on the firm-level profitability of Steel sector and Chemical sector (which are the intrinsic part of BSE-BM among other sub-sectors) were also found to be positive (although statistically insignificant). The underlying reason may be that the firms operating under various sub-sectors within Basic Materials sector were export dependent during the period of study.

6.3.5.4   Price Factor

Price Factor (PF) is the principal component used in the study comprising of IIP, WPI, MS and GP. So, in order to understand the real effect of the PF on the stock prices, the individual effects of its components are to be evaluated. Growth in IIP signals real economic growth in the economy. In the event of rising demand, the corporate houses are able to do better in enhancing their earnings and dividend which exerts a noteworthy positive effect on the stock prices (Liu & Shrestha, 2008; Maysami et al., 2004; Mohammad et al., 2009; Mukherjee & Naka, 1995; Mukhopadhyay & Sarkar, 2003; Naik & Padhi, 2012; Shahbaz et al., 2016). The favourable effect of MS on stock prices can be justified based on pairs of grounds. Firstly, it is empirically observed that with expanding MS, investment gets relocated from non-interest bearing money asset to stocks (Naik & Padhi, 2012). Secondly, with escalating MS, the demand in the economy also gets revamped and ultimately affects stock price favourably (Mukherjee & Naka, 1995). However, it is also contended that as MS surges, inflation also soars which affects the discounting rate in the equity valuation model vis-à-vis stock prices negatively (Liu & Shrestha, 2008; Nishat et al., 2004). The adverse effect of inflation can also be explained using '*Proxy Effect*' (Fama, 1981) where it is put forward that real economic growth is negatively associated with inflation and positively associated with stock prices. Therefore, inflation has negative effect on stock prices. On the contrary, Ram and Spencer (1983) based on '*Philips Curve Theory*' repudiated such theory of negative effect. In addition to it, Marshall (1992) propagated that in the times of inflation the expected return to money reduces along with money demand and thereby affects the stock price favourably. Further, the possibility of enlarging the corporate profitability gets widened during inflation resulting in a surge in stock price (Khan et al., 2017; Mukherjee & Naka, 1995; Shahbaz et al., 2016). On one hand, the investment in stock is contemplated as a fence against inflation whereas the investment in gold is regarded as the cushion against the eccentricity of stock prices leading to a negative association between GP and stock prices (Hasanzadeh & Kianvand, 2012). The scrutiny of Table 6.5 reveals that the effect of PF was positive and found to be statistically noticeable in all the sectoral stock indices during the study period. The fundamental reasons may be that, firstly the effect of IIP was favourable; secondly, the catalytic effect of stimulus brought in by increasing MS abrogated the negative effect on stock prices. As the effects of three out of the four factors were positive, the overall implications of PF towards all the sectoral indices were also found to be favourable.

6.3.5.5 Oil Price

Like exchange and interest rates, the COP was also found to be an insignificant factor in the selected sectoral stock indices except BSE-CDGS. Automobiles, auto parts and equipment and consumer durable companies are the primary constituents of BSE-CDGS which are generally susceptible to the volatility of COP. Therefore, it is obvious that the repercussions of COP are expected to be negative on BSE-CDGS and such consequence is in line with the conclusions of the studies carried out by Basher et al. (2012) and Chancharat et al. (2008).

6.3.6 Step 5—Measurement of Short-Run Elasticity

Existence of long-run relationship necessitated the examination short-run dynamics. In the ARDL framework, Unrestricted Error Correction Model (UECM) was employed to estimate Error Correction Term (ECT) yielding the estimates of short-run adjustment speed to restore long-run equilibrium without losing the long-run information. The ARDL-UECM was expressed as follows:

$$\Delta \ln BSE_t^k = \alpha_0 + \sum_{i=1}^{n} \alpha_1 \Delta \ln BSE_{t-i}^k + \sum_{i=1}^{n} \alpha_2 \Delta \ln EPU_{t-i}$$
$$+ \sum_{i=1}^{n} \alpha_3 \Delta \ln FPIR_{t-i} + \sum_{i=1}^{n} \alpha_4 \Delta \ln INT_{t-i}$$
$$+ \sum_{i=1}^{n} \alpha_5 \Delta \ln REER_{t-i} + \sum_{i=1}^{n} \alpha_6 \Delta \ln PF_{t-i}$$
$$+ \sum_{i=1}^{n} \alpha_7 \Delta \ln COP_{t-i} + \lambda ECT_{t-1} + \varphi_t$$

where, k = BM, FMCG, HC, CDGS and IND.

In this equation, ECT stands for error correction term and λ is the speed of adjustment. A negative value of λ signifies that the variables are coming close to each other at the speed of λ in each period to converge in the long run. Thus a negative and statistically significant value of λ is desirable in establishing short-run and long-run relationships among the variables.

Table 6.4 measures the short-run elasticities from the relationships between the sector-specific BSE manufacturing indices and the selected macroeconomic factors. As anticipated, it is noticed that the values of

ECT_{t-1} corresponding to all the sectoral indices were negative and found to be statistically significant. Thus with the adjustment speed to the magnitude of 6.37% (BSE-HC) to 16.84% (BSE-BM) took place in short run to ensure equilibrium in the long-run relationship. Thus the finding is consistent with the findings of Liu and Shrestha (2008), Shahbaz et al. (2016) and Khan et al. (2017) (Table 6.6).

The robustness of the empirical results can be inferred from the favourable outcomes of different diagnostic tests such as no heteroscedasticity problem in the error terms were observed and the error terms were noticed to be orthogonal of the independent variables as reflected in ARCH test; residuals in all the models were found to be normally distributed as depicted by J-B test; all the models were correctly specified as indicated by Ramsey's RESET test; and ARDL-UEC models were stable as exhibited by CUSUM and CUSUM of Squares plots.

Table 6.6 Short-run elasticities

Variables	$\Delta lnBSE^{BM}$	$\Delta lnBSE^{CDGS}$	$\Delta lnBSE^{FMCG}$	$\Delta lnBSE^{HC}$	$\Delta lnBSE^{IND}$
$\Delta lnEPU_t$	−0.031	−0.032	−0.012	−0.028	−0.035
$\Delta lnEPU_{t-1}$	0.070[a]	0.098[a]	–	0.057[a]	0.085[a]
$\Delta lnEPU_{t-2}$	0.059[b]	0.062[a]	–	0.030[c]	0.052[b]
$\Delta lnEPU_{t-3}$	0.033	0.049[a]	–	–	0.039[c]
$\Delta lnFPIR_t$	0.342[a]	0.302[a]	0.161[a]	0.157[a]	0.333[a]
$\Delta lnFPIR_{t-1}$	–	–	−0.063[b]	–	–
$\Delta lnINT_t$	−0.051[c]	0.020	0.032	0.069[c]	−0.013
$\Delta lnINT_{t-1}$	–	–	–	0.086[b]	–
$\Delta lnREER_t$	0.297	0.081	0.074	−0.118	0.137
$\Delta lnPF_t$	0.090[a]	−0.427	−0.363	−0.523[c]	−0.714
$\Delta lnPF_{t-1}$	–	−0.727[b]	–	−0.578[c]	−0.713[c]
$\Delta lnCOP_t$	0.172[b]	−0.077	−0.023	−0.035	0.057
$\Delta lnCOP_{t-1}$	0.192[b]	0.217[a]	–	0.13649[b]	0.161[c]
$\Delta lnCOP_{t-2}$	–	0.115[c]	–	–	0.119
ECT_{t-1}	−0.168[a]	−0.146[a]	−0.109[a]	−0.064[c]	−0.118[a]
R^2	0.544	0.545	0.278	0.384	0.521
$\bar{R}^2$	0.489	0.481	0.219	0.297	0.453
F-statistics	12.514[a]	10.446[a]	5.843[a]	5.923[a]	9.468[a]
$DW Statistics$	1.96	1.78	1.92	2.01	1.75

Source Author's own calculation

Note a, b and c indicate statistically significant at 1, 5 and 10% respectively

6.4   Structural Break

After establishing short-run and long-run relationships, it is pertinent to identify the structural break in the relationship. Multiple break point methodology (as executed in Bai-Perron Test) is quite helpful in a situation where the break points are unknown.

6.4.1   First Stage

The study identified the multiple break points in the relationship (between sectoral stock indices and macroeconomic factors). Empirical evidences suggest that there was one break point in the ARDL specification of Basic metal sector (December 2008), three break points in Consumer goods and services (December 2007; July 2009; May 2014), one break point in Fast moving consumer goods (November 2008), three break points in case of Health care (December 2007; February 2010; June 2014) and also three break points in case of Industrial equipment (October 2007; December 2009; February 2014) (Table 6.7).

Table 6.7 Determination of structural break points

Sector-specific ARDL models	Identification of multiple break points (Bai-Perron test)	Significance of the break pints (Chow Test)
BSE-BM	December 2008	3.126[a]
BSE-CDGS	December 2007	0.698
	July 2009	2.233[a]
	May 2014	1.403
BSE-FMCG	November 2008	3.113[a]
BSE-HC	December 2007	0.884
	February 2010	3.148[a]
	June 2014	1.873[b]
BSE-IND	October 2007	1.176
	December 2009	2.733[a]
	February 2014	1.424

Source Author's own calculation
Note a and b indicate statistically significant at 1 and 5% respectively

6.4.2   Second Stage

Once the multiple break points were identified, Chow test was used in the next stage to determine the significance of the already determined break points. Out of 11 break points (as identified by Bai-Perron test), six break points were found to be statistically significant (as shown by Chow Test). It is evident that US sub-prime crisis had the most deepening and contagious effects across stock indices of all manufacturing sectors, except health care. Resilience of the health care sector even in the face of global financial meltdown during 2008–2009 was a notable phenomenon. In the health care sector, structural breaks appeared in February 2010 and June 2014. The first structural break can be explained by the Government's decision of huge investment of about Rs. 3000 crore (venture capital fund) in the field of pharmaceutical sector for research and development for new drug discovery.[5] Second structural break can be explained by the formation of NDA Government with full majority, which signalled the political stability and upcoming economic reforms.

6.5   A Sum Up

This study attempted to examine the relationships between stock market indices in the Indian manufacturing sectors and the different macroeconomic variables. The empirical evidences suggest a stable long-run interrelation between all the stock indices and the selected macroeconomic variables. In the short run, a negative and statistically significant error correction term indicates the occurrence of short-run adjustment (at a speed of approximately 6–16%) to ensure long-run equilibrium.

The assessment of long-run relationship between the major macroeconomic variables and the sectoral manufacturing indices demonstrated that all the macroeconomic variables were not equally important for every sector as postulated earlier. For example, except COP, all the selected macroeconomic factors were found to be sensitive in BSE-BM whereas BSE-IND got affected by only EPU, FPIR and PF. Similarly, EPU, FPIR, PF and COP were established as the major long-term determinants of BSE-CDGS. The result of the study also revealed that BSE-FMCG got affected by three macroeconomic factors (namely, FPIR, PF and COP)

---

[5] http://pharmaceuticals.gov.in/industry-news/archieve/2323;   http://pharmaceutic als.gov.in/sites/default/files/pg204.pdf.

whereas only two macroeconomic variables (such as EPU and PF) were found to be relevant to the BSE-HC during the study period. In aggregate, it can be inferred that EPU, FPIR and PF established themselves as the most sensitive macroeconomic variables in the selected sectoral indices during the period under study.

A far-reaching implication of the emergence of the financial meltdown in 2008–2009 was evident cutting across all manufacturing sectors, except the health care sector. In fact, the health care sector remained more or less insulated from the effect of the financial crisis of 2008–2009.

REFERENCES

Acharya, V. V., Anshuman, V. R., & Kumar, K. K. (2016). *Foreign fund flows and asset prices: Evidence from the Indian stock market*. http://pages.stern. nyu.edu/~sternfin/vacharya/public_html/pdfs/Foreign%20Fund%20Flows% 20May_2016.pdf

Agrawalla, R. K., & Tuteja, S. K. (2008). Share prices and macroeconomic variables in India. *Journal of Management Research, 8*(3), 1–12.

Al-Sharkas, A. (2004). The dynamic relationship between macroeconomic factors and the Jordanian stock market. *International Journal of Applied Econometrics and Quantitative Studies, 1*, 97–114.

Antonakakis, N., Chatziantoniou, I., & Filis, G. (2013). Dynamic co-movements of stock market returns, implied volatility and policy uncertainty. *Economics Letters, 120*(1), 87–92.

Arouri, M., & Roubaud, D. (2016). On the determinants of stock market dynamics in emerging countries: The role of economic policy uncertainty in China and India. *Economics Bulletin, 36*(2), 760–770.

Baker, S. R., Bloom, N., & Davis, S. J. (2016). Measuring economic policy uncertainty. *The Quarterly Journal of Economics, 131*(4), 1593–1636.

Basher, S. A., Haug, A. A., & Sadorsky, P. (2012). Oil prices, exchange rates and emerging stock markets. *Energy Economics, 34*(1), 227–240.

Bhargava, V., & Malhotra, D. K. (2015). Foreign institutional investment and the Indian stock market. *The Journal of Wealth Management, 17*(4), 101–116.

Bhattacharya, S. N., Bhattacharya, M., & Basu, S. (2019). Stock market and its liquidity: Evidence from ARDL bound testing approach in the Indian context. *Cogent Economics & Finance, 7*, 1–12.

Bilson, C. M., Brailsford, T. J., & Hooper, V. C. (2002). The explanatory power of political risk in emerging markets. *International Review of Financial Analysis, 11*(1), 1–27.

Cenedese, G., Payne, R., Sarno, L., & Valente, G. (2015). What do stock markets tell us about exchange rates? *Review of Finance, 20*(3), 1045–1080.

Chancharat, S., Valadkhani, A., & Havie, C. (2008). *The influence of international stock markets and macroeconomic variables on the Thai stock market.* Retrieved from https://ro.uow.edu.au/cgi/viewcontent.cgi?referer=https://scholar.google.com/&httpsredir=1&article=1397&context=commpapers

Chen, N. F., Roll, R., & Ross, S. A. (1986). Economic forces and the stock market. *Journal of Business, 59*(3), 383–403.

Cherian, J. A., & Perotti, E. (2001). Option pricing and foreign investment under political risk. *Journal of International Economics, 55*(2), 359–377.

Cheung, Y. W., & Ng, L. K. (1998). International evidence on the stock exchange and aggregate economic activity. *Journal of Empirical Finance, 5*(3), 281–296.

Darrat, A. F., & Dichens, R. N. (1999). On the inter-relationship among real monetary and financial indicators. *Applied Financial Economics, 9*(3), 289–293.

Easterly, W., & Rebelo, S. (1993). Fiscal policy and economic growth. *Journal of Monetary Economics, 32*(3), 417–458.

Fama, E. F. (1981). Stock returns, real activity, inflation, and money. *The American Economic Review, 71*(4), 545–565.

Fama, E. F., & French, K. R. (1989). Business conditions and expected returns on stocks and bonds. *Journal of Financial Economics, 25*(1), 23–49.

Fama, E. F., & Schwert, W. G. (1977). Asset returns and inflation. *Journal of Financial Economics, 5*(2), 115–146.

Ferdows, S. S., & Roy, A. (2012). A study on the international diversification in the emerging equity market and its effect on the Indian capital market. *International Journal of Contemporary Business Studies., 3*(4), 79–96.

Gokmenoglu, K. K., & Fazlollahi, N. (2015). The interactions among gold, oil, and stock market: Evidence from S&P500. *Procedia Economics and Finance, 25*, 478–488.

Gujarati, D. N. (2009). *Basic econometrics.* Tata McGraw-Hill Education.

Hasanzadeh, A., & Kianvand, M. (2012). The impact of macroeconomic variables on stock prices: The case of Tehran Stock Exchange. *Money and Economy, 6*(2), 171–190.

Hassan, M. M. S., & Sangmi, M. U. D. G. (2013). *Macro-economic variables and stock prices in India* (Doctoral dissertation).

Herve, D. B. G., Chanmalai, B., & Shen, Y. (2011). The study of causal relationship between Stock Market Indices and macroeconomic variables in Cote d'Ivoire: Evidence from error-correction models and Granger Causality Test. *International Journal of Business & Management, 6*(12), 146–167.

Hillman, A. J., & Hitt, M. A. (1999). Corporate political strategy formulation: A model of approach, participation, and strategy decisions. *Academy of Management Review, 24*(4), 825–842.

Hillman, A. J., Zardkoohi, A., & Bierman, L. (1999). Corporate political strategies and firm performance: Indications of firm-specific benefits from personal service in the US government. *Strategic Management Journal, 20*(1), 67–81.

Ibrahim, M., & Musah, A. (2014). An econometric analysis of the impact of macroeconomic fundamentals on stock market returns in Ghana. *Research in Applied Economics, 6*(2), 47–72.

Joint Research Centre-European Commission. (2008). *Handbook on constructing composite indicators: Methodology and user guide (OECD).* https://www.oecd.org/sdd/42495745.pdf

Kaneko, T., & Lee, B. S. (1995). Relative importance of economic factors in the US and Japanese stock markets. *Journal of the Japanese and International Economies, 9*(3), 290–307.

Khan, M. K., Teng, J. Z., Parvaiz, J., & Chaudhary, S. K. (2017). Nexuses between economic factors and stock returns in China. *International Journal of Economics and Finance, 9*(9), 182–191.

Ko, J. H., & Lee, C. M. (2015). International economic policy uncertainty and stock prices: Wavelet approach. *Economics Letters, 134,* 118–122.

Lima, L., Vasconcelos, C. F., Simão, J., & de Mendonça, H. F. (2016). The quantitative easing effect on the stock market of the USA, the UK and Japan: An ARDL approach for the crisis period. *Journal of Economic Studies, 43*(6), 1006–1021.

Liu, L., & Zhang, T. (2015). Economic policy uncertainty and stock market volatility. *Finance Research Letters, 15,* 99–105.

Liu, M. H., & Shrestha, K. M. (2008). Analysis of the long-term relationship between macro-economic variables and the Chinese stock market using heteroscedastic cointegration. *Managerial Finance, 34*(11), 744–755.

Maji, S. K., Laha, A., & Sur, D. (2020). Dynamic Nexuses between Macroeconomic Variables and Sectoral Stock Indices: Reflection from Indian Manufacturing Industry. *Management and Labour Studies, 45*(3), 239–269.

Malkiel, B. G., & Fama, E. F. (1970). Efficient capital markets: A review of theory and empirical work. *The Journal of Finance, 25*(2), 383–417.

Marshall, D. A. (1992). Inflation and asset returns in a monetary economy. *The Journal of Finance, 47*(4), 1315–1342.

Maysami, R. C., Howe, L. C., & Hamzah, M. A. (2004). Relationship between macroeconomic variables and stock market indices: Cointegration evidence from stock exchange of Singapore's All-S sector indices. *Jurnal Pengurusan, 24,* 47–77.

Misra, P. (2018). An investigation of the macroeconomic factors affecting the Indian Stock Market. *Australasian Accounting, Business and Finance Journal, 12*(2), 71–86.

Mohammad, S. D., Hussain, A., & Ali, A. (2009). Impact of macroeconomics variables on stock prices: Empirical evidence in case of KSE (Karachi Stock Exchange). *European Journal of Scientific Research, 38*(1), 96–103.

Msindo, Z. H. (2016). *The impact of interest rates on stock returns: empirical evidence from the JSE securities exchange* [Doctoral dissertation]. http://wiredspace.wits.ac.za/bitstream/handle/10539/22148/Zet hu'sFinal%20Researchpaper14Sept.pdf?sequence=1&isAllowed=y

Mukherjee, P., & Roy, M. (2016). What drives the stock market return in India? An exploration with dynamic factor model. *Journal of Emerging Market Finance, 15*(1), 119–145.

Mukherjee, T. K., & Naka, A. (1995). Dynamic relations between macroeconomic variables and the Japanese stock market: An application of a vector error correction model. *Journal of Financial Research, 18*(2), 223–237.

Mukhopadhyay, D., & Sarkar, N. (2003). *Stock return and macroeconomic fundamentals in model specification framework: Evidence from Indian stock market.* https://www.isical.ac.in/~eru/erudp/2003-05.pdf

Naik, P. K., & Padhi, P. (2012). The impact of macroeconomic fundamentals on stock prices revisited: Evidence from Indian data. *Eurasian Journal of Business and Economics, 5*(10), 25–44.

Nishat, M., Shaheen, R., & Hijazi, S. T. (2004). Macroeconomic factors and the Pakistani equity market. *The Pakistan Development Review, 43*(4), 619–637.

Nkoro, E., & Uko, A. K. (2016). Autoregressive Distributed Lag (ARDL) cointegration technique: Application and interpretation. *Journal of Statistical and Econometric Methods, 5*(4), 63–91.

Patel, S. (2012). The effect of macroeconomic determinants on the performance of the Indian stock market. *NMIMS Management Review, 22*(1), 117–127.

Pesaran, M. H., & Shin, Y. (1998). An autoregressive distributed-lag modelling approach to cointegration analysis. *Econometric Society Monographs, 31*, 371–413.

Pesaran, M. H., Shin, Y., & Smith, R. J. (2001). Bounds testing approaches to the analysis of level relationships. *Journal of Applied Econometrics, 16*(3), 289–326.

Pethe, A., & Karnik, A. (2000). Do Indian stock markets matter? Stock market indices and macro-economic variables. *Economic and Political Weekly, 35*(5), 349–356.

Ram, R., & Spencer, D. E. (1983). Stock returns, real activity, inflation, and money: Comment. *The American Economic Review, 73*(3), 463–470.

Rao, K. N., & Bhole, L. M. (1990). Inflation and equity returns. *Economic and Political Weekly, 25*(21), 91–96.

Ross, S. A. (1976). The arbitrage theory of capital asset pricing. *Journal of Economic Theory, 13*(3), 341–360.

Shabbir, M. S. (2018). *The impact of foreign portfolio investment on stock prices of Pakistan.* https://www.researchgate.net/publication/325257541_M_P_RA_The_Impact_of_Foreign_Portfolio_Investment_on_Stock_Prices_of_Pak istan_The_Impact_of_Foreign_Portfolio_Investment_on_Stock_Prices_of_Pak istan

Shahbaz, M., Rehman, I. U., & Afza, T. (2016). Macroeconomic determinants of stock market capitalization in an emerging market: Fresh evidence from cointegration with unknown structural breaks. *Macroeconomics and Finance in Emerging Market Economies, 9*(1), 75–99.

Srinivasan, P. (2011). Causal nexus between stock market return and selected macroeconomic variables in India: Evidence from the National Stock Exchange (NSE). *IUP Journal of Financial Risk Management, 8*(4), 7.

Srivastava, A., & Behl, K. (2015). Macroeconomic variables on Indian stock market interactions: An analytical approach. *JIM Quest: Journal of Management and Technology, 11*(2), 1–8. http://jaipuria.edu.in/jim/wp-content/upl oads/2012/06/jim_quest_july_dec_2015a.pdf#page=5

Suganthi, P., & Dharshanaa, C. (2014). Interrelationship between FII and stock market and their causal relationship with selected macroeconomic variables in India. *TSM Business Review, 2*(1), 29–46.

Sultana, S. T., & Pardhasaradhi, S. (2012). Impact of flow of FDI & FII on Indian stock market. *Finance Research, 1*(3), 4–10.

Sultana, S. T., & Reddy, K. S. (2017). The effect of macroeconomic factors on Indian stock market: An empirical evidence. *FIIB Business Review, 6*(1), 68–76.

Talla, J. T. (2013). *Impact of macroeconomic variables on the stock market prices of the Stockholm stock exchange* [Master's thesis]. Jonkoping International Business School. https://pdfs.semanticscholar.org/531c/af1a5eded 883d4a663b9f200bb9b666abcb5.pdf

Thornton, J. (1993). Money, output and stock prices in the UK: Evidence on some (non) relationships. *Applied Financial Economics, 3*(4), 335–338.

Tripathi, V., & Seth, R. (2014). Stock market performance and macroeconomic factors: The study of Indian equity market. *Global Business Review, 15*(2), 291–316.

Tursoy, T. (2019). The interaction between stock prices and interest rates in Turkey: Empirical evidence from ARDL bounds test cointegration. *Financial Innovation, 5*(1), 1–12.

Vardhan, H., & Sinha, P. (2014). *Influence of foreign institutional investments (FIIs) on the Indian stock market.* https://mpra.ub.uni-muenchen.de/53611/1/MPRA_paper_53611.pdf

Wada, I. (2017). Dynamic causality in energy production and output growth in Nigeria revisited: ARDL bounds test approach. *Energy Sources, Part b: Economics, Planning, and Policy, 12*(11), 945–951.

CHAPTER 7

Summary and Policy Implications

Abstract Effort was made in the earlier chapters of this book in highlighting the growth of the manufacturing sector under alternative policy regimes. Firm-level efficiency and profitability has been delved into thoroughly to understand how these are conditioned upon the microeconomic and macroeconomic factors. Examination of the dynamic relationship between important macroeconomic factors and the manufacturing sector-specific stock indices was a special interest of the whole exercise. This chapter is dedicated towards summarizing the outcome of study in a holistic manner. Policy implications of such results are highlighted in detail along with the scope of future research towards the end of the chapter.

Keywords Manufacturing · Efficiency · Profitability · Microeconomic factor · Macroeconomic factors · Stock Indices

7.1 Overview of the Book

The pivotal role played by the manufacturing sector in promoting economic growth and development is theoretically well established especially in the context of the emerging economies like India. At least, the rise of many of the East Asian economies based on manufacturing sector is a

© The Author(s), under exclusive license to Springer Nature   133
Singapore Pte Ltd. 2022
S. K. Maji et al., *Indian Manufacturing Sector in Post-Reform Period*,
https://doi.org/10.1007/978-981-19-2666-2_7

testimony to that. Higher-level productivity and technological progress potentiality, large-scale employment creation, favourable backward and forward linkage effects make manufacturing sector the back bone of any economy. However, in order to have a strong and resilient manufacturing sector, the firms operating within various sub-sectors must be efficient and profitable. Moreover, with the advent of liberalization measures since late 1980s, although the growth possibilities have stepped up, at the same time the externalities and competition have also escalated manifold during the post-reform era. In order to survive in such a highly competitive business environment, it is of utmost importance that firms operating in the manufacturing industry perform efficiently as well as profitably. The numerous variables which influence the firm performance can be clustered into firm-specific, industry-specific and macroeconomic factors. Therefore, the development of business policies in the post-reform era demands consideration of all these three factors together.

The review of the existing literature clearly indicates that there is a paucity of research studies at both international and national levels which have attempted to account for these factors simultaneously in explaining the efficiency and profitability of the firms especially belonging to the Indian manufacturing sector. Further, the existing studies have only concentrated upon unearthing the impact of different macroeconomic factors on the stock market in general by using market index (not on manufacturing sub-sectorspecific stock indices). It is very much possible that the dynamic relationship between the manufacturing sub-sector specific indices may be completely different from the relationship between market index and the macroeconomic factors.

In this backdrop, the present study makes an attempt to comprehensively investigate into the growth of the Indian manufacturing industry under the various policy regimes in order to understand the implications of the policies taken up from time to time to revamp the manufacturing industry in India. Secondly, the study seeks to ascertain the firm-level efficiency and the various factors affecting such efficiency. Thirdly, the level of profitability of the manufacturing firms has been assessed and the microeconomic and macroeconomic determinants of such profitability have also been explored. It must be noted that only the microeconomic and macroeconomic factors have been considered in this study to explain the firm-level efficiency and profitability. Industry-specific factors have not been taken into account. Since the analysis of firm-level efficiency and profitability has been separately made for each of the manufacturing industry sub-groups, the industry effect has automatically been nullified. Therefore, only the microeconomic and macroeconomic factors have been considered in the present study as the major determinants of the firm-level efficiency and profitability. Finally, the interactions and dynamic relationships between the major macroeconomic variables and the manufacturing sector-specific stock indices in both long run and short run have also been examined in this study.

7.2   SUMMARY OF THE FINDINGS AND CONCLUDING OBSERVATIONS

The various dominant variables affecting the efficiency, profitability and share price of the firms belonging to the various sub-sectors of the Indian manufacturing industry are presented in Table 7.1. It is also to be reckoned that the same set of microeconomic and macroeconomic factors were not taken into consideration in order to explain the efficiency, profitability and share price. The existing literature guides us in selecting the list of variables. After making such selection, the impact of these variables on the efficiency, profitability and share price was assessed. However, for analysing the factors affecting the share price, the representative sector-specific indices were considered instead of firm-level share prices. Hence, it was not possible to consider the firm-specific factors rather the macroeconomic variables were only taken into account to examine their impact on the sectoral stock indices. Therefore, it would not be equitable to presuppose that the same set of variables was considered in explaining variation in efficiency, profitability or share price.

Table 7.1 discloses a holistic list of macroeconomic, firm-specific and other factors influencing the efficiency and profitability of the different manufacturing sub-sectors and the share price of the corresponding sectors. The outcome derived from this table indicates that leverage, size, age openness and inflation established themselves as the predominant determinants of the firm-level efficiency of the majority manufacturing sub-sectors during the period of study while leverage, age, growth, openness, VAIC, liquidity, economic growth and inflation were emerged to be the instrumental factors influencing profitability of the Indian manufacturing firms. As far as the sectoral indices were concerned, they were mostly affected by the dynamism in the economic policy uncertainty,

Table 7.1 Factor-wise impact on efficiency, profitability and share price of various manufacturing sub-sectors

Factors		Variables		
		Efficiency	Profitability	Share Price
Microeconomic	leverage	Construction Engineering, Electrical Equipment, Industrial Machinery, Food Products	Cement, Chemicals, Electrical Equipment, Industrial Machinery, Pharmaceutical & biotechnology	
	Size	Steel, Cement, Chemicals, Construction Engineering, Industrial Machinery, Pharmaceutical & biotechnology, Auto Parts & Equipment, Textiles	Electrical Equipment, Industrial Machinery	
	Age	Steel, Cement, Chemicals, Construction Engineering, Industrial Machinery, Food Products, Pharmaceutical & biotechnology, Auto Parts & Equipment	Steel, Cement, Chemicals, Construction Engineering, Pharmaceutical & biotechnology,	
	Growth	Cement, Auto Parts & Equipment	Cement, Industrial Machinery, Pharmaceutical & biotechnology, Auto Parts &Equipment, Textiles	
	Openness	Steel, Cement, Construction Engineering, Electrical Equipment, Industrial Machinery, Food Products, Pharmaceutical & biotechnology, Auto Parts & Equipment	Cement, Industrial Machinery, Pharmaceutical & biotechnology, Auto Parts & Equipment	

| Factors | Variables | | |
	Efficiency	Profitability	Share Price
VAIC	NOT INCLUDED IN EFFICIENCY ANALYSIS	Steel, Cement, Construction Engineering, Food Products, Pharmaceutical & biotechnology, Auto Parts & Equipment, Textiles	
Liquidity		Steel, Construction Engineering, Electrical Equipment, Industrial Machinery, Food Products,	INCLUDED IN PRICE FACTOR (PRINCIPAL COMPONENT)
Macroeconomic Economic Growth		Cement, Construction Engineering, Electrical Equipment, Industrial Machinery,	
Inflation	Steel, Cement, Chemicals, Construction Engineering, Electrical Equipment, Industrial Machinery, Food Products, Pharmaceutical & biotechnology, Auto Parts & Equipment	Steel, Cement, Construction Engineering, Electrical Equipment, Industrial Machinery, Pharmaceutical & biotechnology, Auto Parts & Equipment, Textiles	
Exchange Rate	Chemicals	Cement, Electrical Equipment, Textiles	BSE-BM
Price Factor	NOT INCLUDED IN EFFICIENCY & PROFITABILITY ANALYSIS		BSE-BM, BSE-IND, BSE-FMCG, BSE-HC, BSE-CDGS
Foreign Investment			BSE-BM, BSE-IND, BSE-FMCG, BSE-CDGS

(continued)

Table 7.1 (continued)

| Factors | Variables | | Share Price |
	Efficiency	Profitability	
	Rate of Interest		BSE-BM,
	Crude Oil Price		BSE-CDGS
Others	Economic Policy	NOT INCLUDED IN EFFICIENCY & PROFITABILITY	BSE-BM, BSE-IND,
	Uncertainty	ANALYSIS	BSE-HC, BSE-CDGS

Source Author's own compilation

foreign portfolio investment and the price factor during the period of study. A summary of the sector-wise results is presented in the following paragraphs:

7.2.1   Basic Metal

It can be inferred that the age, growth, openness and inflation influenced the efficiency and profitability of the firms belonging to BSE-BM sector (inclusive of Steel, Cement and Chemicals sub-sectors). Further, exchange rate was found to be another factor which affected the level of efficiency of the Chemicals sub-sector, profitability of the Steel sub-sector and BSE-BM index at large.

7.2.2   Industrials

Efficiency and profitability of manufacturing firms belonging to BSE-IND covering Construction Engineering, Electrical Equipment, and Industrial Machinery sub-sectors got primarily affected by leverage, age, size and openness during the study period. On the other hand, inflation significantly explained the level of efficiency and profitability and the BSE-IND index as a whole.

7.2.3   Fast Moving Consumer Goods

Inflation was also found to be a major antecedent of the efficiency, profitability and share price of the Food Products firms.

7.2.4   Health Care

While the age and openness were the sensitive firm-specific factors affecting the efficiency and profitability, inflation was also established as the major macroeconomic variable affecting the efficiency, profitability and share price of the firms under BSE-HC.

7.2.5   Consumer Discretionary Goods and Services

Leverage, growth, openness and inflation emerged to be the prime determinants of the level of efficiency, profitability and the share prices of the firms belonging BSE-CDGS sector (encompassing Auto Parts & Equipment and Textile sub-sectors) in general.

7.3   Policy Implications of the Study

The policy implications of the results obtained from the study are as follows:

First, the study revealed that the growth of GDP, capital formation and productivity of the Indian manufacturing sector at large enhanced impressively during the post-reform vis-à-vis pre-reform period. It is very much apparent that the growth of the manufacturing sector demands more liberal economic environment to flourish and sustain in the market. Therefore, it is proposed that a suitable ecosystem needs to be nurtured by implementing appropriate pro-manufacturing sector policies.

Secondly, it is evident from the results of the study that the firms belonging to diverse manufacturing sub-sectors were overburdened with huge debt in their capital structure which can impact the productivity and profitability adversely. It is an established fact that with more debt, the financial risk associated with the firm also steps up. So, it is advised that the firms overburdened with debt-overhang should make effort to reduce the excessive dependence on the external equity. Further, managerial efficiency is desirable to ensure improvement in the operational activities vis-à-vis financial performance. Theoretically, it is also propagated that firms with more debt should be more efficient as well as profitable. However, higher efficiency and profitability can only be reached if the monitoring system of lending institutions guarantees that the borrowing firms execute operational activities in a disciplined fashion. The study revealed that the effect of leverage on efficiency and profitability was negative in most of the manufacturing sub-sectors. So, intuitively it can be inferred that the managers of the borrowing firms were not disciplined enough to carry out the operating activities appropriately to mitigate their fixed financial obligations to the lenders. In addition, it can also be assumed that the borrowed fund was used by the managers in financially unviable projects. As mentioned earlier, it can occur only when the monitoring process as introduced by the lending institutions is faulty. Therefore, credit monitoring mechanism of the financial institutions needs to be reshaped to enable a fair assessment of the credibility of the firms. To a large extent, it is expected to control the burgeoning non-performing assets problem in India.

Fourthly, although it is generally accepted that learning by experience enables the old firms to be more productive, the result of the study suggested that the old firms pertaining to Cement, Electrical Equipment, Industrial Machinery and Textile sub-sectors were inefficient as compared to the newer firms within the same sub-sectors. Such inefficiency of old firms (as opposed to the theoretical conviction) can be explained by their inertia in adapting to the dynamic business environment. In contrast, relatively experienced firms in the Cement, Electrical Equipment, Industrial Machinery and Textile sub-sectors were able to adjust in the dynamic business environment by means of embracing new technology and encouraging innovation through R & D.

Fifthly, the study also revealed that the increase in import expenditure of the Construction Engineering and Cement sub-sector at large can explain the loss in profitability of firms. Hence, it is encouraged that an attempt should be directed to cut down import. An appropriate self-reliance policy of the Government can strengthen the backward supply chain and thereby can reduce the dependence on imports.

Sixthly, intellectual capital was observed to the most sensitive factor which affects favourably the profitability of firms across various manufacturing sub-sectors during the study period. So, a holistic approach needs to be undertaken for ensuring greater efficiency of the individual components of intellectual capital, i.e. human capital, financial capital and structural capital. Then only intellectual capital can be effectively utilized in achieving higher profitability of the firms at large.

Seventhly, within a group of macroeconomic factors, the wide spread impact of inflation on the productivity of Auto Parts and Equipment, Cement, Electrical Equipment, Pharmaceutical & Biotechnology, Steel and Industrial Machinery sub-sectors was empirically established. The profitability of all sub-sectors (except Textiles) was also influenced by the inflation. Hence, it is important for the firms to augment the operational efficiency by endorsing more disciplined behaviour among the managers and workers of the firms during the inflationary situation. Further, these firms may exercise appropriate cost control system (such as hedging against the volatile input prices, reduction of debt, use of better technology, improvement in productivity of employees, outsourcing from a low cost region, reduction in cost of packaging, etc.) to reduce the overall cost of production.

7.4   FUTURE RESEARCH AGENDA

This book has adopted a comprehensive approach to addressing some of the pertinent issues on manufacturing sector in India. However, a scope of further research in this direction can be listed as follows.

- The study was carried out based on the availability of secondary sources of the data. Depending on the availability of firm-specific data and macroeconomic indicators, the reference period of the study on efficiency and profitability analysis was limited to only 15 years data from 1999–2000 to 2013–2014. Similarly, in the analysis of the manufacturing sector-specific BSE-stock indices, the period April 2000 to March 2015 was considered. A longer period of study may provide more meaningful and generalized insights into the determinants of efficiency, profitability and share price.
- The study considered ten out of thirty three BSE manufacturing industry groups within the broad manufacturing sector. Similarly, the firm-level analysis was conducted by taking into consideration 515 firms as sample out of 1240 firms across the ten manufacturing industry groups. Thus, future research may incorporate more number of industry groups and large sample firms.
- The selected ten industry sub-groups in the study were regrouped into the five broad BSE manufacturing sectors where the BSE-sectoral stock indices are available. Thus in order to maintain the consistency with the selected companies only five stock indices (viz. BSE-BM, BSE-CDGS, BSE-HC, BSE-FMCG and BSE-IND) out of available eight indices (other three indices are BSE-Energy, BSE-Information Technology and BSE-Telecom) were chosen for conducting the final analysis of the relationship between the macroeconomic variables and the sectoral stock indices. Thus, a study can be conducted in future considering other three indices, namely BSE-Energy, BSE-Information Technology and BSE-Telecom indices.
- Presently, some of the BSE industry sub-group specific indices such as BSE-Auto, BSE-Consumer Durable and BSE-Capital Goods are also available. Since broad BSE-secto- based indices were selected for the purpose of the study, BSE industry sub-group specific indices were not considered on two grounds. Firstly, sectoral index data were not uniformly available with reference to a particular time frame. For example some of the sectoral indices were available from

1999 whereas others were available from 2004 to 2008. Therefore only those sectoral indices for which the data of September 2005 to October 2016 were available were selected for the purpose of the study. Secondly, it is right that some of the sub-sector level indices such as BSE-Capital Goods; BSE-CDGS including BSE-Auto and BSE-Consumer Durable are now available. However, all these sub-sectoral indices get automatically included in sectoral index BSE-IND. Therefore, sub-sectoral indices were not considered for the purpose of this study. Hence, the consideration of these BSE industry sub-group specific indices can reflect more in-depth information about those industry sub-groups.

- The important macroeconomic factors that the institutional and retail investors consider in taking their investment decisions can be first identified based on a primary survey which is an intrinsic part of behavioural finance theory and then taken into consideration for secondary level analysis in future research studies.

- The Environmental, Social and Governance (ESG) issues are considered to be the important parameters of sustainability. In fact, an environment friendly company is able to save cost more effectively which enhances its efficiency, profitability and share price. In a similar way, theoretically it is propagated that good governance enables the firm to improve its investment decision-making which exerts positive effect on the efficiency and profitability. Moreover, the positive nexus between profitability vis-à-vis firm value and corporate social responsibility is well accepted. Therefore, further studies can incorporate these ESG factors in analysing efficiency, profitability and share price.

Bibliography

Abdalla I. S. A., & Murinde V. (1997). Exchange rate and stock price interactions in emerging financial markets: Evidence on India, Korea, Pakistan and Philippines. *Applied Financial Economics, 7*, 25–35.

Aburime, T. U. (2009). Impact of corruption on bank profitability in Nigeria. *Euro Economica, 2*, 50–57.

Acharya, V. V., Anshuman, V. R., & Kumar, K. K. (2016). *Foreign fund flows and asset prices: Evidence from the Indian stock market.* http://pages.stern. nyu.edu/~sternfin/vacharya/public_html/pdfs/Foreign%20Fund%20Flows% 20May_2016.pdf

Adjasi, C. K., & Biekpe, N. B. (2006). Stock market development and economic growth: The case of selected African countries. *African Development Review, 18*(1), 144–161.

Afza, T., & Nazir, M. S. (2007). Is it better to be aggressive or conservative in managing working capital. *Journal of Quality and Technology Management, 3*(2), 11–21.

Aggarwal, A., & Sato, T. (2011). *Firm dynamics and productivity growth in Indian manufacturing: Evidence from plant level panel dataset* (Research Institute for Economics and Business Administration, Discussion Paper Series DP2011–07). Kobe University.

Aghion, P., Blundell, R., Griffith, R., Howitt, P., & Prantl, S. (2006). *The effects of entry on incumbent innovation and productivity* (No. National Bureau of Economic Research Working Paper No. w12027). https://www.nber.org/pap ers/w12027.pdf

© The Author(s), under exclusive license to Springer Nature
Singapore Pte Ltd. 2022
S. K. Maji et al., *Indian Manufacturing Sector in Post-Reform Period,*
https://doi.org/10.1007/978-981-19-2666-2

145

Agiomirgianakis, G., Voulgaris, F., & Papadogonas, T. (2006). Financial factors affecting profitability and employment growth: The case of Greek manufacturing. *International Journal of Financial Services Management, 1*(2–3), 232–242.

Agrawalla, R. K., & Tuteja, S. K. (2008). Share prices and macroeconomic variables in India. *Journal of Management Research, 8*(3), 1–12.

Ahluwalia, M. S. (2002). Economic reforms in India since 1991: Has gradualism worked? *The Journal of Economic Perspectives, 16*(3), 67–88.

Ahmad, N., Nadeem, M., Ahmad, R., & Hamad, N. (2014). Impact of family ownership on firm's financial performance a comparison study between manufacturing firms and financial firms in Pakistan. *Journal of Business and Management Review, 2*(8), 51–56.

Ahmed, M. S., & Ahmed, M. D. (2013). Efficiency variation of manufacturing firms: A case study of seafood processing firms in Bangladesh. *Review of Economics and Finance, 3*(2), 45–56.

Ahmed, N., Ahmed, Z., & Usman, A. (2011). Determinants of performance: A case of life insurance sector of Pakistan. *International Research Journal of Finance and Economics, 61*(1), 123–128.

Ali, K., Akhtar, M. F., & Ahmed, H. Z. (2011). Bank-specific and macroeconomic indicators of profitability-empirical evidence from the commercial banks of Pakistan. *International Journal of Business and Social Science, 2*(6), 235–242.

Ali, I., Rehman, K. U., Yilmaz, A. K., Khan, M. A., & Afzal, H. (2010). Causal relationship between macro-economic indicators and stock exchange prices in Pakistan. *African Journal of Business Management, 4*(3), 312–319.

Al-Sharkas, A. (2004). The dynamic relationship between macroeconomic factors and the Jordanian stock market. *International Journal of Applied Econometrics and Quantitative Studies, 1*, 97–114.

Alvarez, R., & Crespi, G. (2003). Determinants of technical efficiency in small firms. *Small Business Economics, 20*(3), 233–244.

Ammer, J. (1994). *Inflation, inflation risk, and stock returns* (International Finance Discussion Paper Number 464 of Board of Governors of the Federal Reserve System). https://www.federalreserve.gov/pubs/ifdp/1994/464/ifd p464.pdf

Antonakakis, N., Chatziantoniou, I., & Filis, G. (2013). Dynamic co-movements of stock market returns, implied volatility and policy uncertainty. *Economics Letters, 120*(1), 87–92.

Apergis, N., & Eleftheriou, S. (2002). Interest rates, inflation, and stock prices: The case of the Athens stock exchange. *Journal of Policy Modeling, 24*(3), 231–236.

Arouri, M., & Roubaud, D. (2016). On the determinants of stock market dynamics in emerging countries: The role of economic policy uncertainty in China and India. *Economics Bulletin, 36*(2), 760–770.

Asaolu, T. O., & Ogunmuyiwa, M. S. (2011). An econometric analysis of the impact of macroecomomic variables on stock market movement in Nigeria. *Asian Journal of Business Management, 3*(1), 72–78.

Asimakopoulos, I., Samitas, A., & Papadogonas, T. (2009). Firm-specific and economy wide determinants of firm profitability: Greek evidence using panel data. *Managerial Finance, 35*(11), 930–939.

Attari, M. I. J., & Safdar, L. (2013). The relationship between macroeconomic volatility and the stock market volatility: Empirical evidence from Pakistan. *Pakistan Journal of Commerce and Social Sciences, 7*(2), 309–320.

Azarmi, T., Lazar, D., & Jeyapaul, J. (2011). Is The Indian stock market a casino? *Journal of Business & Economics Research, 3*(4), 63–72.

Baek, H. Y., & Neymotin, F. (2016). International involvement and production efficiency among startup firms. *Global Economic Review, 45*(1), 42–62.

Baker, S. R., Bloom, N., & Davis, S. J. (2016). Measuring economic policy uncertainty. *The Quarterly Journal of Economics, 131*(4), 1593–1636.

Baliyan, S. K., & Baliyan, K. (2015). Determinants of firm-level performance: A study of Indian manufacturing and service sectors. *Indian Journal of Economics and Development, 11*(3), 701–713.

Banerjee, S. (2015). An analysis of profitability trend in Indian cement industry. *Economic Affairs, 60*(1), 171–179.

Barbee, W. C., Jr., Mukherji, S., & Raines, G. A. (1996). Do sales–price and debt–equity explain stock returns better than book–market and firm size? *Financial Analysts Journal, 52*(2), 56–60.

Barro, R. J. (1996). *Determinants of economic growth: A cross-country empirical study* (National Bureau of Economic Research Working Paper No. w5698). https://www.nber.org/papers/w5698.pdf

Basher, S. A., Haug, A. A., & Sadorsky, P. (2012). Oil prices, exchange rates and emerging stock markets. *Energy Economics, 34*(1), 227–240.

Basu, D., & Das, D. (2015). *Profitability in India's organized manufacturing sector: The role of technology, distribution, and demand* (Working Paper, No. 2015-04). University of Massachusetts, Department of Economics. https://www.econstor.eu/bitstream/10419/145413/1/821606948.pdf

Basu, S., Deepthi, D., & Reddy, J. (2011). *Country risk analysis in emerging markets: The Indian example* (Working Paper No. 326, IIM Bangalore Research Paper). http://research.iimb.ernet.in/bitstream/123456789/482/1/wp.iimb.326.pdf

Batra, R., & Kalia, A. (2016). Rethinking and redefining the determinants of corporate profitability. *Global Business Review, 17*(4), 921–933.

Belo, F., Gala, V. D., & Li, J. (2013). Government spending, political cycles, and the cross section of stock returns. *Journal of Financial Economics, 107*(2), 305–324.

Bhandari, A. K., & Maiti, P. (2007). Efficiency of Indian manufacturing firms: Textile industry as a case study. *International Journal of Business and Economics, 6*(1), 71–88.

Bhargava, V., & Malhotra, D. K. (2015). Foreign institutional investment and the Indian stock market. *The Journal of Wealth Management, 17*(4), 101–116.

Bhat, T. P. (2014). *Manufacturing sector and growth prospect* (Working Paper No. 173). Institute for Studies in Industrial Development. http://111.93. 232.162/pdf/WP173.pdf

Bhattacharjee, A., & Han, J. (2010). *Financial distress in chinese industry: Microeconomic, macroeconomic and institutional influences* (SIRE Discussion Paper Number SIRE-DP-2010-53). http://repo.sire.ac.uk/bitstream/ handle/10943/190/SIRE_DP_2010_53.pdf?sequence=1

Bhattacharya, B. B., & Mitra, A. (1989). Industry-agriculture growth Rates: Widening disparity: An explanation. *Economic and Political Weekly, 24*(34), 1963–1970.

Bhattacharya, B., & Mukherjee, J. (2002). *The nature of the causal relationship between stock market and macroeconomic aggregates in India: An empirical analysis.* Conference Paper Presented at 4th annual conference on money and finance, Mumbai. http://citeseerx.ist.psu.edu/viewdoc/download?doi=10.1. 1.467.4248&rep=rep1&type=pdf

Bhattacharya, S. N., Bhattacharya, M., & Basu, S. (2019). Stock market and its liquidity: Evidence from ARDL bound testing approach in the Indian context. *Cogent Economics & Finance, 7*, 1–12.

Bhavani, T. A. (1991). Technical efficiency in Indian modern small scale sector: An application of frontier production function. *Indian Economic Review, 26*(2), 149–166.

Bhayani, S. J. (2010). Determinant of profitability in Indian cement industry: An economic analysis. *South Asian Journal of Management, 17*(4), 6–20.

Bhutta, N. T., & Hasan, A. (2013). Impact of firm specific factors on profitability of firms in food sector. *Open Journal of Accounting, 2*(2), 19.

Bigsten, A., Collier, P., Dercon, S., Fafchamps, M., Gauthier, B., Willem Gunning, J., Oduro, A., Pattillo, C., Söderbom, M., & Teal, F. (2004). Do African manufacturing firms learn from exporting? *Journal of Development studies, 40*(3), 115–141.

Bilson, C. M., Brailsford, T. J., & Hooper, V. C. (2002). The explanatory power of political risk in emerging markets. *International Review of Financial Analysis, 11*(1), 1–27.

Black, F. (1972). Capital market equilibrium with restricted borrowing. *The Journal of Business, 45*(3), 444–455.

Blomström, M. (1986). Foreign investment and productive efficiency: The case of Mexico. *The Journal of Industrial Economics, 35*(1), 97–110.

Bollard, A., Klenow, P. J., & Sharma, G. (2013). India's mysterious manufacturing miracle. *Review of Economic Dynamics, 16*(1), 59–85.

Bontis, N., Keow, W. C C., & Richardson, S. (2000). Intellectual capital and business performance in Malaysian industries. *Journal of Intellectual Capital, 1*(1), 85–100.

Borensztein, E., De Gregorio, J., & Lee, J. W. (1998). How does foreign direct investment affect economic growth? *Journal of International Economics, 45*(1), 115–135.

Bosworth, B., Collins, S. M., & Virmani, A. (2007). *Sources of growth in the Indian economy* (National Bureau of Economic Research Working Paper No. w12901). https://www.nber.org/papers/w12901.pdf

Boyd, J. H., Levine, R., & Smith, B. D. (2001). The impact of inflation on financial sector performance. *Journal of Monetary Economics, 47*(2), 221–248.

Bulmash, S. B., & Trivoli, G. W. (1991). Time-lagged interactions between stocks prices and selected economic variables. *The Journal of Portfolio Management, 17*(4), 61–67.

Burange, L. G., & Ranadive, R. R. (2014). Inter-state analysis of the organised manufacturing sector in India. *Journal of Indian School of Political Economy, 26*(1–4), 1–83.

Burki, A. A., & Terrell, D. (1998). Measuring production efficiency of small firms in Pakistan. *World Development, 26*(1), 155–169.

Campbell, J. Y. (1987). Stock returns and the term structure. *Journal of Financial Economics, 18*(2), 373–399.

Carpenter, M. D., & Johnson, K. H. (1983). The association between working capital policy and operating risk. *The Financial Review, 18*(3), 106–126.

Castiglione, C., & Infante, D. (2014). ICTs and time-span in technical efficiency gains. A stochastic frontier approach over a panel of Italian manufacturing firms. *Economic Modelling, 41*, 55–65.

Cenedese, G., Payne, R., Sarno, L., & Valente, G. (2015). What do stock markets tell us about exchange rates? *Review of Finance, 20*(3), 1045–1080.

Chan, L. K., Lakonishok, J., & Sougiannis, T. (2001). The stock market valuation of research and development expenditures. *The Journal of Finance, 56*(6), 2431–2456.

Chancharat, S., Valadkhani, A., & Havie, C. (2008). *The influence of international stock markets and macroeconomic variables on the thai stock market*. https://ro.uow.edu.au/cgi/viewcontent.cgi?referer=https://scholar.google.com/&httpsredir=1&article=1397&context=commpapers

Chander, S., & Aggarwal, P. (2008). Determinants of corporate profitability: An empirical study of Indian drugs and pharmaceutical industry. *Paradigm, 12*(2), 51–61.

Chang, S. C., & Wang, C. F. (2007). The effect of product diversification strategies on the relationship between international diversification and firm performance. *Journal of World Business, 42*(1), 61–79.

Chapelle, K., & Plane, P. (2005). Technical efficiency measurement within the manufacturing sector in Côte d'Ivoire: A stochastic frontier approach. *Journal of Development Studies, 41*(7), 1303–1324.

Chari, A. (2007). *License reform in India: Theory and evidence.* https://eco nomics.yale.edu/sites/default/files/files/Workshops-Seminars/International-Trade/chari-071128.pdf

Chen, N. F. (1991). Financial investment opportunities and the macroeconomy. *The Journal of Finance, 46*(2), 529–554.

Chen, N. F., Roll, R., & Ross, S. A. (1986). Economic forces and the stock market. *Journal of Business, 59*(3), 383–403.

Cherian, J. A., & Perotti, E. (2001). Option pricing and foreign investment under political risk. *Journal of International Economics, 55*(2), 359–377.

Cheung, Y. W., & Ng, L. K. (1998). International evidence on the stock exchange and aggregate economic activity. *Journal of Empirical Finance, 5*(3), 281–296.

Chiek, A. N., & Akpan, M. N. (2016). Determinants of stock prices during dividend announcements: An evaluation of firms' variable effects in Nigeria's oil and gas sector. *OPEC Energy Review, 40*(1), 69–90.

Chkili, W., & Nguyen, D. K. (2014). Exchange rate movements and stock market returns in a regime-switching environment: Evidence for BRICS countries. *Research in International Business and Finance, 31*, 46–56.

Choudhry, T. (1997). Stochastic trends in stock prices: Evidence from Latin American markets. *Journal of Macroeconomics, 19*(2), 285–304.

Christopherson, S., Martin, R., Sunley, P., & Tyler, P. (2014). Reindustrialising regions: Rebuilding the manufacturing economy? *Cambridge Journal of Regions, Economy and Society, 7*(3), 351–358.

Chuang, Y. C., & Lin, C. M. (1999). Foreign direct investment, R&D and spillover efficiency: Evidence from Taiwan's manufacturing firms. *The Journal of Development Studies, 35*(4), 117–137.

Clark J. & Berko E. (1997). *Foreign investment fluctuations and emerging market stock returns: The case of Mexico* (Federal Reserve Bank of New York, NY Staff Report Number 24). https://papers.ssrn.com/sol3/papers.cfm?abstract_id= 993813

Click, R. W., & Weiner, R. J. (2007). *Does the shadow of political risk fall on asset prices?* https://business.gwu.edu/sites/g/files/zaxdzs1611/f/dow nloads/Does-the-Shadow-of-Risk-Fall-on-Asset-Prices.pdf

Cochrane, J. H. (1991). Production based asset pricing and the link between stock returns and economic fluctuations. *The Journal of Finance, 46*(1), 209–237.

Croce, M. M., Kung, H., Nguyen, T. T., & Schmid, L. (2012). Fiscal policies and asset prices. *Review of Financial Studies, 25*(9), 2635–2672.

Cunado, J., & DeGracia, F. P. (2014). Oil price shocks and stock market returns: Evidence for some European countries. *Energy Economics, 42*, 365–377.

Dandekar, V. M. (1994). Role of economic planning in India in the 1990s and beyond. *Economic and Political Weekly, 29*(24), 1457–1464.

Darrat, A. F., & Dichens, R. N. (1999). On the inter-relationship among real monetary and financial indicators. *Applied Financial Economics, 9*(3), 289–293.

Dasgupta, S., & Singh, A. (2005). Will services be the new engine of Indian economic growth? *Development and Change, 36*(6), 1035–1057.

Defina, R. H. (1991). Does inflation depress the stock market. *Business Review, 3*, 3–12.

Deloof, M. (2003). Does working capital management affect profitability of Belgian firms? *Journal of Business Finance & Accounting, 30*(3–4), 573–588.

Diamonte, R. L., Liew, J. M., & Stevens, R. L. (1996). Political risk in emerging and developed markets. *Financial Analysts Journal, 52*(3), 71–76.

Doaei, M., Anuar, M. A., & Ismail, Z. (2015). Corporate diversification and efficiency of manufacturing firms listed in Bursa Malaysia. *Iranian Journal of Management Studies, 8*(4), 523–543.

Drew, M. E., Naughton, T., & Veeraraghavan, M. (2003). Firm size, book-to-market equity and security returns: Evidence from the Shanghai stock exchange. *Australian Journal of Management, 28*(2), 119–139.

Driffield, N. L., & Kambhampati, U. S. (2003). Trade liberalization and the efficiency of firms in Indian manufacturing. *Review of Development Economics, 7*(3), 419–430.

Durham, J. B. (2002). The effects of stock market development on growth and private investment in lower-income countries. *Emerging Markets Review, 3*(3), 211–232.

Dwivedi, A. K., & Ghosh, P. (2014*). Efficiency measurement of Indian sugar manufacturing firms: A DEA approach* (Centre for Research in Entrepreneurship Education and Development, Entrepreneurship Development Institute of India, Ahmedabad Working Paper Number (CREED/2014/01). http://library.ediindia.ac.in:8181/xmlui/bitstream/handle/123456789/1834/Eff iciency%20Measurement%20of%20Indian%20Sugar%20Manufacturing%20F irms%20A%20DEA%20Approach.pdf?sequence=1&isAllowed=y

Easterly, W., & Rebelo, S. (1993). Fiscal policy and economic growth. *Journal of Monetary Economics, 32*(3), 417–458.

Edvinsson, L., & Malone, M. S. (1997). *Intellectual capital: Realizing your company's true value by finding its hidden brainpower.* http://readenter.info/intellectual-capital-realizing-your-company-s-true-value-by-finding-its-hidden-brainpower-text-book-past-version-michael-s-malone.pdf

Eljelly, A. M. (2004). Liquidity profitability tradeoff: An empirical investigation in an emerging market. *International Journal of Commerce and Management, 14*(2), 48–61.

Erb, C. B., Harvey, C. R., & Viskanta, T. E. (1996). Political risk, economic risk, and financial risk. *Financial Analysts Journal, 52*(6), 29–46.

Fama, E. F., & Schwert, W. G. (1977). Asset returns and inflation. *Journal of Financial Economics, 5*(2), 115–146.

Fama, E. F. (1981). Stock returns, real activity, inflation, and money. *The American Economic Review, 71*(4), 545–565.

Fama, E. F. (1990). Stock returns, expected returns, and real activity. *The Journal of Finance, 45*(4), 1089–1108.

Fama, E. F., & French, K. R. (1989). Business conditions and expected returns on stocks and bonds. *Journal of Financial Economics, 25*(1), 23–49.

Fama, E. F., & French, K. R. (1992). The cross-section of expected stock returns. *The Journal of Finance, 47*(2), 427–465.

Fama, E. F., & French, K. R. (1995). Size and book-to-market factors in earnings and returns. *The Journal of Finance, 50*(1), 131–155.

Fama, E. F., & French, K. R. (2008). Dissecting anomalies. *The Journal of Finance, 63*(4), 1653–1678.

Felipe, J., Mehta, A., & Rhee, C. (2018). Manufacturing matters... but it's the jobs that count. *Cambridge Journal of Economics, 43*(1), 139–168.

Ferdows, S. S., & Roy, A. (2012). A study on the international diversification in the emerging equity market and its effect on the Indian capital market. *International Journal of Contemporary Business Studies, 3*(4), 79–96.

Fernandes, A. M. (2006). *Firm productivity in Bangladesh manufacturing industries* (World Bank Policy Research Working Paper No. 3988). https://openknowledge.worldbank.org/bitstream/handle/10986/8363/wps3988.pdf;sequence=1

Ferrantino, M. J. (1992). Technology expenditures, factor intensity, and efficiency in Indian manufacturing. *The Review of Economics and Statistics, 74*(4), 689–700.

Firth, M., Leung, T. Y., Rui, O. M., & Na, C. (2015). Relative pay and its effects on firm efficiency in a transitional economy. *Journal of Economic Behavior & Organization, 110*, 59–77.

Forlani, E. (2012). *Competition in services and efficiency of manufacturing firms: does' liberalization' matter?* (Katholieke Universiteit Leuven, LICOS Discussion Paper Number 311). https://www.econstor.eu/bitstream/10419/74898/1/dp311.pdf

Froot, K. A., O'Connel, P. G., & Seasholes, M. S. (2001). The portfolio flows of international investors. *Journal of Financial Economics, 59*(2), 151–194.

Fujita, N. (1994). Liberalization policies and productivity in India. *The Developing Economies, 32*(4), 509–524.

Gambhir, D., & Sharma, S. (2015). Productivity in Indian manufacturing: Evidence from the textile industry. *Journal of Economic and Administrative Sciences, 31*(2), 71–85.

Gan, C., Lee, M., Yong, H. H. A., & Zhang, J. (2006). Macroeconomic variables and stock market interactions: New Zealand evidence. *Investment Management and Financial Innovations, 3*(4), 89–101.

Gatsi, J. G., Okpoti, C. A., Gadzo, S. G., & Anipa, C. A. A. (2016). Determinants of market and book based performance of manufacturing companies in Ghana: An empirical study. *International Journal of Economics, Commerce and Management, 4*(1), 393–411.

Gay, R. D., Jr. (2011). Effect of macroeconomic variables on stock market returns for four emerging economies: Brazil, Russia, India, and China. *International Business & Economics Research Journal, 7*(3), 1–8.

Geroski, P. A., Machin, S. J., & Walters, C. F. (1997). Corporate growth and profitability. *The Journal of Industrial Economics, 45*(2), 171–189.

Ghani, E., & O'Connell, S. D. (2016). Can services be a growth escalator in low-income countries? *Revue D'économie Du Développement, 24*(2), 143–173.

Ghosh, A. (1956). Capital output ratio: Its uses and abuses. *The Economic Weekly, 2*(1), 707–710.

Ghosh, S. (2008). Leverage, foreign borrowing and corporate performance: Firm-level evidence for India. *Applied Economics Letters, 15*(8), 607–616.

Gill, A. S., & Biger, N. (2013). The impact of corporate governance on working capital management efficiency of American manufacturing firms. *Managerial Finance, 39*(2), 116–132.

Giokas, D., Eriotis, N., & Dokas, I. (2015). Efficiency and productivity of the food and beverage listed firms in the pre-recession and recessionary periods in Greece. *Applied Economics, 47*(19), 1927–1941.

Goddard, J., Molyneux, P., & Wilson, J. O. (2004). The profitability of European banks: A cross sectional and dynamic panel analysis. *The Manchester School, 72*(3), 363–381.

Goddard, J., Tavakoli, M., & Wilson, J. O. (2005). Determinants of profitability in European manufacturing and services: Evidence from a dynamic panel model. *Applied Financial Economics, 15*(18), 1269–1282.

Gokmenoglu, K. K., & Fazlollahi, N. (2015). The interactions among gold, oil, and stock market: Evidence from S&P500. *Procedia Economics and Finance, 25*, 478–488.

Goldar, B., & Kumari, A. (2003). Import liberalization and productivity growth in Indian manufacturing industries in the 1990s. *The Developing Economies, 41*(4), 436–460.

Goldar, B., Renganathan, V. S., & Banga, R. (2004). Ownership and efficiency in engineering firms: 1990–91 to 1999–2000. *Economic and Political Weekly, 39*(5), 441–447.

Golder, B., & Kumari, A. (2003). Import liberalisation and productivity growth in Indian manufacturing in the 1990s. *Developing Economies, 41*(4), 436–460.

Goldstein, M (1995). *Coping with too much of a good thing: Policy responses to large capital inflows to developing countries* (World Bank Policy Research Working Paper No. WPS 1507). http://www-wds.worldbank.org/external/default/WDSContentServer/WDSP/IB/1995/09/01/000009265_396101 9142948/Rendered/PDF/multi0page.pdf

Gomes, J. F., Kogan, L., & Yogo, M. (2007). *Durability of output and expected stock returns* (National Bureau of Economic Research Working paper No. w12986). https://www.nber.org/papers/w12986.pdf

Granger, C. W. J., Huang, B. N., & Yang, C. W. (2000). A bivariate causality between stock prices and exchange rate: Evidence from recent Asian Flu. *Quarterly Review of Economics and Finance, 40*(3), 337–354.

Grier, K. B., & Tullock, G. (1989). An empirical analysis of cross-national economies 1951–1980. *Journal of Monetary Economics, 24*(2), 259–276.

Grossman, S. J., & Hart, O. D. (1982). Corporate financial structure and managerial incentives. In *The economics of information and uncertainty.* https://www.nber.org/chapters/c4434.pdf

Grubel, H. G. (1968). Internationally diversified portfolios: Welfare gains and capital flows. *The American Economic Review, 58*(5), 1299–1314.

Gujarati, D. N. (2009). *Basic econometrics.* Tata McGraw-Hill Education.

Günay, S. (2016). Is political risk still an issue for Turkish stock market? *Borsa Istanbul Review, 16*(1), 21–31.

Gupta, P. (2002). *Corporate investment and financing in India: Analysis of influencing factors.* KSK Publishers.

Gupta, P., Hasan, R., & Kumar, U. (2008). *What constrains Indian manufacturing?* https://www.econstor.eu/bitstream/10419/176229/1/icr ier-wp-211.pdf

Halkos, G. E., & Tzeremes, N. G. (2007). Productivity efficiency and firm size: An empirical analysis of foreign owned companies. *International Business Review, 16*(6), 713–731.

Hall, B. H., Lotti, F., & Mairesse, J. (2009). Innovation and productivity in SMEs: Empirical evidence for Italy. *Small Business Economics, 33*(1), 13–33.

Hamao, Y. (1988). An empirical examination of the arbitrage pricing theory: Using Japanese data. *Japan and the World Economy, 1*(1), 45–61.

Hanousek, J., Kočenda, E., & Shamshur, A. (2015). Corporate efficiency in Europe. *Journal of Corporate Finance, 32*, 24–40.

Hansen, G. S., & Wernerfelt, B. (1989). Determinants of firm performance: The relative importance of economic and organizational factors. *Strategic Management Journal, 10*(5), 399–411.

Haraguchi, N., Cheng, C. F. C., & Smeets, E. (2017). The importance of manufacturing in economic development: Has this changed? *World Development, 93*, 293–315.

Hasan, R. (2002). The impact of imported and domestic technologies on the productivity of firms: Panel data evidence from Indian manufacturing firms. *Journal of Development Economics, 69*(1), 23–49.

Hasanzadeh, A., & Kianvand, M. (2012). The impact of macroeconomic variables on stock prices: The case of Tehran stock exchange. *Money and Economy, 6*(2), 171–190.

Hassan, M. M. S., & Sangmi, M. U. D. G. (2013). *Macro-economic variables and stock prices in India* [Doctoral dissertation].

Hatemi-J, A., & Roca, E. (2005). Exchange rates and stock prices interaction during good and bad times: Evidence from the ASEAN 4 countries. *Applied Financial Economics, 15*(8), 539–546.

Herve, D. B. G., Chanmalai, B., & Shen, Y. (2011). The study of causal relationship between stock market indices and macroeconomic variables in Cote d'Ivoire: Evidence from error-correction models and granger causality test. *International Journal of Business & Management, 6*(12), 146–167.

Hill, H., & Kalirajan, K. P. (1993). Small enterprise and firm-level technical efficiency in the Indonesian garment industry. *Applied Economics, 25*(9), 1137–1144.

Hillman, A. J., & Hitt, M. A. (1999). Corporate political strategy formulation: A model of approach, participation, and strategy decisions. *Academy of Management Review, 24*(4), 825–842.

Hillman, A. J., Keim, G. D., & Schuler, D. (2004). Corporate political activity: A review and research agenda. *Journal of Management, 30*(6), 837–857.

Hillman, A. J., Withers, M. C., & Collins, B. J. (2009). Resource dependence theory: A review. *Journal of Management, 35*(6), 1404–1427.

Hillman, A. J., Zardkoohi, A., & Bierman, L. (1999). Corporate political strategies and firm performance: Indications of firm-specific benefits from personal service in the US government. *Strategic Management Journal, 20*(1), 67–81.

Hitt, M. A., Hoskisson, R. E., & Kim, H. (1997). International diversification: Effects on innovation and firm performance in product-diversified firms. *Academy of Management Journal, 40*(4), 767–798.

Hondroyiannis, G., & Papapetrou, E. (2001). Macroeconomic influences on the stock market. *Journal of Economics and Finance, 25*(1), 33–49.

Hooley, R. W. (1967). The measurement of capital formation in underdeveloped countries. *The Review of Economics and Statistics, 49*(2), 199–208.

Hosseini, S. M., Ahmad, Z., & Lai, Y. W. (2011). The role of macroeconomic variables on stock market index in China and India. *International Journal of Economics and Finance, 3*(6), 233–243.

Hou, K., & Robinson, D. T. (2006). Industry concentration and average stock returns. *The Journal of Finance, 61*(4), 1927–1956.

Hussain, A., Farooq, S. U., & Khan, K. U. (2012). Aggressiveness and conservativeness of working capital: A case of Pakistani manufacturing sector. *European Journal of Scientific Research, 73*(2), 171–182.

Ibrahim, M., & Musah, A. (2014). An econometric analysis of the impact of macroeconomic fundamentals on stock market returns in Ghana. *Research in Applied Economics, 6*(2), 47–72.

Ismail, R., & Sulaiman, N. (2007). Technical efficiency in Malay manufacturing firms. *International Journal of Business and Society, 8*(2), 47–62.

Issahaku, H., Ustarz, Y., & Domanban, P. B. (2013). Macroeconomic variables and stock market returns in Ghana: Any causal link? *Asian Economic and Financial Review, 3*(8), 1044–1062.

Iyer, A. V., Koudal, P., Saranga, H., & Seshadri, S. (2011). *Indian manufacturing–strategic and operational decisions and business performance* (IIM Bangalore Working Paper No Number 338). https://s3.amazonaws.com/academia.edu.documents/30720563/Indian_Manufacturing-_Strategic_and_Operational_Decisions_and_Business_Performance1_WP_338.pdf?AWSAcc essKeyId=AKIAIWOWYYGZ2Y53UL3A&Expires=1551869392&Signature=88fkpmJLcZJEyO%2BFcQMPlTdj0vU%3D&response-content-disposition=inline%3B%20filename%3DIndian_Manufacturing_Strategic_and_Opera.pdf

Jaffe, J., Keim, D. B., & Westerfield, R. (1989). Earnings yields, market values, and stock returns. *The Journal of Finance, 44*(1), 135–148.

Jain, N. K., Kundu, S. K., & Newburry, W. (2015). Efficiency seeking emerging market firms: Resources and location choices. *Thunderbird International Business Review, 57*(1), 33–50.

Jensen, G. R., & Mercer, J. M. (2002). Monetary policy and the cross-section of expected stock returns. *Journal of Financial Research, 25*(1), 125–139.

Jensen, G. R., Johnson, R. R., & Mercer, J. M. (1997). New evidence on size and price-to-book effects in stock returns. *Financial Analysts Journal, 53*(6), 34–42.

Jensen, M. C. (1986). Agency costs of free cash flow, corporate finance, and takeovers. *The American Economic Review, 76*(2), 323–329.

Jeon, B. N., & Chiang, T. C. (1991). A system of stock prices in world stock exchanges: Common stochastic trends for 1975–1990. *Journal of Economics and Business, 43*(4), 329–338.

John, M. (1993). Emerging equity markets in the global economy. *Quarterly Review-Federal Reserve Bank of New York, 18*(2), 54–83.

Joint Research Centre-European Commission. (2008). *Handbook on constructing composite indicators: Methodology and user guide (OECD).* https://www.oecd.org/sdd/42495745.pdf

Kakani, R. K., Saha, B., & Reddy, V. N. (2001). *Determinants of financial perfor-mance of Indian corporate sector in the post-liberalization era: An exploratory study* (National Stock Exchange of India Limited Research Initiative Paper Number 5). https://www.nseindia.com/content/research/Paper18.pdf

Kalaitzandonakes, N. G., Wu, S., & Ma, J. C. (1992). The relationship between techinical efficiency and firm size revisited. *Canadian Journal of Agricultural Economics/revue Canadienne D'agroeconomie, 40*(3), 427–442.

Kaldor, N. (1967). *Strategic factors in economic development.*

Kambhampati, U. S., & Parikh, A. (2005). Has liberalization affected profit margins in Indian industry? *Bulletin of Economic Research, 57*(3), 273–304.

Kaneko, T., & Lee, B. S. (1995). Relative importance of economic factors in the US and Japanese stock markets. *Journal of the Japanese and International Economies, 9*(3), 290–307.

Kaplan, R. S. (1983). Measuring manufacturing performance: A new challenge for managerial accounting research. *The Accounting Review, 58*(4), 686–705.

Kathuria, V., Raj, S. R., & Sen, K. (2013). The effects of economic reforms on manufacturing dualism: Evidence from India. *Journal of Comparative Economics, 41*(4), 1240–1262.

Khan, M. K., Teng, J. Z., Parvaiz, J., & Chaudhary, S. K. (2017). Nexuses between economic factors and stock returns in China. *International Journal of Economics and Finance, 9*(9), 182–191.

Ko, J. H., & Lee, C. M. (2015). International economic policy uncertainty and stock prices: Wavelet approach. *Economics Letters, 134*, 118–122.

Kochhar, K., Kumar, U., Rajan, R., Subramanian, A., & Tokatlidis, I. (2006). India's pattern of development: What happened, what follows? *Journal of Monetary Economics, 53*(5), 981–1019.

Kosmidou, K., Pasiouras, F., & Tsaklanganos, A. (2007). Domestic and multina-tional determinants of foreign bank profits: The case of Greek banks operating abroad. *Journal of Multinational Financial Management, 17*(1), 1–15.

Kothari, S. P., Shanken, J., & Sloan, R. G. (1995). Another look at the cross-section of expected stock returns. *The Journal of Finance, 50*(1), 185–224.

Kotwal, A., Ramaswami, B., & Wadhwa, W. (2011). Economic liberalization and Indian economic growth: What's the evidence? *Journal of Economic Literature, 49*(4), 1152–1199.

Kraft, J., & Kraft, A. (1977). Determinants of common stock prices: A time series analysis. *Journal of Finance, 32*(2), 417–425.

Kumar, S. (2006). A decomposition of total productivity growth. *International Journal of Productivity and Performance Management, 55*(3–4), 311–331.

Kumbhakar, S. C., Ghosh, S., & McGuckin, J. T. (1991). A generalized produc-tion frontier approach for estimating determinants of inefficiency in US dairy farms. *Journal of Business & Economic Statistics, 9*(3), 279–286.

Kundi, M., & Sharma, S. (2015). Efficiency analysis and flexibility: A case study of cement firms in India. *Global Journal of Flexible Systems Management, 16*(3), 221–234.

Kundi, M., & Sharma, S. (2016). Efficiency of glass firms in India: An application of data envelopment analysis. *Journal of Advances in Management Research, 13*(1), 59–74.

Kwon, C. S., & Shin, T. S. (1999). Cointegration and causality between macroeconomic variables and stock market returns. *Global Finance Journal, 10*(1), 71–81.

Lastrapes, W. D., & Selgin, G. (1995). The liquidity effect: Identifying short-run interest rate dynamics using long-run restrictions. *Journal of Macroeconomics, 17*(3), 387–404.

Le, V., & Harvie, C. (2010). *Firm performance in Vietnam: Evidence from manufacturing small and medium enterprises* (Economics Working Paper No. 4-10). University of Wollongong Faculty of Business. https://ro.uow.edu.au/cgi/viewcontent.cgi?article=1223&context=commwkpapers

Lee, C. Y. (2014). The effects of firm specific factors and macroeconomics on profitability of property-liability insurance industry in Taiwan. *Asian Economic and Financial Review, 4*(5), 681–691.

Leibenstein, H. (1976). *Beyond economic man.* Harvard University Press.

Leigh, M. L. (1997). *Stock market equilibrium and macroeconomic fundamentals.* https://www.elibrary.imf.org/abstract/IMF001/06510-978145184 3224/06510-9781451843224/06510-9781451843224_A001.xml?redirect= true&redirect=true

Lessard, D. R. (1976). World, country, and industry relationships in equity returns: Implications for risk reduction through international diversification. *Financial Analysts Journal, 32*(1), 32–38.

Lev, B. (1989). On the usefulness of earnings and earnings research: Lessons and directions from two decades of empirical research. *Journal of Accounting Research, 27*, 153–192.

Lima, L., Vasconcelos, C. F., Simão, J., & de Mendonça, H. F. (2016). The quantitative easing effect on the stock market of the USA, the UK and Japan: An ARDL approach for the crisis period. *Journal of Economic Studies, 43*(6), 1006–1021.

Linter, J. (1969). The valuation of risky assets and the selection of risky investments in stock portfolios and budget constraints. *Review of Economics and Statistics, 51*(2), 222–224.

Liu, L., & Zhang, T. (2015). Economic policy uncertainty and stock market volatility. *Finance Research Letters, 15*, 99–105.

Liu, M. H., & Shrestha, K. M. (2008). Analysis of the long-term relationship between macro-economic variables and the Chinese stock market using heteroscedastic cointegration. *Managerial Finance, 34*(11), 744–755.

Lokanathan, P. S. (1944). The Bombay plan. *Foreign Affairs, 23*(4), 680–686.

Lu, J. W., & Beamish, P. W. (2004). International diversification and firm performance: The S-curve hypothesis. *Academy of Management Journal, 47*(4), 598–609.

Lundvall, K., & Battese, G. E. (2000). Firm size, age and efficiency: Evidence from Kenyan manufacturing firms. *The Journal of Development Studies, 36*(3), 146–163.

Lyroudi, K., & Lazaridis, Y. (2000). *The cash conversion cycle and liquidity analysis of the food industry in Greece.* https://papers.ssrn.com/sol3/papers.cfm? abstract_id=236175

Ma, C. K., & Kao, G. W. (1990). On exchange rate changes and stock price reactions. *Journal of Business Finance and Accounting, 17*(3), 441–449.

MacDonald, R., & Power, D. (1991). Persistence in UK stock market returns: Aggregated and disaggregated perspectives. In M. P. Taylor (Ed.), *Money and financial markets* (pp. 277–296). Basil Blackwell.

Madheswaran, S., Liao, H., & Rath, B. N. (2007). Productivity growth of Indian manufacturing sector: Panel estimation of stochastic production frontier and technical inefficiency. *The Journal of Developing Areas, 40*(2), 35–50.

Maji, S. G., & Goswami, M. (2016). Intellectual capital and firm performance in emerging economies: The case of India. *Review of International Business and Strategy, 26*(3), 4–24.

Maji, S. K., Laha, A., & Sur, D. (2020a). Dynamic Nexuses between Macroeconomic variables and sectoral stock indices: Reflection from Indian manufacturing industry. *Management and Labour Studies, 45*(3), 239–269.

Maji, S. K., Laha, A., & Sur, D. (2020b). Macroeconomic and microeconomic determinants of efficiency of Indian construction & engineering firms: An investigation. *Ramanujan International Journal of Business and Research, 5*, 105–121.

Majumdar, S. K. (1997). The impact of size and age on firm-level performance: Some evidence from India. *Review of Industrial Organization, 12*(2), 231–241.

Majumdar, S. K., & Bhattacharjee, A. (2010). *The profitability dynamics of Indian firms.* https://www.isid.ac.in/~pu/conference/dec_10_conf/Papers/SumitK Majumdar.pdf

Malkiel, B. G. (1982). *Risk and return: A new look* (National Bureau of Economic Research Working Paper No. 700). https://www.nber.org/papers/ w0700.pdf

Malkiel, B. G., & Fama, E. F. (1970). Efficient capital markets: A review of theory and empirical work. *The Journal of Finance, 25*(2), 383–417.

Marshall, A. (1920). *Industry and trade.* McMaster University Archive for the History of Economic Thought. https://socialsciences.mcmaster.ca/~econ/ ugcm/3ll3/marshall/Industry&Trade.pdf

Marshall, D. A. (1992). Inflation and asset returns in a monetary economy. *The Journal of Finance, 47*(4), 1315–1342.

Mathuva, D. M. (2009). Capital adequacy, cost income ratio and the performance of commercial banks: The Kenyan scenario. *The International Journal of Applied Economics and Finance, 3*(2), 35–47.

Maysami, R. C., Howe, L. C., & Hamzah, M. A. (2004). Relationship between macroeconomic variables and stock market indices: Cointegration evidence from stock exchange of Singapore's All-S sector indices. *Jurnal Pengurusan, 24*, 47–77.

McConaughy, D. L., Walker, M. C., Henderson, G. V., & Mishra, C. S. (1998). Founding family controlled firms: Efficiency and value. *Review of Financial Economics, 7*(1), 1–19.

McGahan, A. M., & Porter, M. E. (2002). What do we know about variance in accounting profitability? *Management Science, 48*(7), 834–851.

Mehralian, G., Rajabzadeh, A., Reza Sadeh, M., & Reza Rasekh, H. (2012). Intellectual capital and corporate performance in Iranian pharmaceutical industry. *Journal of Intellectual Capital, 13*(1), 138–158.

Mensi, W., Hammoudeh, S., Yoon, S. M., & Nguyen, D. K. (2016). Asymmetric linkages between BRICS stock returns and country risk ratings: Evidence from dynamic panel threshold models. *Review of International Economics, 24*(1), 1–19.

Mishra, S. (2013). Relationship between macroeconomic variables and corporate health of manufacturing firms in India. *Journal of Quantitative Economics, 11*(1&2), 230–249.

Misra, P. (2018). An investigation of the macroeconomic factors affecting the Indian stock market. *Australasian Accounting, Business and Finance Journal, 12*(2), 71–86.

Mistry, D. S. (2012). Determinants of profitability in Indian automotive industry. *Tecnia Journal of Management Studies, 7*(1), 20–23.

Mitra, A. (1999). Total factor productivity growth and technical efficiency in Indian industries. *Economic and Political Weekly, 34*(31), M98–M105.

Mitra, A., Sharma, C., & Veganzones, M. A. (2011). *Total factor productivity and technical efficiency of Indian manufacturing: The role of infrastructure and information & communication technology.* https://www.researchgate.net/profile/Marie_Ange_Veganzones/publication/228433873_Total_Factor_Productivity_and_Technical_Efficiency_of_Indian_Manufacturing_The_Role_of_Infrastructure_and_Information_Communication_Technology/links/02bfe50d1fc204595f000000.pdf

Mitra, A., Sharma, C., & Véganzonès, M. A. (2012). Estimating impact of infrastructure on productivity and efficiency of Indian manufacturing. *Applied Economics Letters, 19*(8), 779–783.

Mitra, A., Varoudakis, A., & Veganzones-Varoudakis, M. A. (2002). Productivity and technical efficiency in Indian states' manufacturing: The role of infrastructure. *Economic Development and Cultural Change, 50*(2), 395–426.

Mitra, D., & Ural, B. P. (2008). Indian manufacturing: A slow sector in a rapidly growing economy. *The Journal of International Trade & Economic Development, 17*(4), 525–559.

Mohammad, S. D., Hussain, A., & Ali, A. (2009). Impact of macroeconomics variables on stock prices: Empirical evidence in case of KSE (Karachi stock exchange). *European Journal of Scientific Research, 38*(1), 96–103.

Mongid, A., & Tahir, I. M. (2011). Impact of corruption on banking profitability in ASEAN countries: An empirical analysis. *Banks and Bank Systems, 6*(1), 41–48.

Msindo, Z. H. (2016). *The impact of interest rates on stock returns: empirical evidence from the JSE securities exchange* [Doctoral dissertation]. http://wiredspace.wits.ac.za/bitstream/handle/10539/22148/Zethu'sFinal%20Researchpaper14Sept.pdf?sequence=1&isAllowed=y

Mukherjee, K., & Mishra, R. K. (2010). Stock market integration and volatility spillover: India and its major Asian counterparts. *Research in International Business and Finance, 24*(2), 235–251.

Mukherjee, K., & Ray, S. C. (2005). Technical efficiency and its dynamics in Indian manufacturing: An inter-state analysis. *Indian Economic Review*, 101–125.

Mukherjee, P., & Roy, M. (2016). What drives the stock market return in India? An exploration with dynamic factor model. *Journal of Emerging Market Finance, 15*(1), 119–145.

Mukherjee, T. K., & Naka, A. (1995). Dynamic relations between macroeconomic variables and the Japanese stock market: An application of a vector error correction model. *Journal of Financial Research, 18*(2), 223–237.

Mukhopadhyay, D., & Sarkar, N. (2003). *Stock return and macroeconomic fundamentals in model specification framework: Evidence from Indian stock market.* https://www.isical.ac.in/~eru/erudp/2003-05.pdf

Muradoglu, G., Taskin, F., & Bigan, I. (2000). Causality between stock returns and macroeconomic variables in emerging markets. *Russian & East European Finance and Trade, 36*(6), 33–53.

Myers, S. C. (1984). The capital structure puzzle. *Journal of Finance, 39*(3), 575–592.

Naifar, N., & Al Dohaiman, M. S. (2013). Nonlinear analysis among crude oil prices, stock markets' return and macroeconomic variables. *International Review of Economics & Finance, 27*, 416–431.

Naik, P. K., & Padhi, P. (2012). The impact of macroeconomic fundamentals on stock prices revisited: Evidence from Indian data. *Eurasian Journal of Business and Economics, 5*(10), 25–44.

Nanda, S., & Panda, A. K. (2018). The determinants of corporate profitability: An investigation of Indian manufacturing firms. *International Journal of Emerging Markets, 13*(1), 66–86.

Nandi, S., Majumder, D., & Mitra, A. (2015). *Is exchange rate the dominant factor influencing corporate profitability in India* (RBI Working Paper 04/2015). http://rbidocs.rbi.org.in/rdocs/Publications/PDFs/WP0 49A3B62D596234C97B8CD1B2CC9CBC1CE.PDF

Nayar, B. R. (1971). Business attitudes toward economic planning in India. *Asian Survey, 11*(9), 850–865.

Neogi, C., & Ghosh, B. (1994). Intertemporal efficiency variations in Indian manufacturing industries. *Journal of Productivity Analysis, 5*(3), 301–324.

Nishat, M., Shaheen, R., & Hijazi, S. T. (2004). Macroeconomic factors and the Pakistani equity market. *The Pakistan Development Review, 43*(4), 619–637.

Nkoro, E., & Uko, A. K. (2016). Autoregressive Distributed Lag (ARDL) cointegration technique: Application and interpretation. *Journal of Statistical and Econometric Methods, 5*(4), 63–91.

Nomura, K. (2005). *Turn the tables! Reframing measurement of capital in Japanese national accounts.* Presented at the Conference on the Next Steps for the Japanese SNA. http://www.esri.go.jp/jp/workshop/050325/050 325paper03-1.pdf

Nugent, J. (1999). Corporate profitability in Ireland: Overview and determinants: Discussion. *Journal of the Statistical and Social Inquiry Society of Ireland, 28*(1), 80–81.

Omran, M., & Pointon, J. (2001). Does the inflation rate affect the performance of the stock market? The case of Egypt. *Emerging Markets Review, 2*(3), 263–279.

Opler, T., & Titman, S. (1993). The determinants of leveraged buyout activity: Free cash flow vs. financial distress costs. *The Journal of Finance, 48*(5), 1985–1999.

Ouattara, W. (2010). Economic efficiency analysis in Cte dIvoire. *Journal of Development and Agricultural Economics, 2*(9), 316–325.

Padachi, K. (2006). Trends in working capital management and its impact on firms' performance: An analysis of Mauritian small manufacturing firms. *International Review of Business Research Papers, 2*(2), 45–58.

Pallegedara, A. (2012). *Dynamic relationships between stock market performance and short term interest rate-empirical evidence from Sri Lanka.* https://mpra. ub.uni-muenchen.de/40773/1/MPRA_paper_40773.pdf

Pan, M. S., Fok, R. C. W., & Liu, Y. A. (2007). Dynamic linkages between exchange rates and stock prices: Evidence from East Asian markets. *International Review of Economics & Finance, 16*(4), 503–520.

Panagariya, A. (2004a). Growth and Reforms during 1980s and 1990s. *Economic and Political Weekly, 39*(25), 2581–2594.

Panagariya, A. (2004b). *India's trade reform: Progress, impact and future strategy.* https://econwpa.ub.uni-muenchen.de/econ-wp/it/papers/0403/0403004.pdf

Papadogonas, T. A. (2006). The financial performance of large and small firms: Evidence from Greece. *International Journal of Financial Services Management, 2*(1–2), 14–20.

Pastor, L., & Veronesi, P. (2012). Uncertainty about government policy and stock prices. *The Journal of Finance, 67*(4), 1219–1264.

Patel, S. (2012). The effect of macroeconomic determinants on the performance of the Indian stock market. *NMIMS Management Review, 22*(1), 117–127.

Pattnayak, S. S., & Thangavelu, S. M. (2005). Economic reform and productivity growth in Indian manufacturing industries: An interaction of technical change and scale economies. *Economic Modelling, 22*(4), 601–615.

Pelham, A. M. (2000). Market orientation and other potential influences on performance in small and medium-sized manufacturing firms. *Journal of Small Business Management, 38*(1), 48.

Peng, M. W., & Luo, Y. (2000). Managerial ties and firm performance in a transition economy: The nature of a micro-macro link. *Academy of Management Journal, 43*(3), 486–501.

Pesaran, M. H., & Shin, Y. (1998). An autoregressive distributed-lag modelling approach to cointegration analysis. *Econometric Society Monographs, 31*, 371–413.

Pesaran, M. H., Shin, Y., & Smith, R. J. (2001). Bounds testing approaches to the analysis of level relationships. *Journal of Applied Econometrics, 16*(3), 289–326.

Pethe, A., & Karnik, A. (2000). Do Indian stock markets matter? Stock market indices and macro-economic variables. *Economic and Political Weekly, 35*(5), 349–356.

Phylaktis, K., & Ravazzolo, F. (2005). Stock prices and exchange rate dynamics. *Journal of International Money and Finance, 24*(7), 1031–1053.

Piesse, J., & Thirtle, C. (2000). A stochastic frontier approach to firm level efficiency, technological change, and productivity during the early transition in Hungary. *Journal of Comparative Economics, 28*(3), 473–501.

Pilinkus, D. (2015). Stock market and macroeconomic variables: Evidences from Lithuania. *Economics and Management, 14*, 884–891.

Pitt, M. M., & Lee, L. F. (1981). The measurement and sources of technical inefficiency in the Indonesian weaving industry. *Journal of Development Economics, 9*(1), 43–64.

Poterba, J. M., & Summers, L. H. (1988). Mean reversion in stock prices: Evidence and implications. *Journal of Financial Economics, 22*(1), 27–59.

Pradhan, R. P., Arvin, M. B., & Ghoshray, A. (2015). The dynamics of economic growth, oil prices, stock market depth, and other macroeconomic variables:

Evidence from the G-20 countries. *International Review of Financial Analysis*, *39*, 84–95.

Pratheepan, T. (2014). A Panel data analysis of profitability determinants: Empirical results from Sri Lankan manufacturing companies. *International Journal of Economics, Commerce and Management*, *2*(12).

Pucci, T., Simoni, C., & Zanni, L. (2015). Measuring the relationship between marketing assets, intellectual capital and firm performance. *Journal of Management & Governance*, *19*(3), 589–616.

Pulic, A. (1998). *Measuring the performance of intellectual potential in knowledge economy*. http://www.academia.edu/download/35277685/pulic_1998.doc

Purohit, H., & Tandon, K. (2015). Intellectual capital, financial performance and market valuation: A study on IT and pharmaceutical companies in India. *IUP Journal of Knowledge Management*, *13*(2), 7.

Rajan, R. G. (2006). India: The past and its future. *Asian Development Review*, *23*(2), 36.

Ram, R., & Spencer, D. E. (1983). Stock returns, real activity, inflation, and money: Comment. *The American Economic Review*, *73*(3), 463–470.

Ramya, M., & Mahesha, M. (2012). Impact of financial crisis on profitability of Indian banking sector-panel evidence in bank-specific and macroeconomic determinants. *Asian Journal of Research in Banking and Finance*, *2*(12), 27–43.

Rao, K. N., & Bhole, L. M. (1990). Inflation and equity returns. *Economic and Political Weekly*, *25*(21), 91–96.

Raza, S. A., Jawaid, S. T., & Shafqat, J. (2013). *Profitability of the banking sector of Pakistan: Panel evidence from bank-specific, industry-specific and macroeconomic determinants*. https://mpra.ub.uni-muenchen.de/48485/1/MPRA_p aper_48485.pdf

Reinganum, M. R. (1981). Misspecification of capital asset pricing: Empirical anomalies based on earnings' yields and market values. *Journal of Financial Economics*, *9*(1), 19–46.

Riahi-Belkaoui, A. (2003). Intellectual capital and firm performance of US multinational firms: A study of the resource-based and stakeholder views. *Journal of Intellectual Capital*, *4*(2), 215–226.

Ripley, D. M. (1973). Systematic elements in the linkage of national stock market indices. *The Review of Economics and Statistics*, *55*(3), 356–361.

Rodriguez, P., Siegel, D. S., Hillman, A., & Eden, L. (2006). Three lenses on the multinational enterprise: Politics, corruption, and corporate social responsibility. *Journal of International Business Studies*, *37*(6), 733–746.

Rodrik, D. (2016). Premature deindustrialization. *Journal of Economic Growth*, *21*(1), 1–33.

Rodrik, D., & Subramanian, A. (2005). From "Hindu growth" to productivity surge: The mystery of the Indian growth transition. *IMF Staff Papers, 55*(2), 193–228.

Ross, S. A. (1976). The arbitrage theory of capital asset pricing. *Journal of Economic Theory, 13*(3), 341–360.

Rostow, W. W. (1990). *The stages of economic growth: A non-communist manifesto.* Cambridge University Press.

Rudra, A. (1985). Planning in India: An evaluation in terms of its models. *Economic and Political Weekly, 20*(17), 758–764.

Rumelt, R. P. (1982). Diversification strategy and profitability. *Strategic Management Journal, 3*(4), 359–369.

Sanyal, A. (2011). The curious case of the Bombay plan. *Contemporary Issues and Ideas in Social Sciences, 6*(1), 1–31.

Schuler, D. A. (1996). Corporate political strategy and foreign competition: The case of the steel industry. *Academy of Management Journal, 39*(3), 720–737.

Schumpeter, J. A. (1912). 1934. *The theory of economic development: An inquiry into profits, capital, credit, interest and the business cycle.* Harvard University Press.

Selling, T. I., & Stickney, C. P. (1989). The effects of business environment and strategy on a firm's rate of return on assets. *Financial Analysts Journal, 45*(1), 43–52.

Serrasqueiro, Z. S., & Nunes, P. M. (2008). Performance and size: Empirical evidence from Portuguese SMEs. *Small Business Economics, 31*(2), 195–217.

Shabbir, M. S. (2018). *The impact of foreign portfolio investment on stock prices of Pakistan.* https://www.researchgate.net/publication/325257541_M_P_RA_The_Impact_of_Foreign_Portfolio_Investment_on_Stock_Prices_of_Pakistan_The_Impact_of_Foreign_Portfolio_Investment_on_Stock_Prices_of_Pakistan

Shahbaz, M., Rehman, I. U., & Afza, T. (2016). Macroeconomic determinants of stock market capitalization in an emerging market: Fresh evidence from cointegration with unknown structural breaks. *Macroeconomics and Finance in Emerging Market Economies, 9*(1), 75–99.

Sharma, C., & Sehgal, S. (2010). Impact of infrastructure on output, productivity and efficiency: Evidence from the Indian manufacturing industry. *Indian Growth and Development Review, 3*(2), 100–121.

Sharma, S. K., & Sehgal, S. (2015). Productivity, innovations and profitability of manufacturing industries in India: A regional study of Haryana state. *International Journal of Business Excellence, 8*(6), 700–723.

Sharpe, W. F. (1964). Capital asset prices: A theory of market equilibrium under conditions of risk. *The Journal of Finance, 19*(3), 425–442.

Sheng, H. C., & Tu, A. H. (2000). A study of cointegration and variance decomposition among national equity indices before and during the period of the

Asian financial crisis. *Journal of Multinational Financial Management, 10*(3), 345–365.

Shin, H. H., & Soenen, L. (1998). Efficiency of working capital management and corporate profitability. *Financial Practice and Education., 8*(2), 37–45.

Siddharthan, N. S., Pandit, B. L., & Agarwal, R. N. (1994). Growth and profit behavior of largescale Indian firms. *The Developing Economies, 32*(2), 188–209.

Siddiqui, K. (2009). Financial crisis and its impact on the economies of China and India. *Research in Applied Economics, 1*(1), 1–28.

Siggel, E., & Agrawal, P. (2009). *The impact of economic reforms on Indian manufacturers: Evidence from a small sample survey* (Institute of Economic Growth, University of Delhi Working Paper Series No. E/300/2009). http://iegindia.org/upload/pdf/wp300.pdf

Singh, J. (2012). *Impact of the surge in Chinese import on Indian manufacturing sector.* http://eaindustry.nic.in/discussion_papers/Impact_Chinese_Import.pdf

Singh, R. D., & Narwal, K. P. (2018). Examining the relationship between intellectual capital and financial performance: An empirical study of service and manufacturing sector of India. *International Journal of Learning and Intellectual Capital, 15*(4), 309–340.

Sinha, A. (2019). A theory of reform consolidation in India: From crisis-induced reforms to strategic internationalization. *India Review, 18*(1), 54–87.

Söderbom, M., & Teal, F. (2004). Size and efficiency in African manufacturing firms: Evidence from firm-level panel data. *Journal of Development Economics, 73*(1), 369–394.

Soenen, L. A., & Hennigar, E. S. (1988). An analysis of exchange rates and stock prices-the U.S. experience between 1980 and 1986. *Akron Business and Economic Review, 19*(4), 7–16

Solnik, B. (1987). Using financial prices to test exchange rate models: A note. *Journal of Finance, 42*(1), 141–149.

Soo, K. T. (2008). From licence Raj to market forces: The determinants of industrial structure in India after reform. *Economica, 75*(298), 222–243.

Spanos, Y. E., Zaralis, G., & Lioukas, S. (2004). Strategy and industry effects on profitability: Evidence from Greece. *Strategic Management Journal, 25*(2), 139–165.

Srinivasan, P. (2011). Causal nexus between stock market return and selected macroeconomic variables in India: Evidence from the National Stock Exchange (NSE). *IUP Journal of Financial Risk Management, 8*(4), 7.

Srivastava, A., & Behl, K. (2015). Macroeconomic variables on Indian stock market interactions: An analytical approach. *JIM Quest: Journal of Management and Technology, 11*(2), 1–8. http://jaipuria.edu.in/jim/wp-content/uploads/2012/06/jim_quest_july_dec_2015a.pdf#page=5

Subbarao, D. (2009). *Impact of the global financial crisis on India: Collateral damage and response*. In Speech delivered at the Symposium on The Global Economic Crisis and Challenges for the Asian Economy in a Changing World. https://rbidocs.rbi.org.in/rdocs/Speeches/PDFs/Speech% 20-%20as%20sent-%20Modified%20_4_.pdf

Sufian, F. (2009). Determinants of bank efficiency during unstable macroeconomic environment: Empirical evidence from Malaysia. *Research in International Business and Finance, 23*(1), 54–77.

Sufian, F., & Habibullah, M. S. (2009a). Bank specific and macroeconomic determinants of bank profitability: Empirical evidence from the China banking sector. *Frontiers of Economics in China, 4*(2), 274–291.

Sufian, F., & Habibullah, M. S. (2009b). Determinants of bank profitability in a developing economy: Empirical evidence from Bangladesh. *Journal of Business Economics and Management, 10*(3), 207–217.

Sufian, F., & Habibullah, M. S. (2010a). Assessing the impact of financial crisis on bank performance: Empirical evidence from Indonesia. *ASEAN Economic Bulletin, 27*(3), 245–262.

Sufian, F., & Habibullah, M. S. (2010b). Does economic freedom fosters banks' performance? Panel evidence from Malaysia. *Journal of Contemporary Accounting & Economics, 6*(2), 77–91.

Suganthi, P., & Dharshanaa, C. (2014). Interrelationship between FII and stock market and their causal relationship with selected macroeconomic variables in India. *TSM Business Review, 2*(1), 29–46.

Sultana, S. T., & Pardhasaradhi, S. (2012). Impact of flow of FDI & FII on Indian stock market. *Finance Research, 1*(3), 4–10.

Sultana, S. T., & Reddy, K. S. (2017). The Effect of macroeconomic factors on Indian stock market: An empirical evidence. *FIIB Business Review, 6*(1), 68–76.

Sur, D., Maji, S. K., & Banerjee, D. (2014). Working capital management in Select Indian pharmaceutical companies: A Cross-sectional analysis. In N. Ray & K. Chakraborty (Eds.), *Handbook of research on strategic business infrastructure development and contemporary issues in finance* (pp. 1–11). IGI Global.

Szewczyk, S. H., Tsetsekos, G. P., & Zantout, Z. (1996). The valuation of corporate R&D expenditures: Evidence from investment opportunities and free cash flow. *Financial Management, 25*(1), 105–110.

Tahir, M., & Anuar, M. B. A. (2015). The determinants of working capital management and firms performance of textile sector in Pakistan. *Quality & Quantity, 50*(2), 605–618.

Talla, J. T. (2013). *Impact of macroeconomic variables on the stock market prices of the Stockholm stock exchange* [Master's thesis]. Jonkoping International Business School. https://pdfs.semanticscholar.org/531c/af1a5eded 883d4a663b9f200bb9b666abcb5.pdf

Thatcher, M. E., & Oliver, J. R. (2001). The impact of technology investments on a firm's production efficiency, product quality, and productivity. *Journal of Management Information Systems, 18*(2), 17–45.

Thomas, D. E. (2006). International diversification and firm performance in Mexican firms: A curvilinear relationship? *Journal of Business Research, 59*(4), 501–507.

Thornton, J. (1993). Money, output and stock prices in the UK: Evidence on some (non) relationships. *Applied Financial Economics, 3*(4), 335–338.

Tripathi, V., & Seth, R. (2014). Stock market performance and macroeconomic factors: The study of Indian equity market. *Global Business Review, 15*(2), 291–316.

Tursoy, T. (2019). The interaction between stock prices and interest rates in Turkey: Empirical evidence from ARDL bounds test cointegration. *Financial Innovation, 5*(1), 1–12.

Van Biesebroeck, J. (2005). Exporting raises productivity in sub-Saharan African manufacturing firms. *Journal of International Economics, 67*(2), 373–391.

Van der Eng, P. (2009). Capital formation and capital stock in Indonesia, 1950–2008. *Bulletin of Indonesian Economic Studies, 45*(3), 345–371.

Vardhan, H., & Sinha, P. (2014). *Influence of foreign institutional investments (FIIs) on the Indian stock market.* https://mpra.ub.uni-muenchen.de/ 53611/1/MPRA_paper_53611.pdf

Vejzagic, M., & Zarafat, H. (2014). An analysis of macroeconomic determinants of commercial banks profitability in Malaysia for the period 1995-2011. *Asian Economic and Financial Review, 4*(1), 41–57.

Vikramasinghe, B. G. (2006). *Macro economic forces and stock prices: Some empirical evidence from an emerging market* (Working Paper Series 06/14). University of Wollongong. https://ro.uow.edu.au/cgi/viewcontent.cgi?ref erer=https://scholar.google.co.in/&httpsredir=1&article=1029&context=acc finwp

Vining, A. R., & Boardman, A. E. (1992). Ownership versus competition: Efficiency in public enterprise. *Public Choice, 73*(2), 205–239.

Vong, P. I., & Chan, H. S. (2009). Determinants of bank profitability in Macao. *Macau Monetary Research Bulletin, 12*(6), 93–113.

Voulgaris, F., Doumpos, M., & Zopounidis, C. (2000). On the evaluation of Greek industrial SME's performance via multicriteria analysis of financial ratios. *Small Business Economics, 15*(2), 127–136.

Wada, I. (2017). Dynamic causality in energy production and output growth in Nigeria revisited: ARDL bounds test approach. *Energy Sources, Part b: Economics, Planning, and Policy, 12*(11), 945–951.

Wagner, J. (1995). Exports, firm size, and firm dynamics. *Small Business Economics, 7*(1), 29–39.

Wang, Y., Wu, C., & Yang, L. (2013). Oil price shocks and stock market activities: Evidence from oil-importing and oil-exporting countries. *Journal of Comparative Economics, 41*(4), 1220–1239.

Weston, J. F., & Mansinghka, S. K. (1971). Tests of the efficiency performance of conglomerate firms. *The Journal of Finance, 26*(4), 919–936.

Widyastuti, M., Oetomo, H. W., & Riduwan, A. (2017). Working capital and macroeconomic variables as value creation in Indonesian textile companies. *International Journal of Business and Finance Management Research, 5*, 7–16.

Willett, T. D., Liang, P., & Zhang, N. (2011). Global contagion and the decoupling debate. In Y.-W. Cheung, V. Kakkar, & G. Ma (Eds.), *The evolving role of Asia in global finance* (pp. 215–234). Emerald Group.

Williams, B. (2003). Domestic and international determinants of bank profits: Foreign banks in Australia. *Journal of Banking & Finance, 27*(6), 1185–1210.

Wilson, P. (1994). Don't frighten the horses—The political economy of Singapore's foreign exchange rate regime since 1981. *Economist*, 15–57.

Won, J., & Ryu, S. L. (2015). Determinants of operating efficiency in Korean construction firms: Panel data analysis. *International Information Institute (Tokyo). Information, 18*(5B), 1885–1892.

Wong, W. K., Agarwal, A., & Du, J. (2005). *Financial integration for India stock market, a fractional cointegration approach* (Working Paper No. WP0501). National University of Singapore. https://www.researchgate.net/profile/Wing-Keung_Wong/publication/5201388_Financial_Integration_for_India_Stock_Market_a_Fractional_Cointegration_Approach/links/0c960515e7f5 9a9018000000.pdf

Wu, T. P., Liu, S. B., & Hsueh, S. J. (2016). The causal relationship between economic policy uncertainty and stock market: A panel data analysis. *International Economic Journal, 30*(1), 109–122.

Yang, C. H., & Chen, K. H. (2009). Are small firms less efficient? *Small Business Economics, 32*(4), 375–395.

Yang, J. C. (2006). The efficiency of SMEs in the global market: Measuring the Korean performance. *Journal of Policy Modelling, 28*(8), 861–876.

Yu, Y. S., Barros, A., Yeh, M. L., Lu, M. J., & Tsai, C. H. (2012). A study of estimating the technical efficiency of optoelectronic firms: An application of data envelopment analysis and tobit analysis. *International Journal of Academic Research in Business and Social Sciences, 2*(7), 192.

Zantout, Z. Z. (1997). A test of the debt monitoring hypothesis: The case of corporate R&D expenditures. *Financial Review, 32*(1), 21–48.

Zhang, A., Zhang, Y., & Zhao, R. (2003). A study of the R&D efficiency and productivity of Chinese firms. *Journal of Comparative Economics, 31*(3), 444–464.

Zhang, X., & Daly, K. (2013). The Impact of bank specific and macroeconomic factors on China's bank performance. *Global Economy and Finance Journal, 6*(2), 1–25.

Index

© The Author(s), under exclusive license to Springer Nature Singapore Pte Ltd. 2022

S. K. Maji et al., *Indian Manufacturing Sector in Post-Reform Period*, https://doi.org/10.1007/978-981-19-2666-2

Lightning Source UK Ltd.
Milton Keynes UK
UKHW050018060722
405379UK00014B/120